Badiou, Poem and Subject

Also available from Bloomsbury

Badiou and His Interlocutors: Lectures, Interviews and Responses, ed. A.J. Bartlett and Justin Clemens
Badiou and Indifferent Being: A Critical Introduction to Being and Event, William Watkin
Badiou and the German Tradition of Philosophy, ed. Jan Völker
The Pornographic Age, Alain Badiou, trans. A.J. Bartlett and Justin Clemens

Badiou, Poem and Subject

Tom Betteridge

BLOOMSBURY ACADEMIC
LONDON • NEW YORK • OXFORD • NEW DELHI • SYDNEY

BLOOMSBURY ACADEMIC
Bloomsbury Publishing Plc
50 Bedford Square, London, WC1B 3DP, UK
1385 Broadway, New York, NY 10018, USA
29 Earlsfort Terrace, Dublin 2, Ireland

BLOOMSBURY, BLOOMSBURY ACADEMIC and the Diana logo are trademarks of
Bloomsbury Publishing Plc

First published in Great Britain 2020
This paperback edition published in 2021

Copyright © Tom Betteridge, 2020

Tom Betteridge has asserted his right under the Copyright, Designs and Patents Act, 1988, to be identified as Author of this work.

For legal purposes the Acknowledgements on p. viii constitute
an extension of this copyright page.

Cover design by Maria Rajka
Cover image: Arnica Montana from *Phytographie Medicale* by Joseph Roques (1772–1850), published in 1821 (engraving), Hoquart, L.F.J. (fl 1821) /
Private Collection / The Stapleton Collection / Bridgeman Images

All rights reserved. No part of this publication may be reproduced or transmitted in any form or by any means, electronic or mechanical, including photocopying, recording, or any information storage or retrieval system, without prior permission in writing from the publishers.

Bloomsbury Publishing Plc does not have any control over, or responsibility for, any third-party websites referred to or in this book. All internet addresses given in this book were correct at the time of going to press. The author and publisher regret any inconvenience caused if addresses have changed or sites have ceased to exist, but can accept no responsibility for any such changes.

A catalogue record for this book is available from the British Library.

A catalog record for this book is available from the Library of Congress.

ISBN: HB: 978-1-3500-8585-5
PB: 978-1-3502-6227-0
ePDF: 978-1-3500-8586-2
eBook: 978-1-3500-8587-9

Typeset by Integra Software Services Pvt. Ltd.

To find out more about our authors and books visit www.bloomsbury.com
and sign up for our newsletters.

For Emilia Weber, with love.

Contents

Acknowledgements	viii
Abbreviations	ix
Introduction	1
Badiou's intervention	1
Heidegger and the German heritage	5
Argument and methodology	10
'This restrained intensity': Dance as a metaphor for thought	13
1 Silence Being Thought	19
Paul Celan's ineloquence	19
Poetic and subtractive ontologies: *Phusis* and *Idea*	36
Heidegger's nothing	45
The void and poetry's idea	52
2 The Poem Becoming-Prose	69
Desacralization and authenticity	69
Hölderlin's 'The Journey'	78
Lacoue-Labarthe: The poem becoming-prose	89
Poem and subject	103
3 Anabasis	113
Anabasis and homecoming	113
Reading Celan's 'Homecoming'	121
Reading Celan's 'Anabasis'	129
4 Subtraction and Love	137
Badiou and Adorno	137
Adorno's *Endgame*	142
Beckett's generic prose	154
The latent poem and love	163
Conclusion	181
Notes	189
Bibliography	219
Index	227

Acknowledgements

This book is based on the doctoral research I undertook in the School of Critical Studies at the University of Glasgow between 2010 and 2015. Without my supervisors, Vassiliki Kolocotroni and Paddy Lyons, none of that work would have been possible, and I am immeasurably grateful to them for their guidance and inspiration, and for their solidarity. My warmest thanks to my examiners Jane Goldman and Nina Power, whose generous and critical comments and suggestions were a constant source of encouragement and reassurance in revising this work for publication. A very early version of the first part of Chapter 1 was first published in 2012 as 'Silence Being Thought: Badiou, Heidegger, Celan', in *Evental Aesthetics*, 1 (2): 17–48. Chapter 3 was published in 2016 as 'Alain Badiou's Anabasis: Rereading Paul Celan against Heidegger', in *Textual Practice*, 30 (1): 45–68. My thanks to the editors. Many thanks to Carcanet Press Ltd too for their permission to reproduce extracts from Michael Hamburger's translations of Paul Celan. All efforts have been made to trace copyright holders. In the event of errors or omissions, please notify the publisher in writing of any corrections that will need to be incorporated in future editions of this book.

I would also like to thank Ellen Dillon and Andrew Rubens for their invaluable help with knotty questions of translation, Lila Matsumoto and Georgina Brückner for all of the Celan-talk and Dominic Smith for recommending Badiou's *The Century* in 2007 – this is all your fault. Thank you as well to the anonymous readers of both my initial book proposal and the resulting manuscript for their belief in the project and for their insightful suggestions, and to the editors at Bloomsbury, Liza Thompson, Frankie Mace and Lucy Russell, for their patience, advice and support throughout the process of bringing this work to publication.

My sincere gratitude to my friends and colleagues over the years for their innumerable kindnesses, inspiration and generosity, and to my parents, Chris and John, and my sister, Sally, for their unwavering support throughout my studies. This book is for Emilia Weber, with love.

Abbreviations

All works by Alain Badiou

AP	*The Age of Poets: And Other Writings on Twentieth-Century Poetry and Prose*
BE	*Being and Event*
BOE	*Briefings on Existence: A Short Treatise on Transitory Ontology*
C	*Conditions*
E	*Ethics: An Essay on the Understanding of Evil*
FP	*The Adventure of French Philosophy*
HI	*Handbook of Inaesthetics*
IT	*Infinite Thought: Truth and the Return to Philosophy*
OB	*On Beckett*
M	*Metapolitics*
MP	*Manifesto for Philosophy*
ISLP	'In Search of Lost Prose'
LW	*Logics of Worlds: Being and Event, II*
PL	*In Praise of Love*
PM	*Philosophy for Militants*
PP	*Pocket Pantheon*
TC	*The Century*
TW	*Theoretical Writings*
W	*Five Lessons on Wagner*
WA	*Wittgenstein's Antiphilosophy*

Introduction

Badiou's intervention

Recalling one of his early encounters with Richard Wagner's operas, Alain Badiou offers an arresting image of cultural exchange between France and Germany in the wake of the Second World War:

> As early as the summer of 1952, my father, as the Oberbürgermeister of Toulouse, was invited to the 'New Bayreuth' under the direction of Wieland Wagner. We travelled through a defeated, dreary Germany that was still in ruins. The sight of these big cities reduced to piles of rubble insidiously prepared us for the disasters of the *Ring* or the derelictions of *Tannhäuser* that we would be seeing on the stage. I was enthralled by Wieland's quasi-abstract productions, which were aimed at doing away with all the 'Germanic' particularism that for a time had associated Wagner with the horrors of Nazism.[1]

Badiou's father, Raymond Badiou, was a mathematics professor and the mayor of Toulouse from 1944 to 1958, the city's first following its liberation by the French Resistance in 1944. By naming his father the 'Oberbürgermeister of Toulouse', 'Badiou prefaces his account of Wieland Wagner's productions with wariness towards this German invitation that would presume to lay claim to French territory after its liberation. Nonetheless, Badiou's father, as both French leftist mayor of Toulouse and German 'Oberbürgermeister', here is made to stand as something of a figure of cultural exchange between France and Germany, a site of reciprocity from which Badiou embarks on his own process of intellectual formation. More concretely, Wagner's operas were also, Badiou claims, his mother's 'great musical passion' (*W*, ix–x). For the young Badiou, there is a renewed promise in this exchange, reflected in Wieland Wagner's 'quasi-abstract' productions, unsullied by '"Germanic" particularism'.[2] Badiou's relation to Wagner is one of reverence, but this is a Wagner 'rid ... of any references to a national mythology'. For Badiou, Wieland Wagner purges his grandfather's work of what had only 'for a time ... associated Wagner with the horrors of Nazism' (W, 5),³ intending to reveal something in these operas capable of persistence beyond the social and historical context of their creation – a provocation to those philosophers and theorists for whom, as Badiou begins to articulate his mature philosophical project thirty years later, the Holocaust and its ruins remain a fundamental rupture for thought.⁴ That Badiou's guide in the journey above is a leftist mathematician is not arbitrary in this respect, then, for it anticipates the alternative path Badiou follows out of the ruins: the conjunction of radical politics and the rigorous abstractions of formal mathematics.

The broad context of this book is the relation of French philosophy to its German heritage following the Second World War. It explores Alain Badiou's intervention in twentieth-century French philosophy, taking as its focus his decisive break from the continuing importance this latter affords to the writing of Martin Heidegger, notoriously a member of the Nazi party from 1933 until its disintegration after the Second World War. This study's specific site of enquiry is the new relation Badiou poses between philosophy and the poem, and especially its participation in his attempt to think a category of 'subject' adequate to the demands of contemporary political resistance. Initially exploring these questions through the lens offered by the poems of Paul Celan, who lost his parents to the Holocaust yet maintained an avid interest in Heidegger's philosophy, this book sustains its focus on French philosophy's relation to Germany by comparing at its close Badiou and Theodor W. Adorno's respective readings of Samuel Beckett.

Badiou's philosophical output spans some sixty years, though scholarship today recognizes three distinct periods in his philosophy's development. The early Badiou's Maoist interventions prior to and immediately following the student- and worker-led protests in Paris in May 1968 comprise the first period, reaching its fulfilment and closure with the 1982 publication of Badiou's *Théorie du sujet* (translated by Bruno Bosteels and published in 2009 as *Theory of the Subject*). During this period, Badiou's philosophy is almost exclusively tethered to militant politics, though the continuing importance to Badiou's project of both Stéphane Mallarmé's poetry and Jacques Lacan's psychoanalytic writing is anticipated in this text too: Badiou dedicates significant portions of *Theory of the Subject* to Mallarmé and Lacan, 'The two great modern French dialecticians'.⁵ The second period is bound to the publication of Badiou's most influential work to date, *L'être et l'événement* in 1988, published in English in 2006 as *Being and Event* (translated by Oliver Feltham). This was followed by prolific publication and translation of texts throughout the 1990s and into the twenty-first century in which Badiou explored the consequences of his magnum opus's major claims across philosophy's four 'conditions': art, love, politics and science. This second period features many of the most influential of Badiou's works from an Anglophone perspective, including the companion book to *Being and Event*, *Manifesto for Philosophy* (1992/1999), the important essay collection *Conditions* (1992/2008) and the 'trilogy' expanding on three of the four conditions (art, politics and science/mathematics), *Handbook of Inaesthetics* (1998/2005), *Metapolitics* (1998/2005), and *Briefings on Existence: A Short Treatise on Transitory Ontology* (1998/2006). This period in Badiou's work takes its point of departure from his central philosophical claim in *Being and Event*, that 'mathematics equals ontology', and the restitution of the categories of 'truth', 'subject' and 'event' on that proposition's basis. The third period in Badiou's work is anticipated by *Briefings on Existence* and the English essay collection *Theoretical Writings* (2004), but finds its inauguration with the publication of *Logiques des Mondes* in 2006 (*Logics of Worlds: Being and Event II*, appears in English in 2009). Though the appearance of Badiou's third systematic work of philosophy, following *Theory of the Subject* and *Being and Event*, was long awaited, Badiou scholarship is still coming to terms with the consequences of this work which, having split 'being qua being' from 'appearance', seeks the systematic formalization of the latter via recourse to the logical expressions of contemporary category theory. A fourth period in Badiou's work and its reception is now due, with the publication of the third and final volume of *L'être et l'événement*, *L'immanence des vérités* in France in September 2018, soon to be published in English as *The Immanence of Truths*.

This monograph's focus on Badiou's ontological commitments, his departure from Heidegger and the attendant consequences for the relations between philosophy, the poem and the category of the subject demand a focused analysis of the thought associated with the second period in his work, the elaboration of his main philosophical intervention in *Being and Event*. *Being and Event* remains the bedrock of Badiou's philosophy: *Logics of Worlds* and later *The Immanence of Truths*, though addressing several technical issues with their predecessor, modulate and push forward *Being and Event*'s material towards a 'full' or 'complete' articulation of the philosophical project it inaugurates. *Logics of Worlds* moves from the ontological commitments of *Being and Event* towards an examination of truths' 'appearance', broadly, and *The Immanence of Truths* addresses, again broadly, the subjective apprehension of the world from the standpoint of truth. Published during a period 'in full intellectual regression' (*BE*, xi), *Being and Event* marks Badiou's intervention in twentieth-century French philosophy and in the history of philosophy more broadly. However, Badiou's point of departure in *Being and Event* is neither twentieth-century French philosophy nor classical philosophy, but 'the last universally recognized philosopher', Martin Heidegger. It is my contention that there is still much to explore in this point of departure, and that Badiou's relation to literature, on the basis of both his supposed rejection of Heideggerian thinking and his peculiar, often reverent readings of Paul Celan and Samuel Beckett, is a field of investigation still in its relative infancy, especially insofar as it relates to the philosophical category of the subject. I gesture in the conclusion of this study to the ways in which I think a re-examination of Badiou's 'second period' illuminates his most up-to-date work too, especially given the increasing importance of 'love', as he conceives it, in his thought and the emergence of Philippe Lacoue-Labarthe as his most valued interlocutor.

Badiou's mature project from the late 1980s onwards seeks nothing less than the complete reinvigoration of philosophy following its supposed end or completion. In his introduction to *Being and Event*, Badiou diagnoses, in the France of the late 1980s, the 'current global state of philosophy' via recourse to three statements: that, firstly, 'Heidegger is the last universally recognized philosopher'; secondly, that contemporary Analytic philosophy, taking its premises from the work of the Vienna Circle, '[has] succeeded in conserving the figure of scientific rationality as a paradigm for thought'; and finally, that 'a post-Cartesian doctrine of the subject is unfolding', bound to the 'non-philosophical' discourses of psychoanalysis and militant politics, and indexed to Freud and Lacan on the one hand and Marx and Lenin on the other. 'They all indicate', Badiou writes, 'the closure of an entire epoch of thought and its concerns' (*BE*, 1). For Badiou, the supposed 'disparity' between these statements and their resistance to formal unification outlaws the possibility of a speculative and systematic philosophical project.

More than simple 'unification', however, Badiou's project, conceived as an intervention in this global philosophical situation, 'draws a diagonal'[6] through these three points, modulating their concerns and drawing them into systematic relation. Recast at the outset of *Being and Event* to offer a schema for the orientation of his philosophical system, Badiou rearticulates these three points as follows: (i) 'philosophy as such can only be re-assigned on the basis of the ontological question' (following Heidegger); (ii) the Cantorian *event* in formal mathematics 'sets new orientations for thought'; (iii) any new 'conceptual apparatus', the kind of which Badiou seeks, must imbricate itself with the 'theoretico-practical orientations of the modern doctrine of the subject', despite this latter's most forceful presentations occurring resolutely within the non-philosophical discourses of clinical/political 'practical processes' (BE, 2).[7]

Defying claims to the end of philosophy, Badiou 're-assigns' its future course by re-assigning in turn the ontological question itself. For Badiou, philosophy must relinquish its hold on ontology. Cantor's innovations in set-theoretical mathematics, Badiou claims, allow the articulation of being qua being in set-theoretical discourse, thought as 'the infinity of pure multiples' (BE, xiii). Badiou is committed to an ontology that precludes any instance of the 'One' at the level of being qua being. He finds in set-theoretical mathematics following Cantor an articulation of the multiple in which the One only ever figures as the result of a secondary operation, or what Badiou calls the 'count-as-one', by which inconsistent multiples are made consistent. Transcendent or mystical evocations of an originary, ungraspable wholeness at the level of being are foreclosed in advance, then, by the adoption of set-theory as the discourse that writes being. Following this shift, 'new orientations for thought' bind the practice of philosophy not to being per se but to the formal rupture of novelty, or to what Badiou famously calls 'events'. However, it is not only radical innovations in mathematics like Cantor's that come to condition the efforts of philosophy in this way[8] but innovations in philosophy's other 'conditions' – art, politics and love – too. The rejuvenation of the category of subject in Badiou's philosophy, for example, arises from philosophy's encounter with the 'practical processes' of the subject offered by both emancipatory political sequences and psychoanalytic practice. The theoretical re-articulation of philosophy's relation to being, as well as to non-being and event, is then concomitant with the conceptualization of new forms of practical resistance. For Peter Hallward, Badiou's conceptualization of the familiar problem of theory's relation to practice is one of his most important innovations: 'We might say that Badiou's great achievement is to have reconceptualised for our times the relation between the real (of immediate action or declaration) and the ideal (of formal consistency), where the latter is composed over time, as the consequences of the former.'[9]

Heidegger and the German heritage

Given Badiou's nomination of Heidegger as 'the last universally recognisable philosopher' in Being and Event, and the importance afforded to the latter's thought in Manifesto for Philosophy, whose fourth chapter is titled 'Heidegger Viewed as Commonplace', it is of course no secret that Heidegger is of great importance to how Badiou understands his own philosophical project.¹⁰ However, beyond the strictly philosophical import of the 'ontological question', detailed above, Heidegger also assumes a central place in Badiou's thinking concerning the relation between literature and philosophy. The opening essay of Badiou's *Handbook of Inaesthetics*, 'Art and Philosophy', begins by contrasting Plato's expulsion of the poets from his republic, or 'the judgment of ostracism that Plato directed against poetry, theatre, and music', with what Badiou calls 'the other extreme', at which 'we find a pious devotion to art, a contrite prostration of the concept – regarded as a manifestation of technical nihilism – before the poetic word'.¹¹ This latter extreme, by which philosophy relinquishes its claim to the concept, neatly encapsulates Badiou's reading of Heidegger, but it also opens the question of each thinker's relation towards both 'art', or 'the poem' more specifically, and the historical tension between philosophy and language.

This study's point of departure is Badiou's relation to Heidegger: it asks how Badiou, in providing a new direction for philosophy, seeks to overcome Heidegger's understandings of ontology and philosophy's relation to 'the poem', as well as assessing the broadly political implications of this decision insofar as it concerns the material body of practical change, or the subject. This is also to stage an encounter between twentieth-century French philosophy and its German heritage, especially where the question of literature is concerned. It is interesting in this regard that Badiou conceives his own work as perhaps the last in a determinately French philosophical sequence. In Badiou's preface to his relatively recent collection *The Adventure of French Philosophy*,¹² he claims the existence of a 'French moment' in the history of philosophy, running from the publication of Jean-Paul Sartre's *Being and Nothingness* in 1943 to the last writings of Gilles Deleuze in the 1990s (his *What Is Philosophy?*, with Felix Guattari).¹³ For Badiou, this sequence is of a significance only rivalled by the classical philosophy of Ancient Greece and the works of Kant, Hegel and German Idealism more broadly. Badiou's claim is not intended to aggrandize a period of thought coming to its close, however, but to emphasize the specificity of the extended philosophical investigations therein. He begins, then, by outlining the sites of enquiry common to French philosophy during this time, nominating its persistent exploration of the category of subject, expressed by the tension maintained throughout between 'the concept' and 'interior life' or consciousness, as its main unifying feature.

Beyond 'subject', however, Badiou also claims four 'intellectual operations' common to the French moment: its sustained engagements with German philosophy, with 'Science', with 'Politics' and with modernity or 'new forms of living' (*FP*, liv–lvi). Before returning briefly to the question of subject, it is important to note two of the ways in which by nominating a 'French moment' in philosophy Badiou offers an account of the influence of an ostensibly German line of thinking on his own philosophical endeavours. Badiou's uncertainty when it comes to claiming his own work as a contribution to this 'moment' – 'Time will tell', he writes, 'though if there has been such a French philosophical moment, my position would be as perhaps its last representative' (*FP*, lii) – only serves to emphasize the decisive impact he deems his philosophical project to have had on what is retrospectively claimed as a saturated or closed sequence of thinking, which is to claim, also, the singularity of his own engagement with 'the German heritage'.

Badiou claims that the French philosophical moment is inextricable from the German philosophy preceding it:

> The first move is a German one – or rather, a French move upon German philosophers. All contemporary French philosophy is also, in reality, a discussion of the German heritage. Its formative moments include Kojève's seminars on Hegel, attended by Lacan and also influential on Lévi-Strauss, and the discovery of phenomenology in the 1930s and 40s, through the works of Husserl and Heidegger. (*FP*, liv)

Contemporary French philosophy, Badiou makes clear, is always a discussion of its German precedent, whether the former's focus is the contemporary importance of the Hegelian dialectic (we might think of Jean-Paul Sartre's two-volume work *Critique of Dialectical Reason*) or the shift from phenomenology to deconstruction in Derrida's readings of Husserl and Heidegger, or Lacoue-Labarthe's sustained questioning of Heidegger's thought in its relation to National Socialism, to name but three examples. Badiou makes a further claim regarding the French moment, then: that this 'first operation ... is effectively a French appropriation of German philosophy' (*FP*, lv) – an appropriation, for Badiou, because German philosophy is elevated as French philosophy's sole resource in the quest for a new relation between concept and existence, between the rational and the vital. Badiou's inability to claim his own contribution as a part of this sequence is perhaps due to the decisiveness with which his philosophy chooses the concept over existence as the privileged site of philosophical enquiry. The absolutely fundamental role of mathematics in Badiou's philosophy, for example, is intended, in part, to revivify philosophy's claim to the universality of reason, privileging the rational over the vital (a distinction maintained in his rivalry with Deleuze).[14] Beyond the French moment's adoption and transformation of

German philosophy, however, Badiou argues that the innovation sought by the latter in its encounter with its German precedent also had an impact on the form of philosophy's transmission: 'one could not displace the concept without inventing new philosophical forms' (*FP*, lvii), Badiou writes. The second essential element for understanding the relation between French and German philosophy, then, concerns the interaction between philosophy and literature: 'if the surrealists were the first representatives of a twentieth-century convergence between aesthetic and philosophical projects in France', Badiou argues,

> by the 1950s and 60s it was philosophy that was inventing its own literary forms in an attempt to find a direct expressive link between philosophical style and presentation, and the new positioning of the concept that it proposed. (*FP*, lviii)

Just as Badiou claims an abiding influence of the Heideggerian proximity of philosophy and poem, or 'the contrite prostration of the concept' above, he also claims a peculiar intimacy between philosophy and literature throughout the 'French moment'. Of Deleuze, Foucault, Derrida and Lacan in particular, he claims, 'these thinkers were bent upon finding a style of their own, inventing a new way of creating prose; they wanted to be writers' (*FP*, lviii). Though the respective developments of these emergent 'philosophical styles' reveal divergent commitments – to genealogy, text or slips in signification – Badiou claims a shared feature here: the collapse of philosophy as a self-same discourse oriented by a sense of its own resolutely singular work. Badiou does not intend to enshrine philosophy in a Hegelian move at the centre and foundation of all other discourses, though, of course, this may be the result of his endeavours nonetheless. Instead, Badiou wishes to revitalize philosophy as the pursuit of 'truths' by emphasizing, firstly, the intensity with which particular discourses outwith philosophy's bounds produce thought on their own terms and, secondly, philosophy's role in 'thinking that thought' at a remove; 'literature' and 'philosophy', for example, remain irreducible sites of thought, at times drawn into productive local encounters by which 'truths' are unveiled – a relation Badiou calls 'inaesthetics'. Reflecting the maintenance of this distinction between literature and philosophy, Badiou is both 'writer' (novelist and playwright)[15] and 'philosopher'.

The relation between philosophy and literature, however, carries important consequences for the political too, especially insofar as it concerns the category of 'subject', to which Badiou alludes as his argument proceeds:

> One could even say that one of the goals of French philosophy has been to construct a new space from which to write, one where literature and philosophy would be indistinguishable; a domain which would be neither specialized

philosophy, nor literature as such, but rather the home of a sort of writing in which it was no longer possible to disentangle philosophy from literature. A space, in other words, where there is no longer a differentiation between concept and life, for the invention of this writing ultimately consists in giving a new life to the concept: a literary life. (*FP*, lviii- lix)

The prostration of the concept Badiou reads from Heidegger persists here in modulated form. Badiou argues that in the space of thinking proposed by French philosophy the concept is revitalized textually, given a 'literary life'. The concept becomes inextricable from the workings of language, and the subject carried through this space of enquiry becomes the individual that writes. Badiou deploys a strategic reductiveness here in order to anticipate his own philosophy's intervention in this philosophical/literary scene, an intervention receiving its most explicit and rigorous expression in *Being and Event*, most notably in its insistence on the results of philosophy's revived relationship with formal mathematics, an insistence, moreover, that influences Badiou's own distinct philosophical 'style'.

Peter Hallward's translation notes in the first Badiou monograph, *Badiou: A Subject to Truth*, reveal the distance Badiou's writing takes from his contemporaries and predecessors: 'Although it is often difficult to convey the remarkable concision of Badiou's prose (to say nothing of the power of his voice)', Hallward writes, 'to translate Badiou is not fundamentally problematic. Unlike Heidegger or Derrida, say, he makes no appeal to a mysterious "gift of language." On the contrary, as a matter of firm principle he insists that "the transmission of thought is indifferent to language".[16] For Badiou, that thought subtracts itself from the play of language, and perhaps more importantly from the latter's hold upon identification, as will become clear, is a necessary prerequisite of any thought of universal address. Weaving together his departures from Heidegger and his legacy in French philosophy, Badiou makes the following claim for the French language: 'Against the fascination for the word and for etymology, that is, for the origin and for substance', Badiou writes, 'the French language plays up the primacy of syntax, that is, of the relation and the assertion. *And this is why, once more, philosophy in the French language is political*: between axiom and sentence, against consensus and ambiguity, the French language imprints its certainty and its authority, which also make up its persuasive beauty.'[17] The political is now tethered to the rational cut of transmissible thought, to the concept, against the textual life afforded to the latter throughout the French moment.

To make this sense of the political a little more concrete prior to the investigations undertaken in the main body of this book requires a small tangent.

Beneath both Badiou's sustained critique of Heidegger and his claim that the French moment begins in the middle of the Second World War with Sartre's *Being and Nothingness* lies the historical impact of what French philosophy calls 'Auschwitz' upon both philosophy and literature, as well as upon the possibility of their participation in thinking new categories of political resistance for the future. The majority of this book, working from Hölderlin and Heidegger through Celan and on to Adorno and Beckett, takes such questions as its primary concern, but for now, Badiou's prologue to *Metapolitics* offers an insight into his personal involvement in the question of Auschwitz and its legacy. Therein, Badiou laments the murder of the philosophers Albert Lautman and Jean Cavaillès by the Nazis in 1944, claiming that, with their passing, the 'course of philosophy in France was enduringly altered'. Both thinkers demanded mathematics' centricity in philosophical endeavour: Lautman attempts to 'found a modern Platonism', and Cavaillès through his work in formal mathematics seeks 'the internal necessity of notions'.[18] What Badiou argues, however, is that in both thinkers, the rigour with which they approach the work of philosophy – their commitments to formal mathematics, to logic, to the concept – is inextricable from their militant resistance in the face of Nazi occupation; Badiou invokes Georges Canguilhem's comment here, that 'Cavaillès was resistant *by logic*' (*M*, 4). With their deaths, this conjunction of political militancy and formal necessity falters 'for quarter of a century', replaced by 'the Sartrean theory of Commitment' (*M*, 5). There is a very real sense in which the trajectory of French philosophy, in relation to the concept of 'resistance' especially, is radically altered for Badiou by Auschwitz. This lends nuance to Badiou's own attempts towards the century's close to enshrine the formal deductions of mathematics at the centre of philosophy once more. This commitment is bound to the history of philosophical militancy and offers too a means of departure from the pervasive coextension of philosophy and language in twentieth-century examinations of 'text' and 'the poem', as well as from structuralism, hermeneutics and deconstruction more broadly.

Argument and methodology

This study examines the relation between philosophy, the poem and the subject in the mature philosophy of Alain Badiou. It investigates Badiou's decisive contribution to these questions primarily by means of comparison, especially to Martin Heidegger, Philippe Lacoue-Labarthe and Theodor Adorno, as well as by analysing Badiou's readings of poems and prose by Paul Celan and

Samuel Beckett, respectively, as sites of potential dialogue with his immediate predecessors. The study stresses the importance of French philosophy's German heritage, emphasizing not only Badiou's radical departure from Heidegger and his legacy but also the former's wholesale rejection of philosophies that would, in the wake of twentieth-century violence and beyond, proclaim their own end or completion. The book argues Badiou's innovative readings of Celan and Beckett to be crucial to understanding this endeavour: for Badiou, both writers use the poem to affirm novel conceptions of subjectivity capable of transcending the historical conditions of their presentation.

Chapter 1, 'Silence Being Thought', argues that Badiou's fragmentary readings of Celan's poems are of especial significance when it comes to interpreting Badiou's departure from Heidegger with regard to philosophy and the poem. As well as opening up this study's central questions – of ontology, language and politics – it also offers an in-depth reading of Badiou's account of the 'poetic idea' as a way of distinguishing Heideggerian and Badiouian conceptions of ontology. This groundwork is necessary to bring Badiou's idiosyncratic and complicated account of subjectivity – on which the second half of the study focuses – into relief. Chapter 2 builds significantly on the preceding chapter's primarily philosophical work by arguing that the way into thinking about the political consequences of the relation between philosophy and the poem in the twentieth century is through the role of 'myth' in the poem, a topic explored at length by Philippe Lacoue-Labarthe. In this chapter, I offer the first sustained examination of Badiou's discussion with Lacoue-Labarthe, anticipating the emergence in 2017 of Lacoue-Labarthe as one of Badiou's most important interlocutors, with the publication of Badiou's piece on Lacoue-Labarthe, 'In Search of Lost Prose'. This chapter consolidates my argument about the role of myth by introducing the category of the political subject so prevalent in the study's closing chapters. Finally, it argues that the resources Badiou offers to contemporary understandings of the relation between philosophy and the poem are bound to his maintenance of the political subject as an active agent. Chapter 3 works to unfold the movement of Badiou's political subject by returning to Paul Celan's poem 'Anabasis'. It argues that, for Badiou's philosophy, Celan is central in anticipating novel conceptions of the political subject pushing beyond the historical bounds of the Holocaust and, importantly, beyond Heideggerian complicities in National Socialism. This chapter emphasizes the processual nature of the Badiouian political subject and stresses its resistance towards prevailing conceptions of subjectivity bound to particular regimes of identification. Chapter 4 extends this discussion of philosophy, poem and the subject by presenting a comparative analysis of

Badiou and Theodor Adorno's respective readings of Samuel Beckett. It argues that Badiou's focus on the affirmation of the subject of love in Beckett's work is especially significant in moving beyond, in philosophy, the impact of the Holocaust on subjectivity. It also argues that Badiou's adoption of Beckett's mistrust of language in any thinking of subjectivity capable of persisting into the twenty-first century comprises a significant departure from Lacanian psychoanalysis' understanding of sexual difference.

Finally, my conclusion argues broadly for the importance of Celan and Beckett to Badiou's project of conceptualizing a subject capable of moving beyond the historical strictures of the twentieth century into the twenty-first century. More specifically, the conclusion stresses the immanence of this new subject, its inner dynamism, closing a narrative woven throughout the book from the 'restrained intensity' of dance, through 'anabasis', to the fragile subject of 'the Two' of love. My conclusion concretizes the book's arguments in dialogue with Louise Burchill's recent work on Badiou and the emerging importance of 'Love', 'difference' and Lacoue-Labarthe to his project at large.

One of the challenges confronting Badiou's exegetes is his philosophy's systematic arrangement, in which each concept finds its life only by virtue of its imbrication with other terms of his system and with the system as a whole. Badiou's reader is unable to conceive of 'event', for example, without 'truths' or 'subject'; they are, in Hallward's words, 'aspects of a single process'.[19] This system poses difficult questions for any reader seeking both to pass through it and to demonstrate their results without reduction or confusion. Responding to such difficulties by eschewing, in part, the strictures of linear exegesis, this book pursues a single thread through Badiou's work, but unfolds the full content of the relevant conceptual innovations in his philosophy gradually, not only over the course of each chapter's development but across the entire study too. Each of the four chapters claims one or two taut philosophical fragments of Badiou's as its starting point: 'Celan completes Heidegger' and 'The modern poem harbours a central silence'; 'the poem's becoming-prose'; the subjective movement of 'anabasis'; and the 'latent poem' beneath Beckett's prose; and, it is hoped that the submission of these compactions to close scrutiny produces an in-depth, faithful and fresh reading of Badiou's philosophy, much of which deals with points in his writing that have received little to no critical attention. Despite this methodological difficulty, recurrent themes and ideas of course persist throughout – the process of 'subtraction', for example, as well as the key triumvirate of concepts in Badiou's philosophy, event, truth and subject – and these are lent some initial elaboration in the following prologue examining

Badiou's essay from *Handbook of Inaesthetics*, 'Dance as a Metaphor for Thought'. The essay has been offered little sustained attention, but it offers an excellent initial account of the imbrication of thought and the category of the subject in Badiou's work of the period immediately after *Being and Event*, and gives, in their most abstract form, the shapes of 'inaesthetics', 'thought', 'knowledge' and 'subtraction' that inform so many of the more concrete, particular investigations across this book's four chapters.

'This restrained intensity': Dance as a metaphor for thought

'Dance as a Metaphor for Thought' is the sixth essay in Badiou's collection, *Handbook of Inaesthetics* (1998/2005). Ostensibly a reading of dance in Friedrich Nietzsche's *Thus Spake Zarathustra*, 'Dance as a Metaphor for Thought' supplements Nietzsche's ideas concerning dance's *affirmative* potential with six 'principles of dance' extrapolated from Stéphane Mallarmé's essays, 'Ballets' and 'Another Dance Study'. In his initial reading of Nietzsche, Badiou conceives the subjective process immanent to dance as a 'restrained intensity'. Dance is thought here as an internally driven process that actively fights the demands of external verification, whether the strictures of choreography or the desirous excitability of the dancing body itself.

Badiou's 'Dance as a Metaphor for Thought' presents a localized encounter between philosophy, which Badiou refers to as 'my doctrine' (*HI*, 61), and the 'thought' that dance produces on its own terms. The model for such 'encounters' between philosophy and art is given in the epigraph to *Handbook of Inaesthetics*:

> By "inaesthetics" I understand a relation of philosophy to art that, maintaining that art is itself a producer of truths, makes no claim to turn art into an object for philosophy. Against aesthetic speculation, inaesthetics describes the strictly intraphilosophical effects produced by the independent existence of some works of art. (*HI*, n.p.)

The stakes of this 'inaesthetic' model are extrapolated and discussed at length throughout this book, but it would be imprudent not to provide here at least the shape of this relation, with which Badiou intends to reinvigorate philosophy's persistent attachment to art broadly thought. Seeking to overcome philosophy's appropriation of the artwork in the discourse known as 'aesthetics', as well as the blurring of the boundaries between philosophy and literature so prevalent in twentieth-century Continental thought from Blanchot and Heidegger onwards, Badiou emphasizes the 'local' nature of the working relation between philosophy and art, stressing the importance of reciprocity between the two: philosophy reads the thought produced in art, and is read back in turn, whereby 'intraphilosophical effects' are produced, the forced modulation of the concepts philosophy deploys.[20]

Badiou begins 'Dance as a Metaphor for Thought' in the language of Nietzsche's *Thus Spake Zarathustra*:

> Why does dance dawn on Nietzsche as a compulsory metaphor for thought? It is because dance is what opposes itself to Nietzsche-Zarathustra's great enemy, an enemy he designates as the 'Spirit of Gravity'. Dance is, first and foremost, the image of a thought subtracted from every spirit of heaviness. (*HI*, 57)

From the outset, Badiou divorces 'thought' from the realm of 'objects' and 'objectivity'. Dance provides an image of thought to oppose the sphere in which gravity exerts its force, grounding its objects, lending them weight. Implicit in this 'subtraction' of thought from 'every spirit of heaviness' lies a corresponding shift from thought's apprehension of 'things in the world', bearing what we might understand as 'knowledge' broadly construed, towards 'thought' as a process that interrupts knowledge's organization.[21] More simply, thought impinges upon what is already known, the latter unable to account for the former. There is a sense in which thought is isolated from the world it intervenes in, opening a space beyond knowledge's bounds.

However, dance is initially unable to isolate itself in this way. Badiou continues, 'it is important to register the *other* images of this subtraction, for they inscribe dance into a compact metaphorical network' (*HI*, 57). Reading Nietzsche, Badiou claims 'metaphorical connections' between dance and 'the bird', and more generally, 'the image of flight', as well as 'the child', 'the fountain' and 'the air' (*HI*, 58). Dance is not simply inscribed within this series of images but arises from the network as a process able to actively 'work on' those images to which it is metaphorically linked; dance is the active subject of Badiou's first sentence – 'Dance *dawns on* Nietzsche' (*HI*, 57). In Badiou's reading of Nietzsche, then, we find that 'there is a germination, or a dancing birth, of what we would call the bird in the body'; that 'dance, which is both bird and flight, is also everything that the infant designates'; that 'dance is innocence, because it is a body before the body'; that 'the dancing body [like the fountain] is always leaping, out of the ground, out of itself'; and finally, that 'in dance, the earth is thought as if it were endowed with a constant airing' (*HI*, 57–58). Dance carries the images of the series within itself, 'traversing' them in the process, recapitulating them, reworking them.

Badiou's claim is that the moment of dance, that is, dancing itself, does 'subtractive' work. Dance articulates what is essential to each image of the series, so that, for example, beneath the potential 'mawkishness' of the series (potentially like a 'childish tale', Badiou writes), the affirmative, decisive import of 'innocence', 'birth' or 'flight', unfolds through the dancing body. Evolving this conception of dance as an active, transformative process, Badiou writes:

> Dance lends a figure to the traversal of innocence by power. It manifests the secret virulence of what initially appeared as fountain, bird, child-hood. In actual fact, what justifies the identification of dance as the metaphor for thought is Nietzsche's conviction that thought is an *intensification*. (*HI*, 58)

One important aspect of dance's 'intensification' is its ability to manifest the 'secret virulence' of the images discussed above. However, what 'intensification' 'primarily opposes', for Badiou, is 'the thesis according to which thought is a principle whose mode of realization is external'. Just as thought must impinge upon knowledge, dance must resist by its own immanence the structures that would lay claim to its efficient transmission: 'Dance is like a circle in space, but a circle that is its own principle, a circle that is not drawn from the outside, but rather draws itself' (*HI*, 58).

The main structure of external verification that would threaten dance's 'immanent intensification' is choreography, and dance's main site of resistance to choreography is of course the dancing body itself. The relation of metaphor between dance and thought, Badiou explains, 'works only if we put aside every representation of dance that depicts it as an external constraint imposed upon a supple body or as a gymnastics of a dancing body controlled from the outside'. Representations of dance that seek its depiction impose themselves upon an otherwise immanent, internally driven *presentation* of the dancing body. Badiou reveals the broadly political implications of dance's relation to thought at this point: the body which submits to external restraints finds its archetype in what Badiou calls the 'servile and sonorous body' of the (specifically German) military parade, following Nietzsche's 'bad German', his 'Obedience and long legs'. The dancing body is not a resonant body to be sounded from the outside but a light, singular body of resistance. The negative imperatives for dance as a metaphor for thought then include its resistance to any presentation of a body relying on external verification. However, as it stands, this provides little help in understanding dance's 'affirmative' capacity. Any internally dynamic process of intensification must surely present itself as an investigation, a procedure. That is, dance cannot remain still; there must be conflicts and tensions by which dance (conceived as a process) derives its energy. Following Nietzsche, Badiou addresses this question by introducing 'the theme of mobility': 'What Nietzsche sees in dance ... is the theme of a mobility that is firmly fastened to itself, a mobility that is not inscribed within an external determination, but instead moves without detaching itself from its own centre.' Crucially, Badiou continues, 'this mobility is not imposed, it unfolds as if it were an expansion of its own centre'. The figure of the 'bad German' above is borne by an external imposition that dance must resist, but the body mobilized by dance is never straightforwardly free of other impositions capable of manifesting themselves internally, impositions that would prevent such 'unfoldings' and 'expansions'.

For Badiou, the most important 'internal' imposition the dancing body needs to overcome is the fulfilment of quick desire, or put another way, the primacy of 'self' expression. In order to avoid this, dance's intensification requires restraint: more than the simple 'active becoming' of the body, dance must designate 'the capacity of bodily impulse not so much to be projected onto a space outside of itself, but rather to be caught up in an affirmative attraction *that restrains it*' (*HI*, 59). The most important 'internal' imposition to be overcome then is the bodily capacity for impulsiveness, for the cathartic purging of tension. Again, this is a negative imperative for dance: the freedom of the dancing body depends, counter-intuitively, on resisting any obedience to bodily impulse. Reading Nietzsche again, Badiou proclaims that 'for the unrestrained impulse – the bodily entreaty that is immediately obeyed and manifested – is precisely what Nietzsche calls *vulgarity*' (*HI*, 60). The vitalizing force of bodily impulse is not the site of freedom from oppression but merely a course resulting in submission to external constraints. But in the struggle between bodily impulse and its restraint, dance finds its own affirmative capacity, the disjunctive site of its own self-propulsion. Dance then becomes a 'restrained intensity': 'perhaps Nietzsche's most important insight', Badiou writes, is that 'beyond the exhibition of movements or the quickness of their external designs, dance is what testifies to the force of restraint at the heart of these movements' (*HI*, 59–60). For dance's lightness to persist, the impulses of the body need to be restrained. Submission to spontaneous impulse or cathartic purging hands the dancing body over to the regime of visibility its task is to oppose. Dance is not the 'liberated bodily impulse', Badiou concludes, but 'the bodily manifestation of the *disobedience* to an impulse' (*HI*, 60).

This opposition between intensity and restraint, an opposition which constitutes the true freedom or lightness of dance, is explored and evolved by Badiou in a series of disjunctive images:

> Dance, in its most extreme and virtuosic quickness, exhibits this hidden slowness that makes it so that what takes place is indiscernible from its own restraint. At the summit of its art, dance would therefore demonstrate the strange equivalence not only between quickness and slowness, but also between gesture and nongesture. It would indicate that, even though movement has taken place, this taking place is indistinguishable from a virtual nonplace. Dance is composed of gestures that, haunted by their own restraint, remain in some sense undecided. (*HI*, 61)

Dance produces and sustains a moment in which a 'strange equivalence' takes place between quickness and slowness, between gesture and non-gesture, between being and non-being. The assertion that in dance what takes place might be indiscernible from its own restraint highlights the ephemerality of the real moment of dance, the moment in which dance threatens its own appearance with disappearance, a moment in which being is threatened by non-being. This is perhaps the most forceful point in Badiou's exegesis, then, for what he reads from Nietzsche is that dance provides 'the metaphor for the fact that every genuine thought depends upon an event' (*HI*, 61). What he means by this is that dance, in its capacity as a metaphor for thought, must sustain 'an emergence that is indiscernible from its own disappearance', a sudden, chance supplement to the situation for which the latter cannot account.

There is an incisive question operating throughout 'Dance as a Metaphor for Thought' concerning the characteristics of the contemporary subject. Badiou is asking what material support is necessary in order to sustain this ephemeral, 'undecidable' element. Undecidability is described in *Being and Event* as an uncertainty about whether a supplement to a situation 'belongs' or not, asserting a radical lack of knowledge when it comes to embracing a novel rupture and the attendant risk of commitment to it: 'Undecidability is a fundamental attribute of the event: its belonging to the situation in which its eventual site is found is undecidable. The intervention consists in deciding at and from the standpoint of this undecidability' (*BE*, 525). The main question Badiou is asking, then, concerns the kind of body this undecidable requires. If we try and approach Badiou's ideas here concretely by considering dance insofar as we might witness it on stage or elsewhere, what is being emphasized is precisely the capacity for dance to produce in its witnesses the feeling of being co-opted into an ephemeral new present which is precariously affirmed and at every point threatens to collapse. There is a dancing body on stage which must sustain a tension, its 'restrained intensity', against its own impulses that with every movement run the risk of reducing the body either to a choreographed puppet or to a figure of saturated desire. The dancing body threatens to submit to external verification or to fall back on the cathartic expression of an individual self, the already visible in other words.

The material support on which dance depends then must aspire to be non-visible. Or more precisely, because it must be visible – must appear on stage – it must depict as close to nothing as possible. For Badiou, the 'dancing body' is subtracted towards a 'thought-body' that 'depicts nothing' in order to ensure that the undecidable it supports be sustained. We move then from the individual body, the body of the dancer, as well as its knowledge of the dance danced, or from the body's expression of its interiority, towards the fragile appearance of interiority itself in the thought-body. For Badiou, 'the dancing body does not express any kind of interiority. Entirely on the surface, as a visibly restrained intensity, it is itself interiority' (*HI*, 64).

Dance provides a compulsory metaphor for thought, in Badiou's words, because in the dancing body it presents and sustains the undecidable. By doing so, it ruptures the structures of external verification – choreography, most obviously, but also the dancer's knowledge of the dance, as well as the dancer's individual identity and concomitant self-expression. For Badiou, event, thought and subject are drawn together in dance. But, sustaining an undecidable element requires a material support, a body (or 'subject') subtracted from knowledge and identity, orientating itself towards the appearance of something singular and universal. It is important in this regard that the subject does not precede the event, then; rather, the subject is only able to compose itself following an event and insofar as it draws out this event's consequences.

1

Silence Being Thought

Paul Celan's ineloquence

In an endnote to *Logics of Worlds* (2006/2009), Alain Badiou declares his philosophical debts to Samuel Beckett and Stéphane Mallarmé. He asserts that two concepts fundamental to his philosophy – 'generic truth' and 'subtractive ontology', respectively – continue to be shifted, modified, 'sharpened' by his readings of these writers; Badiou's philosophy, he claims, is 'under condition' of Beckett's prose and Mallarmé's poetry. Further, without irony, Badiou declares that understanding the 'stories' produced by Beckett's late prose work *How It Is* and Mallarmé's poem 'A la nue accablante tu ... ' is 'perhaps the only goal of [his] philosophy'.[1] Badiou's writings on these two figures comprise a book-length collection, published in English as *On Beckett*, and a sustained engagement with Mallarmé spread out over the course of thirty years, from *Theory of the Subject* (1982/2009) to *Being and Event* (1988/2005) and the books of the 1990s that would further elaborate its central claims, especially *Handbook of Inaesthetics* (1998/2005), and then throughout the philosophical shift marked by *Logics of Worlds* (2007/2010) and *Second Manifesto for Philosophy* (2009/2011). In stark contrast, the page-time afforded to the German-Jewish poet Paul Celan over this writing period consists of about twenty pages, disparately placed among ten or so publications. And, this is to be further contrasted with the time dedicated to Celan by certain of Badiou's philosophical contemporaries, most notably Jacques Derrida, both in his posthumously published *Sovereignties in Question: The Poetics of Paul Celan* and at a distance through his friendship with Celan's close friend and interpreter Peter Szondi.[2] As well, Philippe Lacoue-Labarthe has dedicated a book, *Poetry as Experience*, to Celan and his strained relationship with Heidegger.[3] Badiou's relatively modest engagement with Celan is not in proportion to the overall importance of his poetry to Badiou's project at large, especially when they are used as interface with which to open up the complexities of Badiou's departure from Heideggerian thinking. Badiou's most thorough investigations of Celan's poetry take place in *Handbook of Inaesthetics* (1998/2005) and *The Century* (2005/2007). It is more useful to start, however, with the importance afforded to Celan in *Being and Event*'s complementary treatise, Badiou's *Manifesto for Philosophy* (1989/1999). One of Badiou's most provocative claims therein is that, following Hegel, the willingness of philosophy to relinquish its independence to the imperatives of science or politics, or in Peter Hallward's words, philosophy's preoccupation with 'the sterile hypotheses of scientific positivism and historical materialism',[4] gave rise to an 'Age of Poets' in which poetry was burdened with an ostensibly philosophical task. For Badiou, the Age of Poets is a philosophical category pertaining to a specific 'epoch', stretching from Stéphane Mallarmé to Paul Celan, for which 'poetic saying not only constitutes a form of thought and instructs a truth, but also finds itself constrained to *think this thought*'.[5] A moribund philosophy finds its central theses concerning being, truth and subject outsourced, then, to a specific poetic enterprise engaged in the reflexive interrogation of its own thinking. For Badiou, this operation, by which philosophy settles itself within the bounds of the poem, is termed a 'suture': philosophy stiches itself to, or perhaps within, the poem.

Beneath these claims lies an important theory concerning how philosophy relates to, broadly speaking, that which is not philosophy. Oriented by the desire to restore the question of 'Truth' to the centre of philosophical endeavour, Badiou insists that, far from having 'truths' of its own with which to work, philosophy 'thinks' the truths produced by its 'conditions', of which there are four: love, science, art and politics. For Badiou, an adequately contemporary philosophy must be able to think its own time, by engaging not only the singular instances of truth produced by its conditions but also their 'compossibility', or how the truths produced by local experiments in emancipatory politics might interact with those borne by innovations in formal mathematics, or those produced in poetry or theatre with psychoanalytic accounts of love, for example. When Badiou claims that philosophy following Hegel has subsumed itself to science or politics, then, he is gesturing towards, for example, the elevation of scientific knowledge in nineteenth-century scientific positivism and its legacy in contemporary Analytic philosophy from Gottlob Frege and Bertrand Russell to Rudolf Carnap and Willard Van Orman Quine or the exclusive relation between philosophy and politics expressed during the development of orthodox Marxism from Marx through to György Lukács and Bertolt Brecht. Badiou's claim is that the danger of these intimacies between philosophy and either one of its conditions is its confinement of 'truth' to the chosen productive discourse. This is detrimental both to the other conditions, whose own productions of what philosophy would call 'truth' are passed over, and philosophy itself, which gives up its autonomy, or its ability to learn from and traverse multiple fields of thought.

The claim of any 'sutured' philosophy is that 'truth' may only arise within the condition it binds itself to. In its 'sutures' to politics and science, philosophy relinquishes its vocation, but for Badiou, it is the poem that then takes on the role of philosophical thinking. Although one of the desires central to Badiou's own philosophical intervention is to ensure that philosophy is restored, as he has it, to its role as the 'thinker' of the compossibility of truths produced elsewhere, the 'Age of Poets' is still an 'epoch' of significant importance. Badiou's 'Age of Poets', in which poetry does philosophical work, is anticipated by Friedrich Hölderlin, begins in earnest in the work of Stéphane Mallarmé and Arthur Rimbaud and is then borne by Georg Trakl, Osip Mandelstam and Fernando Pessoa, before finishing, crucially, with Paul Celan. Against philosophical assertions of a fundamental consistency, whether via scientific method or in the teleological promise of 'History', these poets, for Badiou, understood the essential disorientation and 'inconsistency' of their time:

> The fact is that there really was an *Age of Poets*, in the time of the sutured escheat of philosophers. There was a time between Hölderlin and Paul Celan when the quavering sense of what that time itself was, the most open approach to the question of Being, the space of compossibility least caught-up in brutal sutures and the most informed formulation of modern Man's experience were all unsealed and possessed by the poem. A time when the enigma of Time was caught up in the enigma of the poetic metaphor, wherein the process of unbinding was itself bound within the 'like' of the image. An entire epoch was represented in short philosophies as a consistent and especially *oriented* one. There was progress, the sense of History, the millenarian foundation, the approach of another world and other men. But the real of this epoch was on the contrary inconsistency and disorientation. Poetry alone, or at least "metaphysical" poetry, the most concentrated poetry, the most intellectually strained poetry, the most obscure also, designated and articulated this essential disorientation.[6]

For Badiou, these poets 'submitted to a kind of intellectual pressure' to take on the role of philosophy itself (i.e. devoid of its 'suturing' to science or politics), and their work is 'recognizable as a work of thought ... at the very locus where philosophy falters, a locus of language wherein a proposition about being and about time is enacted' (*MP*, 69). Not only this, such poetry '[constructs] the space of thinking which defines philosophy'. Badiou's general claim concerning Paul Celan, then, is that his poetry 'thinks' (like those of the other figures in this

Age of Poets) and that this poetic thought, through 'the art of binding Word and experience', is guided by 'the question of Being', by 'the real of the epoch'. However, a further claim specific to Celan's poetry is that it closes or ends the Age of Poets, and this is a claim inextricably bound to the philosophy of Martin Heidegger: for Badiou, indeed, Celan's poetry 'completes Heidegger'(*MP*, 77).

Badiou admits that Heidegger was successful in 'philosophically *touching* an unnoticed point of thought detained in poetic language'. Yet, in order to go beyond the 'power of Heideggerian philosophy', Badiou claims, it is imperative to reconsider the 'couple formed by the saying of poets and the thought of thinkers' profuse in Heidegger (*C*, 36). That is, following a period of near-exclusive intimacy between poetry and thought (or philosophy, as Badiou would insist), it is once more necessary to radically distinguish their respective discourses; there is to be an irreducibility between poetic thought and its subsequent thinking in philosophy. It seems clear that, for Badiou, the poetry of Celan embodies this movement through and beyond Heidegger, both in its departure from the '*in*distinction' between the 'poet' and the 'thinker' and in its ultimately disjunctive relation to the exploration of being, pervasive throughout the Age of Poets. Badiou's argument is that the poet/thinker couple is broken by Celan, and in the process of this break the site in which being may be thought is recast beyond Heidegger's demands for poetry. For Badiou, 'the fundamental criticism of Heidegger can only be the following one: the Age of Poets is completed, it is *also* necessary to de-suture philosophy from its poetic condition' (*MP*, 74).

It is worth noting at this point a second temporalizing claim made in Badiou's *The Century*. Badiou understands Celan to be the last to fulfil the poetic task of 'naming the century' the 'short century preceding the Restoration of the last twenty years'.[7] This claim is inextricable from Celan's attempt to construct a poetics capable of engaging with the Holocaust. Celan's engagement with Heidegger, a member of the Nazi party between 1933 and 1945, appears peculiar and compelling in light of this poetic task especially given their protracted relationship, manifest in their long-term correspondence, in Celan's serious theoretical and practical engagement with Heidegger's thought, and finally in their meeting at Todtnauberg in 1967, but it is also helpful when interrogating Badiou's claim that Celan's poetry heralds a fundamental departure from Heidegger's dictates for thought. Badiou's assertion here is of no small importance with regard to his own philosophy too, for Celan marks not only the saturation of Heidegger's thought but also the gateway into Badiou's philosophical break with much that precedes him.

A primarily philosophical encounter with Celan's poetry cannot be exercised without caution, for it threatens to mirror the flippant responses his poetry garnered when it first came to prominence in Germany and France. For a philosopher like Badiou, unafraid to posit 'strong' philosophical readings of the artists he privileges, this is a pressing concern,[8] not least due to the potential resonance of any encounter between philosophy and poetry with Martin Heidegger's notorious readings of Friedrich Hölderlin: poetry is made into the aesthetic vehicle for the grand political inauguration of a specifically 'German' people's hitherto deferred emergence into history – a subject to which this book returns in some depth in Chapters 2 and 3. Describing the German reception of Paul Celan's work in the 1950s, John Felstiner argues that all too often a blind eye was turned towards the trauma and loss at the heart of Celan's poetry, critics choosing to emphasize instead his 'surrealism' or his 'special gift for imagery', 'as if', Felstiner argues, Celan were not 'a Chagall but an effete Whistler', not an artist whose work is grounded in historical trauma but an artist purveying 'art for art's sake'. Felstiner writes that, in the Hamburg journal *Die Zeit*, for instance, 'a German friend of Celan's was sympathetic yet made no mention of "Todesfuge" or the realities conditioning the poetry – loss, death, Jewishness'.[9] Badiou's claims that they produce a 'thought of being' aside, Celan's poems, however, despite this inextricability from concrete experiences of loss, of course address philosophical questions, not least in their rendering of a thorough, dedicated engagement with Heidegger's writings.

This chapter is oriented primarily by Badiou's assertion that 'Celan completes Heidegger' as well as by a broader philosophical attempt to understand the nuances of what Badiou terms the poem's 'thought of being'. But in what immediately follows, I want to give some of the coordinates of Badiou's engagement with Celan, starting with one of his two most in-depth readings of Celan's poetry from Badiou's collection of lectures *The Century*, including passages to which I will return at some length in Chapter 3 when discussing the particular subjective movement at stake in Badiou's encounter with Celan here. In *The Century*, Badiou extrapolates his understanding of some of the constituent parts of Celan's poetics from a comparative study of his poem 'Anabasis' (1963) and an earlier poem of the same name (from 1924) by the francophone poet Saint-John Perse.[10] There are several ways in which Badiou specifies the divergence in poetics across this forty-year span, and across languages, though at all times such difference is conditioned by their respective experiences of twentieth-century violence. Badiou presents, perhaps reductively, an essentially pre-Holocaust poetics in Perse, in which a 'disjunctive synthesis' of 'spiritual vacancy' and 'epic affirmation' sustains, in poetry, a bathetic encounter with early twentieth-century nihilism, understood by Badiou as a figure of the saturation of 'nineteenth century conditions' (*TC*, 84–85). It is with undisguised disdain, some of it self-deprecating given his own colonial background, that Badiou draws out details of Perse's childhood in Guadeloupe, as the white West-Indian son of plantation owners, followed by his six-year appointment as Secretary-General at the French Ministry of Foreign Affairs, as well as his self-imposed exile in 1940 to the United States. After this, claims Badiou, Perse becomes the heir to Valéry, the 'official poet of the Republic', a writer of state-sanctioned poems. Perse's biography is intended to reveal a certain orientation within language towards the violent innovations in political subjectivity emerging primarily out of Russia from 1917 onwards; he is able, in Badiou's words, to 'clearly perceive' 'the century's epic dimension', but only 'from the recesses of his gilded armchair in a waning republic'.

For Badiou, Perse's poetry represents what is already deemed to exist with a verbose eloquence adequate to the engorged and self-satisfied persistence of 'the era of tranquil imperialism' (*TC*, 85). Though Perse recognizes the century's 'epic' dimension, the qualitative magnitude of the century is imbricated in his work only with the persistence of this imperialist 'benevolence' or of 'what already is'. In Badiou's contemporaneous 'Third Sketch of a Manifesto for Affirmationist Art' (2003), his fifteenth axiom for 'affirmationist' art states, contra Perse, that 'it is better to do nothing than work formally toward making visible what the West declares to exist'.[11] Badiou's claim is that Perse's poetry reinforces what is already deemed visible and is guilty of nihilism in its lack of penetrative critique, its refusal to grant existence to anything beyond what is already deemed to be. Badiou picks out a tiny fragment from Perse's 'Anabasis' to illustrate his point, in which already existing 'roads of the world' are to be followed, already existing 'signs of the earth' course with authoritative power (*TC*, 86). Strawman or no, Badiou declares that Perse 'will praise precisely what there is precisely to the extent that it is' (*TC*, 85) and this corresponds to a particular conception of anabasis, a movement of nihilistic force in the form of the epic. Anticipating the contrast made with Celan's poetics, Badiou at this stage is far more interested by poetry which attempts to approach precisely what is 'not-yet', a poetry that, from within language, seeks the mute points afforded no being, revealing the contingency of the whole.[12] The imperative Badiou reads in Perse's work, then, 'may your force be nihilistic, but your form epic', anticipates the almost exact reversal of this imperative in Celan's poetry, which, we may suppose, for Badiou, carries an affirmative force (especially in the figure of the subject it produces which I investigate in Chapter 3), but in a form that renounces the grandeur we might understandably associate with 'epic' and its role as the support for the historical becoming of a people.

Badiou explores these divergent approaches to poetic language, and its various knotted relations to state power, truth and subjectivity, through the concept of 'eloquence', which he defines, harnessing language invoking settler colonialism, as 'the conviction that language is endowed with resources and cadences that demand to be exploited'. Badiou seeks to correlate 'eloquence' – the opulence of Perse's language, the richness of its images, the 'affirmative', 'epic' grandeur of its form – with a kind of disengaged flippancy and a refusal to really interrogate the century's happenings, all of this bolstered by a prevailing trust towards language, wielded as the means of triumphantly representing what is already deemed visible by power. More broadly, this particular 'anabasis', the journey of which this epic poem provides the account, is, despite the prevalence of other symbolic and formal coherences in play, bound primarily to a seemingly militaristic, 'civilising' venture in central Asia.

To anticipate some of the shapes of subject formation I examine at length in the chapters that follow, what Badiou seems to find in Perse's 'Anabasis' is a movement of subjective development in which the subject determines itself via its militaristic movement through the 'foreign'. And this movement is accompanied and secured by the lyric abundance of a language that lays claim to everything around it. Badiou's argument is that the violence of the 'bare and cruel' twentieth century is only in the distance in Perse's 'Anabasis', just as, from the perspective of imperial subjects, colonial violence takes place at the edges of empire in the far distance. Perse's conception of the century's movement, for Badiou, 'prolongs an imperial dream whose horror is distant and discreet': that is, the 'truth' of the century, even if 'bare and cruel', has no impact on Perse's conception of subjectivity, nor on the form his poetry takes (*TC*, 89). Perse's attempt to think his own time is bound to a nineteenth-century imperial dream. Badiou's key point, then, is that Celan's own 'Anabasis' is forged in a defiant engagement with the violence of the 1930s and 1940s, after which the century 'was forced to change the *direction* of its movement, as well as the words that would articulate it' (*TC*, 90). The epic form of Perse's poem, and the 'spiritual vacancy' at its core, its inability to reckon with the specific desires and specific violences of the early twentieth century, and its 'epic' subjectivity represent for Badiou, especially when reading Perse in retrospect via Celan, an anachronistic, ahistorical propagation of imperialist myth.

At this point it is worth noting the implied, perhaps naive, relationship between ontology and epistemology that this attitude towards language assumes, for language by this schema is deemed capable of representing everything: the fields of ontology and epistemology – what is, or what pertains to being, and what is knowable – are drawn into exclusive relation.[13] Badiou is able to place the question of language's relation to being, cast in terms of language's capacity to approach the 'truth of the century' in this case, under the imperative to push against the boundaries of experience, to move into an 'outside' not yet given to experience. But Badiou's second claim regarding language's relation to this 'truth' is that 'the truth of the century is linguistically impassable' as long as one remains on the schema of 'eloquence'; truth cannot be passed through as long as the poetic imperative to deploy language's abundant resources continues.

Badiou finds Celan far more capable of approaching this 'truth' of the century in concordance with a rejection of the 'eloquence' employed by Perse. Though, for Badiou, Perse produces an 'image of the century' that 'conforms' to the 'imperative' that 'your force be nihilistic, but your form epic', the subsequent events of the 1930s and 1940s require radical, formal innovations adequate to a new situation, a new conception of the century's 'movement' (*TC*, 85). Language's abundance of resources, infinite capacity for ornamentation and means of reflexive glorification all, as Badiou has it, demand to be exploited under this 'eloquent' conception of poetic language. Against 'eloquence', then, for Badiou, Celan's poetics is driven instead by experience of the century's 'hard core': Badiou argues consistently that Celan demonstrates poetry to still be possible after the Holocaust, but also that poetic 'eloquence' is 'obscene' (*TC*, 89). The imperative Celan seems to follow in the wake of the Holocaust according to Badiou and, to differing degrees, many of his precedents and contemporaries, is to craft poems that deny eloquence under immense historical pressure, in order that the poem may once again think its own time. And, this is to dispel the implicit attitudes concerning the ontology/epistemology couple inherent to 'eloquent' poetry. Language is deemed incapable of approaching the truth of the century as long as it remains the vehicle for the triumphant rendering and imaging of reality. We find in Celan then a lapidary carving of language, a cold sparseness in which layers of language are pared away towards a silent kernel. 'Anabasis', for example, to anticipate the more protracted reading of this poem I undertake in Chapter 3, comprises many formal experiments familiar to readers of Celan's poems from the late 1950s onwards, for example, hyphened neologisms and line-breaks across hyphens that reach their apex in the third strophe, stretched as if on a rack, line and image disintegrating into polyglottal stutter:

Then:
buoys,
espalier of sorrow-buoys
with those
breath reflexes leaping and
lovely for seconds only -: light-
bellsounds (dum-
dun-, un-,
unde suspirat
cor),
re-
leased, re-
deemed, ours.[14]

The verbose triumphalism of Perse's poetry is eschewed by Celan in favour of the crystalline and paring effects of syntax and prosody, his poetry always orientated by contraction, reduction and the splintered energy of the broken line, as well as by a broader commitment to plumbing the depths of the German language via paronomasia; near or exact homophones amass at the poem's edges, lending each of these sustained, honed compactions of language a field of resonance beyond its final iteration on the page.

Before some comments concerning this shift in emphasis from eloquence to sparseness, compaction and splintering, from trust of language to suspicion, some conclusive insights on the relation between poetic language and truth are to be found in Badiou's 1993 lecture 'Language, Thought, Poetry' (a reference to Heidegger's collection *Poetry, Language, Thought*) collected in *Theoretical Writings*. Badiou begins his lecture by asserting, in a familiar argument, poetry's autonomy, its status as an 'intransigent exercise', defiant in the face of the contemporary demand for 'the simple message'. Poetic language, the declaration made on the page, opposes itself to the instrumental language of communication or to language in its functional, instrumental capacity: 'The poem does not consist in communication. The poem has nothing to communicate. It is only a saying, a declaration that draws authority from itself alone.'[15] For Badiou, not only does the poem fail to communicate, as a 'unique fragment of speech subtracted from universal reporting' (*TW*, 241);[16] it also refuses to enter into circulation, a correlate of which is the quest in poetry for what lies beyond the language of knowledge, exemplified for Badiou in Celan's defiant rejection of eloquence in his attempt to confront the century's 'dark core'.

Running parallel to this commitment to escaping the functional or instrumental languages of knowledge, Badiou also demonstrates a preoccupation with the relation between poetic language and 'silence', which offers further scope to relate his broad philosophical commitments, even if here detailed thus far in necessarily schematic form, to Paul Celan's poetics. Before returning to Celan to interrogate this seemingly obscure movement towards silence, Badiou offers some comments in 'Language, Thought, Poetry' that serve as a useful preface. The modern poem, emanating from its privileged site as a thing of language apart from any mediation, is described by Badiou as 'folded and reserved'. However, it also 'harbours a central silence' (*TW*, 240). He continues:

> The poem says the opposite of what Wittgenstein says about silence. It says: 'This thing that cannot be spoken of in the language of consensus; I create silence in order to say it. I isolate this speech from the world.' (*TW*, 240)

Far from 'passing over' that which cannot be spoken, the poem creates silence as a means of interrupting communication's noisy carousel across saturated networks. This idea of the modern poem's 'central silence' is absolutely fundamental to Badiou's systematic exposition of the 'inaesthetic' relation between the poem and philosophy for it marks the recession of the object from language, the subtraction of being from presence and the main point of Badiou's departure from Heidegger's ontology, the subject of the next section of this book. For now, though, I want to further explore Celan's poetics, partly to gauge the sensitivity of Badiou's reading, but also to both consolidate and evolve the intricacies of the relations between poetic language, ineloquence and silence before moving into a more overtly philosophical register.

The language of 'consensus' is especially pertinent to Celan's poetics, for the German language he wielded was the language of the oppressor. Celan, however, occupied a peculiar position within the German language, having grown up in Czernowitz, Romania, speaking Romanian, Yiddish and German. Occupied by the Soviets in 1940, at which point Celan started translating from Russian, Czernowitz was then reclaimed by German and Romanian forces and its Jewish population forced into ghettos. Celan continued his studies in German once he moved to Paris in 1948 and then became a lecturer in German literature in 1958.[17] In his comparative study *Paul Celan & Martin Heidegger*, James K. Lyon attests to Celan's 'unconventional' spoken German, 'out of step with current usage'. He also cites Celan's childhood friend Ilana Shmueli who claimed that 'the German of Czernowitz [Celan's birthplace] had a bad reputation because of its twisted linguistic structures, its odd vocabulary, and curious turns of speech'.[18] Celan approaches spoken German as his 'mother tongue', but also from a point of exile outwith the inherited language. More importantly, in Celan's work there is also the articulation of the 'inexpressibility' of the Holocaust through the creation of silence. Celan's engagement with silence is, broadly, twofold. Firstly, he evokes and interrogates those silences bound to German language use specifically, of the victims of the Holocaust who 'dig a grave in the breezes', for example, and others who bore witness to those events.[19] Secondly, there is the silence accompanying language per se, the 'central silence' one approaches in order to escape the din of communication, the 'ambient cacophony'. Celan's poetics oppose, in Badiou's words, 'the obscenity of "all seeing" and "all saying" – of showing, sounding out and commenting everything' (*TW*, 241). In 'The Meridian' speech, given by Celan on receipt of the Georg Büchner Prize in 1960, he speaks of Büchner's own 'terrifying silence' in contrast to Lucile's catastrophic declaration 'Long live the king' from Büchner's play *Danton's Death*: 'It is a terrifying silence', he writes, 'It takes his – and our – breath and words away. Poetry is perhaps this: an *Atemwende*, a turning of our breath.'[20] Celan's poetry, as well as comprising a formal response to the impact of the Holocaust, also seeks an ostensibly philosophical questioning concerning the relations between language and meaning, subjectivity and being, in what Lacoue-Labarthe, following Adorno, calls the 'post-Auschwitz era', during which 'murder is the first thing to count on, and elimination the surest means of identification'.[21]

In his analysis of Celan's 'With a Changing Key' ('*Mit Wechseldndem Schlüssel*') from *Von Schwelle Zu Schwelle* (1955), James K. Lyon traces the explicit influence of Martin Heidegger in Celan's poems by analysing Celan's personal library of Heidegger's philosophical works. Lyon is keen to emphasize that directly prior to the writing of this poem in 1953, Celan was embroiled in intensive reading of both Heidegger's *Wrong Paths* and his *A Letter on Humanism*.[22] In both of these works, language is consistently referred to as the 'house' or the 'temple of being', and it is this image that figures in Celan's poem from the same year, the first three lines of which, in Michael Hamburger's translation, read as follows:

With a variable key
you unlock the house in which
drifts the snow of that left unspoken.

Mit wechselndem Schlüsel
schließt du das Haus auf, darin
der Schnee des Verschwiegenen treibt.[23]

In Hamburger's translation, it is the 'snow of that left unspoken' that drifts (and has drifted) inside the house. John Felstiner's rendering, however, is 'the snow of what's silenced'.[24] The contrast between translations is important, for though it must be acknowledged that Celan's poetry is oriented by concrete experiences of loss – 'snow', as Felstiner points out, may be indexed to Celan's mother's death, for example[25] – the contrast brings much to bear on the relation of being to language as well. In German, 'Verschwiegenen' is formed by suffixing the adjective *verschwiegen* with *-en* to make a noun. This adjective typically means 'discrete' or 'secret' in English, though it pertains to speech too, as 'tight-lipped', for example. The suffix materializes the content of the adjective, forming a noun. By attesting to the 'snow of what's silenced', Felstiner closes off this silence to questions that go beyond real, concrete loss, which is also to threaten the poem's philosophical engagement with Heidegger; 'unspoken', in the Hamburger translation, offers a greater openness towards that which escapes language's bounds. The poet's key unlocks the house of language, in which, from outside, silence's snow drifts. This silence from outside language provides a negative mark of being within language. Two silences marking being are left: one within, the other outside.

Both silences are invoked and evolved in Celan's later poem 'Below' ('Unten') from *Sprachgitter* (1959), of which the first strophe, again in Michael Hamburger's translation, reads:

Led home into oblivion
the sociable talk of
our slow eyes.

Heimgeführt ins Vergessen
das Gast-Gespräch unsrer
langsamen Augen.[26]

'Below' claims that language's inherited condition is the oblivion or forgetting (*Vergessen*) of its 'home'. The migration from 'home' to 'oblivion' (in the German, the poem begins with 'Heim … ') finds its fleeting figuration in the localized 'sociable talk of/our slow eyes'.[27] The idea that this exchange is soon to depart is invited by the familiar rendering of 'Gast' in English as 'guest'; 'sociable talk' then becomes a fleeting discursive intervention upon the blankness of oblivion. But this conversation also serves to encapsulate the movement from home to homelessness, for, in order to present itself as guest (*Gast-Gespräch*), this 'sociable talk' must construct and pass through the bounds of a home, however ephemeral. The conversation is a local figure of the movement towards homelessness, raised upon the background of both its condition and destination, before receding into these latter with inevitability. The seeming inexorability of home's recession in each local instance of 'sociable talk' feels rhythmically present too in the soft, falling cadence of 'langsamen Augen', the repeated 'a' sounds in langsamen rounded out and stunted by their recapitulation in the 'au' of 'Augen', conjured somewhat in English by the slow, spondaic finality of 'slow eyes'.

What is important here is that 'Unten' marks the condition of language: that there is no home, that home is now oblivion and that every instance of light chatter, as the concrete sharing of a language without ground, consolidates this move. The poem scrutinizes the 'our' too: 'unsrer' is tethered to 'langsamen', in which, beneath the slowness, we hear the *lager* of the concentration camps. Taken in isolation, perhaps this is an overreach, but the resonance of *lager* is consolidated in the poem's final strophe by 'angelagert' ('heaped up') – in turn a compacted evolution of 'langsamen Augen'. There is the reminder here that this 'our' is utterly contingent, and that, as an invocation of identity, during the Holocaust at least, its construction depends upon the eradication of those whom it excludes.

The power of speech to mean wilts under the pressure of the inexpressible. As language falls away in the second strophe, 'eyes' find their ultimate destination in the mute dots on the face of each 'dayblind' die:

> Led now, syllable after syllable, shared
> out among the dayblind dice, for which
> the playing hand reaches out, large,
> awakening.

The rudiments of language are disintegrating, falling back into the dark revealing nothing, unless activated by chance, awoken by 'the playing hand'. They are 'led' there, dissected and distributed syllable by syllable 'now'. But the 'now' is ambiguous: the poem responds to its own material, the 'now' of the poem's writing, but also to the historically situated, post-Holocaust experience of inherited language. The image of each syllable being led 'home' one after the other (the invocation of home in the source word for 'led now', 'Heimgeführt' is only repeated in the original German) also ensures the disintegration of language be thought alongside the deployment of technical apparatuses during the Holocaust. A language returning 'home' only to find 'oblivion' must seek an outside point beyond language from which the prospect of a return from exile might be thinkable. Celan's poem asks what becomes of language when the possibility of 'dwelling' within is foreclosed, when the homeland upon which language embarks is abyssal, forgotten.

Following the 'our' ('unsrer') of the opening strophe, the third submits language to the question of alterity, of an 'I' speaking to a 'you':

And the too much of my speaking:
heaped up round the little
crystal dressed in the style of your silence.

Following the imperatives laid for poetic language, it is interesting that specifically 'speaking' fails here. The 'too much of my speaking' reflects perhaps the 'obscenity of "all-seeing" and "all-saying"' offered by Badiou in 'Language, Thought, Poetry'. This excess of speech from an 'I' attempting somehow to approach the other falls around the 'little / crystal dressed in the style of your silence', muffling it, preventing its silence from 'speaking'. Fragments of speech fall around this crystal like dead leaves that elide its light, preventing it from being seen, from 'showing' itself to 'our eyes'. The 'dressing' of this crystal only occurs following 'the too much of my speaking' always already heaped against it; it is this 'too much' which obscures. It is also worth noting that 'too much' is subsumed under 'my speaking' as if speech itself is conditioned by an excess, saturated from within. The task of the poet is to 'undress' this crystal, shrouded in saturated spoken language, the language of communication and the language of the oppressor. In line with Badiou's imperatives for modern poetry to 'harbour a central silence' and for poetic language to oppose itself to 'ambient cacophony', Celan in 'Below' calls for this crystal's undressing, guided by the disintegration of speech, by the condition of language following the erasure of 'home'; Celan prunes and cuts towards a silent point outside, but also towards a silent other. It is telling that in Heidegger's 'What Is Metaphysics?', despite the assertion that 'anxiety reveals the nothing', we find that 'in the malaise of anxiety we often try to shatter the vacant stillness with compulsive talk'.[28] Speech or chatter is a natural response to the anxiety caused by the nothing, a response that both hides the presence of the nothing but also 'proves' its existence.

Celan's poetry does not just render 'eloquent' poetry obscene; it invites us to make a critical conclusion about language, specifically about how much can be said or 'shown'. Following Celan's experiences of the Holocaust a mute point in language is nominated, something beyond it that only a non-instrumental language might begin to approach; to paraphrase Badiou's words above, a silence must be created in order to speak what cannot be said. There is this silence existing alongside language then as the absent faces of a cube might exist alongside our perception of it, a silence that exists on the plane of language. But there is also the assertion in Celan of a more foundational silence, language's 'home' beyond itself. In Celan's Meridian speech he speaks of certain expectations borne by the poem, 'to speak also on behalf of the strange ... *on behalf of the other – who knows, perhaps of an altogether other*'.[29] This seems to be another way of characterizing the two 'silences': 'an other', that particular which does not speak, and an 'altogether other', the grounding silence or nothingness with which the poem must engage, or the 'central silence' the poem must harbour. In seeking these others, the poem must '[hold] its ground on its own margin' and shows a 'strong tendency towards silence'.[30]

Celan's relationship with Heidegger's philosophy is complicated by the account Anthony Mellors offers in his *Late Modernist Poetics: From Pound to Prynne*. There, in a reading of Celan's 'The Meridian', Mellors claims that when Celan refers to poetry as *'einsam und unterwegs* ("lonely and on the way", *en route*)' he is making a clear allusion to 'Heidegger's pastoral lore of the path, the way ... to language and being.'[31] The poem, for Celan, 'takes us towards a clearing, to "an 'open' question 'without resolution', a question which points towards open, empty, free spaces – we have ventured far out"'.[32] However, for Mellors the word 'empty' allows the formulation of an important difference between Celan and Heidegger. 'Only the word "empty" in Celan's account', Mellors argues, 'keeps it from being identified with the positivity of Heidegger's "open"',[33] an idea consolidated by the resonance of 'unweg' beneath 'unterwegs', a negation of the path 'underway' ('unweg' may be glossed in English as 'unpath'). Across *unterwegs* we find the visual and sonic invocation of the 'unpath', *unweg*. Mellors invites a contrast between positive, that is, assertive, openness – 'Truth is the openness of beings' for Heidegger[34]– and a conception of poetic truth oriented instead by the negative and emptiness.[35] On the one hand we find beings unfolding into truth, into openness, and on the other, truth's alignment with open spaces divested of such content, empty spaces. It is in this difference, borne by the assertion of an empty space, that the departure Badiou makes from Heidegger, through Celan, may be anticipated. For, the emptiness to which Celan points is a seemingly negative space beyond the plane upon which Heidegger's considerations of being and language operate. Celan effects a radical subversion of the relation between language and being postulated by Heidegger, and Badiou moves beyond the territory upon which Heidegger operates, from a thought of being arising in poetic language to a thought of being able to arise in poetic language but escaping its strictures, testifying to an empty 'outside' beyond language.

An exegesis of these potentially obscure ideas stems naturally from a critical comparison of Heidegger and Badiou's respective approaches to ontology. An elementary way of characterizing their difference would be to state the primacy of language for the former and of mathematics for the latter, or to state that being and language share an especially intimate relationship in Heidegger, whereas for Badiou being qua being is radically 'subtracted' from knowledge and the language of its transmission. This sharp contrast in ontological approach has yet to show itself in the discussion, for effective exegesis has required Badiou's exploration of silence to be taken at his word, without excavating its full philosophical pertinence. The relatively recent publication of two translated essays of Badiou's on Wittgenstein, in *Wittgenstein's Antiphilosophy*, highlights the danger of foregoing such an excavation, however, for, perhaps surprisingly given the commentary so far, Badiou opposes his philosophical project to the privileging of the plane of silence and speech in philosophical writing. We may of course think here of certain twentieth-century philosophical preoccupations with, broadly, meaning, interpretation and text. When philosophy comes to pay too much heed to questions of the sayable and the unsayable, in Badiou's terms, it does so in the service of sophistry.[36]

In his introduction to *Wittgenstein's Antiphilosophy*, Bruno Bosteels returns to Badiou's collection, *Conditions*, in order to shed some light on the folly inherent to 'sophistic' thought:

> Modern sophists are those who, in the footsteps of the great Wittgenstein, maintain that thought is held to the following alternative: either effects of discourse, language games, or the silent indication, the pure 'showing' of that which is subtracted from the clutches of language. Sophists are those for whom the fundamental opposition is not between truth and error, or errancy, but between speech and silence, that is, between what can be said and what is impossible to say. Or again: between propositions endowed with sense and others devoid of it. (*WA*, 17)

Sophistry for Badiou operates entirely on the surface of language, both at the level of the proposition and at the level of discourse. Language, for the sophist, is hegemonic to the extent that any thought of being is consigned exclusively to its realm; what lies beyond language is deemed non-thought and devoid of sense. The sophistic approach to being or truth is then always directed by this previous assertion of language's primacy, and where language falters or falls silent, the sophist emphasizes that seemingly blank space as a non-thought to be passed over, in line with the final demand of Wittgenstein's *Tractatus*: 'What we cannot speak about we must pass over in silence.'[37]

Badiou is keen to set the early Wittgenstein's early thought apart from sophistry, however, by highlighting the role in this work of the extra-theoretical act through which the 'mystical element' beyond language might be 'shown'. Badiou cites section 6.522 of the *Tractatus* to this end: 'There are, indeed, things that cannot be put into words. They *make themselves manifest*. They are what is mystical' (*WA*, 80). The attempt to present non-thought via an extra-philosophical act, via an aesthetic 'showing' in Wittgenstein, is what sets the 'antiphilosopher' apart from the sophist. Badiou's figure of the 'antiphilosopher', represented also by Rousseau, Nietzsche and Lacan among others, straddles the gap between philosophy and sophistry, retaining the act by which the unspeakable is presented. Nonetheless, despite the aesthetic 'showing' of this mystical element, the absolute coupling of language and thought effected by sophistic and antiphilosophical thinking forces this element to languish in non-thought, to remain mystical beyond the bounds of sense; the act of 'showing' this element in Wittgenstein, for example, replaces the attempt to speak it, to make it rationally transmissible. In Badiou's reading of Wittgenstein, then, the latter places a boundary on thought and by correlation on philosophy, such that the excavation of what lies beyond language becomes a purely aesthetic concern. In Badiou's words, for the antiphilosopher Wittgenstein,

> It is thus a question of firmly establishing the laws of the sayable (of the thinkable), in order for the unsayable (the unthinkable, which is ultimately given only in the form of art) to be situated as the 'upper limit' of the sayable itself: 'Philosophy [that is, antiphilosophy] must set limits to what can be thought; and, in doing so, to what cannot be thought' (4.114). (*WA*, 80)

In stark contrast to this conception of the limits of philosophy, Badiou demands that philosophy speak what cannot be spoken – 'philosophy exists only to defend that the whereof one cannot speak is precisely what it sets out to say' – and this is both to place the remit of thought beyond the strictures of mere language games and to reclaim a conception of truth that is not contingent upon the propositional form and its verification (*MP*, 117). A key distinction between the philosopher and the antiphilosopher then concerns 'truth'. For the former, following Plato, 'truths have no sense whatsoever ... [they] make a "hole" in sense'. Whereas, for the latter, truths must in the first instance 'make sense' as propositions and then be verified according to the state of affairs they purport to describe; truth for the antiphilosopher is consigned to the realm of sense (*WA*, 117).

A twofold claim can now be made concerning Badiou's affirmation of a central silence harboured in modern poetry. Firstly, the 'modern' poem always already harbours and attests to something beyond its own capacity to speak. More, if the modern poem contains a 'thought of being' as Badiou declares, then this central silence is constitutive of that thought. Against philosophical sophistry, then, the second claim is that this silence, as a constituent element of the thought of being, marks what philosophy aims to speak: the unspeakable. Philosophy then, in order to speak the unspeakable, must have the capacity to think beyond the strictures of language. For Badiou, it is in mathematics that philosophy finds the resources to do this. The 'philosophical form', in Badiou's words, 'combines resources borrowed from those procedures of truth that are most clearly disjointed from sense (if "sense" means description of a state of affairs): mathematics ... and poetry' (WA, 117). Further, in Badiou's preface to the English translation of *Being and Event* he outlines his commitment to maintaining an approach to philosophy informed by both mathematics and poetry, in the wake of Plato, Descartes, Liebniz and Hegel: philosophy must know 'how to make thought pass through demonstrations as through plainsong, and thus to steep an unprecedented thinking in disparate springs' (BE, xiv). That thinking 'being' for Badiou requires the transgression of the boundaries of poetic language, privileging as he does mathematics *as* ontology, demands further elaboration of the departure Badiou's 'subtractive ontology' makes from Heidegger's 'poetic ontology'.

Poetic and subtractive ontologies: *Phusis* and *Idea*

The opening pages of Badiou's *Being and Event* (1988/2005) trace a retrospective philosophical bond with Heidegger. 'Along with Heidegger', Badiou asserts, 'it will be maintained that philosophy as such can only be re-assigned on the basis of the ontological question' (BE, 1). The ontological question in this context pertains to the distinction between beings and being qua being. It seeks to account for existence apart from its instantiation in existent things, as well as for how these things are determinately unified, made distinct, similar, heterogeneous or hierarchically placed at the level of being qua being itself. Badiou's own approach to this question is radical. His task in *Being and Event* is to demonstrate that 'mathematics equals ontology'. Badiou deems mathematics, specifically post-Cantorian set-theory, to be 'the science of being qua being', the discourse in which ontology is 'written'. One immediate consequence of this is that ontology is removed from philosophy's remit: though philosophy can think through the intra-mathematical innovations which produce and disrupt the writing of ontology, it is unable itself to claim this latter for its own. By contrast, although 'metaphysics' is the 'history of Being' for Heidegger,[38] his later philosophy claims the site of being's potential return to be the poem. There is of course a clear distinction then between these two thinkers concerning the location of ontological work, over the discourse or kind of thinking in which being may be approached; does the philosopher embark on ontological investigation via the poem or via mathematics? In what follows I will explore this divergence in ontological approach by examining Badiou's most important meditation on Heidegger and ontology from *Being and Event* alongside Heidegger's own thinking concerning the relation between ontology and nature in *Introduction to Metaphysics*, in order to develop my exegesis of Badiou's antipathy towards Heideggerian ontology, and more importantly suggest how this departure from Heidegger impacts Badiou's writings about the poem and about Celan more specifically.

In the eleventh meditation of *Being and Event*, 'Nature: Poem or Matheme?', Badiou lays out a history of the interpretation of being, from the pre-Socratic thought of Parmenides and Heraclitus (and their restoration in Heidegger), to the rational argumentation of Socrates in Plato's dialogues, to, from his own philosophical perspective, the latter-day mathematical innovations of Georg Cantor and Paul Cohen.[39] This is the means by which Badiou comes to distinguish 'ontologies of Presence' from the 'subtractive' ontology he affirms in the formula 'ontology = mathematics', *Being and Event*'s central thesis. Badiou's contention in *Being and Event*'s eleventh meditation, against Heidegger, is that Platonic doctrine, in its rationality, comes to intervene upon approaches to being shrouded in mystery and the potential of poetic revelation. For Badiou, it is this intervention upon poetry that marks the true specificity of 'Western' philosophy's inauguration in Greece or what Badiou calls 'the Greek event'. Though Badiou admits that 'absolutely originary thought occurs in poetics and the letting-be of appearing', from his perspective, such thought prefigures the arrival of mathematics in Greek thought and is an interpretation of being which transcends the site of ancient Greece; the 'immemorial character of the poem and poetry' is 'both far more ancient, and with regard to its original sites, far more multiple (China, India, Egypt ...)' (*BE*, 125). Most specific to the Greek event, for Badiou, is the attempt 'to think being subtractively in the mode of an ideal or axiomatic thought', or to submit being to the 'matheme' (*BE*, 126). The 'matheme', it should be noted immediately, was a term that rose to prominence in Jacques Lacan's seminars of the 1970s, referring to the formulae that became a crucial part of his work's transmission, most notably in his formulae for sexuation in *Seminar XX*.⁴⁰ Applied retrospectively by Badiou, it speaks to the rigorous conceptualization of being qua being, to the fact that being, from his perspective, being qua being can be written in the discourse of set-theoretical mathematics, a move towards mathematics inaugurated by Plato.

Distinguishing the Presocratic orientation towards being from the intervention of the matheme, Badiou's first move is to declare that for 'ontologies of Presence' (here conflated with 'poetic ontologies'), the theme of nature is 'decisive'. For such ontologies, in Badiou's words, φύσις (*phusis*, typically Greek for 'nature', with etymological connotations of growth and emergence) 'resonates' beneath the word 'nature'. Badiou invokes Heidegger's declaration in *Introduction to Metaphysics* that *phusis* is a 'fundamental Greek word for being' in order to anchor his thinking within an overarching philosophical departure from Heidegger's thought (*BE*, 123).

It is worth noting tangentially, however, that Badiou is consciously reductive in choosing *phusis* as the site of his critique of Heidegger. As Mark Hewson points out, *phusis* is just one of many Presocratic words adopted by Heidegger for the way in which they encapsulate seemingly originary interpretations of the question of being. By so closely tying *phusis* alone to 'the theme of nature', Badiou surreptitiously colours Heidegger's investigation of being with a transcendent 'giving' nature close to what Hewson describes as a 'pantheist mystery religion'.⁴¹ For Hewson, Badiou's writing on Heidegger in this case does little to account for the evental aspect of being in Heidegger's work on the Presocratics or the fact that being is 'made to arrive' in poetic work. Accordingly, it is prudent to follow Hewson's advice that if we wish to characterize the Presocratics as the creators of 'poetic ontologies', we might bear in mind that such 'ontologies of the One' are nonetheless *constituted* and 'opened up in poetic thought as the 'setting to work of being', rather than examples of an all-encompassing theological 'One', 'the same noumenon, celebrated in the song and ritual of all lands and peoples'.⁴²

Nonetheless, Badiou's reading, avoidance of Heidegger's 'event' aside, finds much elsewhere to bolster it across Heidegger's works, notably in the relatively late three-part lecture he presented between 1957 and 1958 entitled 'The Nature of Language'. There, Heidegger says:

> The quest for thinking always remains the search for the first and ultimate grounds. Why? Because this, that something is and what it is, the persistent presence of being, has from of old been determined to be the ground and foundation. As all nature has the character of ground, a search for it is the founding and grounding of the ground or foundation.⁴³

Again, thinking is inextricably tied to the question of being, being *as such* having been cleaved by thought from its manifestation in *beings*. In the above, the question of being, that which opens thought to questions of ground or foundation, is then prescribed its own grounding in nature, all of which has, in turn, 'the character of ground', drawing nature and ontology into proximity. For Heidegger, thinking nature provides the ground for thinking in turn the persistent presence of being. While Hewson is correct in asserting that Heidegger excavates a multitude of Greek words for their ontological resonance, especially in *Introduction to Metaphysics* in which he claims '*logos, alētheia, phusis, noein,* and *idea* have been hidden away and covered up in unintelligibility', it is *phusis* nonetheless that attains primacy; the Greek word afforded the most important role after *phusis, logos,* is delineated only insofar as it shares its privileged position with *phusis*.[44]

In *Introduction to Metaphysics*, Heidegger wants to think the being/nature couple within the context of 'the originary essence of Greek philosophy'.[45] Heidegger's interpretation of *phusis* is a response to what he sees as the destruction of its 'authentic philosophical naming force' by the subsequent adoption of the reductive Latin translation 'natura' ('nature'), a translation that, for Heidegger, becomes definitive for modern philosophy.[46] The result of this concealment for Heidegger is the misrepresentation of Greek thought as a 'philosophy of nature', 'a representation of all things according to which they are really of a material nature'.[47] Heidegger wants to return, then, to what he thinks the word *phusis* contained for Greek thought, and therefore to how philosophy might rethink what 'nature' signifies when its supposedly originary tie to being is foregrounded once again.

For Heidegger, the word *phusis* expresses an understanding of the being of beings, where being refers at once to the emergence, the persistent presence, and to the autonomous unfolding of each being in itself:

> Now what does the word *phusis* say? It says what emerges from itself (for example, the emergence, the blossoming, of a rose), the unfolding that opens up, the coming-into-appearance in such unfolding, and holding itself and persisting in appearance – in short, the emerging-abiding sway.[48]

The etymology of *phusis* lies in *phuō*, most commonly 'to grow'. In *phusis*, however, there is not only this character of growth, emergence and becoming 'from itself', of 'the rising of the sun', the 'surging of the sea' or 'the growth of plants',[49] there is also the 'holding sway' (from *walten*, the German verb to 'prevail, to reign, to govern'),[50] the persistence in presence of what appears. *Phusis* is both emergence and holding sway at once, the 'emerging-abiding sway'. Gregory Fried and Richard Polt suggest in their translator's introduction to *Introduction to Metaphysics* that 'to hold sway' and 'the sway', for them, most adequately capture the powerful, prevailing nature of this emergent energy: '"the sway" suggests this powerful upsurge of the presence of beings'.[51] Heidegger, however, is adamant that *phusis* is not synonymous with these processes of emergence and opening which he claims still inform how we think nature today. Rather, he claims:

> This emerging and standing-out-in-itself may not be taken as just one process among others that we observe in beings. *Phusis* is Being itself, by virtue of which beings first become and remain observable.[52]

This original coupling in nature as *phusis* between being itself and its 'bursting forth' in the coming to presence of beings requires that nature, in Badiou's commentary, be conceived neither as 'objectivity nor the given, but rather the gift'. Nature is not the totality of given appearances, not a manifold of perceptions the essence of which remains beyond our grasp. Nor is 'nature' the opposite, the thing in itself. Being coincides with a coming to presence 'in the guise of appearance' (*BE*, 123). Nature conceived in this way is that through which being finds its presentation.

Returning to *Being and Event*, Badiou's attempts to oppose his own philosophy to nature as *phusis* becomes clearer. Writing in Heidegger's terms, Badiou claims:

> Nature is ... not objectivity nor the given, but rather the gift, the gesture of opening which unfolds its own limit as that in which it resides without limitation. (*BE*, 123)

At once, nature appears and unfolds, but also places itself, limits itself, thereby providing the dwelling for its unlimited opening. This unfolding is what Heidegger refers to as ἀλήθεια, *alētheia*, meaning disclosure or clearing (especially with regard to 'truth') or what Badiou calls 'non-latency'. That is, through nature qua *phusis*, the being of beings is disclosed through its coming to presence and its subsequent persistence in presence. Badiou continues by claiming that '[*phusis*] designates being-present according to the offered essence of its auto-presentation'. Being-present is designated by *phusis* according to the 'offered essence' – the essence (or being) that arises within it – of its auto-presentation, that is, being shows *itself* in presence, or rather being is 'the appearing which resides in itself' (*BE*, 123).

A foray into Heidegger's earlier work, *Being and Time*, reveals this conception of being to cohere with Heidegger's conception of phenomenology: 'The phenomenological concept of phenomenon, as self-showing, means the being of beings – its meaning, modifications and derivatives.'[53] In this phenomenon, that which 'shows itself' discloses itself both ontically and ontologically, usurping the binary opposition between objectivity and mere appearance, instead asserting their coming together in the arising of being in presence. For the young Heidegger, '*Ontology is possible only as phenomenology.*'[54] This maxim is intended to overcome the forgetting of being enacted via the development of dogmatic metaphysical systems aiming to approach the figure of objective 'true' reality, often using the resources of mathematics.[55] For Heidegger, mathematics partakes in the elision of phenomena, lending itself to knowledge of mere objective presence, the enduring substantiality of Descartes's *res extensa*: Descartes 'not only goes amiss ontologically in his definition of the world', Heidegger writes, '[but his] interpretation and its foundations lead him to *pass over* the phenomenon of world'.[56] Further, according to Badiou in *Being and Event*, mathematics for Heidegger contributes to our blindness towards being: 'Mathematics … is not, for Heidegger, a path which opens onto the original question [of being] … mathematics is rather blindness itself … the foreclosure of thought by knowledge' (*BE*, 9). Fields of knowledge grounded in the objective presence of beings fail to take into account being itself, thereby guarding against the potential abrasion of knowledge by thinking.

This antipathy towards mathematics is decisive for the relationship between Heidegger and Badiou. Badiou proposes his own privileged 'name' for being, opposing being as *idea* to Heidegger's *phusis*. Quoting Heidegger's *Introduction to Metaphysics*, Badiou writes:

> If 'with the interpretation of being as ἰδέα [*idea*] there is a rupture with regard to the authentic beginning', it is because what gave an indication, under the name of φύσις [*phusis*], of an originary link between being and appearing – presentation's guise of presence – is reduced to the rank of subtracted, impure, inconsistent given, whose sole opening forth is the cut-out of the Idea, and particularly, from Plato to Galileo – and Cantor – the mathematical Idea. (*BE*, 125)

Badiou thus provides a narrative whereby Heidegger's suspicion of mathematics insofar as it relates to the question of being finds its source in what Badiou calls 'the Platonic turn'. It is following Plato that our understanding of the word 'nature', for both Badiou and Heidegger, forgets its originary coupling with *phusis*. This originary thinking of nature is replaced by the contemporary thinking of 'natural objectivity' in the language of mathematics in physics. According to Badiou, our adoption of this thinking, especially following Galileo, depends on a more radical subversion of nature guided by the Platonic interpretation of *phusis* as *idea*.[57]

This is an interpretation supported throughout Heidegger's writings, not least in *Introduction to Metaphysics*. Therein he claims that following Plato, 'being as *idea* was elevated to a supersensory realm. The chasm, *khōrismos*, was torn open between the merely apparent beings here below and the real Being somewhere up there.'[58] Nature no longer stands as that through which the being of appearing presents itself or comes to presence. Rather, the being of appearing is taken to reside solely in the form of the Idea, in the '*evident* aspect of what is offered; it is the "surface", the "façade"', suggests Badiou (*BE*, 124). It is Plato's 'allegory of the cave' from Book VI of *The Republic* that grounds Heidegger's assertion here. Heidegger finds evidence there for the replacement of being as *phusis* by *idea*. Truth conceived as *alētheia* or 'unhiddenness' is then intervened upon by a Platonic 'doctrine' of the essence of truth, whereby 'the essence of unhiddenness' ceases to 'unfold from its proper and essential fullness' and instead 'shifts to the essence of the ιδέα [*idea*]':

> The things that the 'allegory' mentions as visible outside the cave are the image for what the proper being of beings consists in. This, according to Plato, is that by which beings show up in their 'visible form.' Plato does not regard this 'visible form' as a mere 'aspect.' For him the 'visible form has in addition something of a 'stepping forth' whereby a thing 'presents' itself. Standing in its 'visible form' the being shows itself.[59]

There are two mutually implicating connotations of 'the Idea' at work here: one of replacement, the other of falling away. On the one hand, the Idea only presents the evident aspect of the being of appearing, that is, in Badiou's words, its appearing is 'within the delimitation, the cut-out, of a visibility *for us*' (*BE*, 124). Heidegger too emphasizes this 'cut-out' in *Introduction to Metaphysics*: 'The visage offered by the thing and no longer the thing itself, now becomes what is decisive.'[60] The loss of the thing in-itself in this interpretation of being, the thing's inability to show itself in a way that gestures beyond its own visible form, reduces the interpretation of the being of beings to mere appearance. On the other hand, because the Idea is bound by its appearing *for us*, being itself falls away. Following the assertion of the Idea as the 'sole and definitive interpretation of Being', the usurpation of *phusis* by mere 'slices' of appearing, the decline in being's non-latency begins; the possibility of *alētheia* falls away from presentation.[61]

The originary understanding of nature as *phusis* is veiled over, forgotten, and being, in Badiou's interpretation, is then experienced as lack rather than through presence. For Badiou, however, Plato's 'cut' of the Idea is of foundational importance, and it is an innovation whose consequences Badiou is committed to pursuing: 'The singularity of Greece', Badiou writes, 'is ... to have interrupted the narrative about origins through secularized and abstract statements, to have impaired the prestige of the poem in favour of that of the matheme' (*MP*, 31). Once the Idea becomes the sole interpretation of being, being itself is subjugated by the contentless mathematical text. This movement is a correlate of the privileged role Plato affords to mathematics insofar as it relates to knowledge and intelligibility. In *The Republic*, for instance, mathematical reasoning, *dianoia*, operates as the bridge between the visible and the first principles developed by philosophy in 'full understanding' or 'truth'.[62] And, as is well known, poetry and art are consigned to the realm of mere illusion, *eikasa*. In Badiou, following Plato, 'thought' requires a similar element of 'reason': 'Philosophy requires that the *profound* utterance's authority be interrupted by argumentative secularisation.'[63] 'Thought', as that which orientates itself towards being, requires mathematical, 'secular' reason in Badiou, but, in Heidegger, in Hewson's words, we find the '"setting to work of being"' in 'poetic thought'.[64] These contrasting approaches rest on differing interpretations of being, the former asserting being's subtraction from appearance and the latter aiming to revivify being's originary presence in the 'emerging-abiding sway'.

In the wake of this Platonic turn, Heidegger remains steadfast in his rejection of the forgetting of being and wishes to excavate and revivify the originary tie of being to appearing within a primordial understanding of nature's capacity to support the unveiling of being within phenomena. In his later work on Friedrich Hölderlin especially, this unveiling is to take place within the setting to work of being in poetic thought. Heidegger's notorious readings of Hölderlin and their political ramifications are one of the main themes of Chapter 2. For now, however, this 'poetico-natural' orientation towards being and the subsequent 'mathematico-ideal' orientation following the Platonic turn constitute, for Badiou, the directions which 'command the entire destiny of thought in the West':

> One, based on nature in its original Greek sense, welcomes – in poetry – appearing as the coming-to-presence of being. The other, based on the Idea in its Platonic sense, submits the lack, the subtraction of all presence, to the matheme, and thus disjoins being from appearing, essence from existence. (*BE*, 125)

Badiou is keen, however, not to retain these two orientations' absolute separation and thus proposes a different 'disposition' towards their understanding. He is adamant that within the resources of poetry there remains the potential for 'absolutely originary thought' yet at the same time he removes ontology from poetry's remit. Ontology thus conceived cannot be, for Badiou, the naming in poetry of appearing as the non-latency of being (ἀλήθεια, *alētheia*) (*BE*, 125). Rather, Badiou maintains fidelity to the 'event' marked by the Platonic turn and thus conceives ontology's 'infinite text' as 'the historicity of mathematical deductions'. Being, for Badiou, is written in the various mathematical Ideas generated from Plato through Galileo and Cantor and not in the naming power of poetry: 'being is expressible once a decision of thought subtracts it from any instance of presence' (*BE*, 126).

Tensions inherent in Badiou's split from Heidegger here are manifold but the most important concerns the usurpation of the 'mystery' of being (and poetry's power to apprehend it) by a rational, secular history of being written in mathematics. When Badiou writes in 'The Philosophical Recourse to the Poem', in *Conditions*, that 'philosophy requires that the *profound* utterance's authority be interrupted by argumentative secularisation',[65] he aims to shift the point of departure for philosophy from the profundities and mysteries exhibited in poetic language to a rational formalization guaranteeing universality (through ontology's inscription in mathematics). This tension reflects a further split between philosophy's starting from what is 'evident', from what 'bursts forth' in nature, and the affirmation of formal structures devoid of presence (in Badiou's case guaranteeing the universality of 'truth procedures').

Nonetheless, Badiou wishes to make clear that 'the poem' 'has … never ceased'. Further, the poem, fundamentally, remains the exploration of presence in language. However, for Badiou, following the Platonic turn, the poem now figures (in its 'immemorial nature') as the 'temptation' of a return to 'presence and rest'. This nostalgia for presence enacted in poetry is not due to a loss or a forgetting of being as Heidegger would have it, but rather the 'interruption' caused by the advent of mathematics: 'This nostalgia, latent thereafter in every great poetic enterprise, is not woven from the forgetting of being: on the contrary, it is woven from the pronunciation of being in its subtraction by mathematics in its effort of thought' (*BE*, 126). There is a reversal of Heidegger's thought here, for the melancholy 'forgetting of being' testified to by Heidegger is replaced by the very precise 'pronunciation' of being affirmed by Badiou following the subtraction of being from presence. Finally, in its nostalgia for that 'being', subtracted from presence, the poem pursues 'the impossible *filling in* of the void'; in its attempts to once more reveal being in presence, the poem stumbles against being's subtraction, revealing the primacy of the void of being instead and the withdrawal of the object. The epoch in which poetry is conceivable as the abundant representation of being 'bursting forth' within nature, in which poetry's saying is deemed the necessary conduit in re-approaching being, foreclosed and covered over since Plato, is declared over by Badiou.

In a relatively recent account of issues facing the thinking of ontology, Badiou's former student Quentin Meillassoux helps to lend nuance to Badiou's departure from Heidegger. The key distinction here is between a sense of being in which it is 'given' through poetic language's disclosure or otherwise, and being as something that refuses or resists capture by knowledge, subtracts itself from it. Badiou's ontology is a 'subtractive' one in which being is never 'given'; being eludes our grasp. In *After Finitude*, Meillassoux demands that philosophy present an ontology in which '*being* is not co-extensive with *manifestation*'.[66] That is, to present an ontology which, by correlation, does not depend on appearance, an assertion of being that does not depend on its disclosure. This distinction between being in its givenness, its encapsulation in the word, and being qua being's subtraction from presence to a realm beyond language is at the heart of Badiou's relationship with Heidegger. Bearing this distinction in mind, it becomes important to understand poetry's role here, as a sphere dedicated to an ostensibly philosophical 'thought of being', or in other words how poetry itself comes up against this primary 'lack' in being, or being's void in presentation. This void, in testifying to being's inconsistency beyond the bounds of the whole, stands in a peculiar relationship to Heidegger's conception of 'the Nothing' that accompanies being: an investigation of each will help uncover what it is that poetry is actually able to do in Badiou's work, as well as how he conceives its relation to philosophy and especially how it is that, marking the end of the Age of Poets, 'Celan completes Heidegger' (*MP*, 77). In what immediately follows, then, I want to elucidate Heidegger's conception of nothingness in its relation to being before moving on to assessing Badiou's correlative concept of the void and examining how these contrasting approaches to being, nothing, to ontology at large and its relation to poetry impact the sense in which we can understand Badiou's commitment to 'a thought of being' in the poem.

Heidegger's nothing

This section examines Heidegger's conception of 'the nothing' and the relations it holds to thought, to being and to poetic language. It does this in order to anticipate a crucial distinction with Badiou's later philosophy, for which, following the subtraction of being from knowledge delineated above, the concept of 'the void' and its relation to poetic language become fundamental. For the Heidegger of 'The End of Philosophy', metaphysics is the history of being.[67] Through its focus on objectively present beings, however, metaphysics forces the 'forgetting' of being itself. This state of forgetting, or oblivion, is exacerbated by the strict logic imposed on the knowledge such metaphysical investigations produce, for which talk of nothingness is considered nonsensical. For Heidegger, against such logic, metaphysics of its kind is the history of the forgetting of being precisely because it fails to take into account the 'nothing' that performs a constitutive role for being. Being itself is elided precisely where this nothing is not taken into account; ontology becomes the investigation of objectively present beings and is unable to distinguish them from being per se.

In *Introduction to Metaphysics*, Heidegger asserts that the failure to take the nothing into account is based on a fundamental misunderstanding on the part of traditional metaphysical investigation, which 'stems from an *oblivion of Being* that is getting increasingly rigid'.[68] And, this oblivion is manifested in being's contemporary lack of meaning: 'the fact that Being is in fact almost nothing more than a word now, and its meaning an evanescent vapour'.[69] There is circularity at work here: failure to recognize the nothing contributes to a forgetting of being per se, but being's 'oblivion' in turn is further grounds to reject talk of the nothing as nonsensical. More fundamentally, a metaphysics seeking access to objective reality, which Heidegger refers to as 'objective presence' throughout *Being and Time*, seeks to approach being from a standpoint disengaged from *Dasein*, or from the reflection of (human) beings upon being, which for Heidegger must always mark the point of departure for any ontological investigation.[70]

Heidegger begins his 'What Is Metaphysics?' (1929) by supposing that science, as that which 'determines our existence', takes 'solely beings and beyond that – nothing' as its object of study, failing in the process to account for the 'nothing' thus invoked. Science, it is claimed, 'wishes to know nothing of the nothing', yet in expressing what it deems to be its essence – its investigation of beings themselves and nothing more – it calls on 'the nothing' for help.[71] This nothingness is revealed to *Dasein* via a specific mood or 'attunement' Heidegger calls anxiety.[72] Between *Being and Time* and 'What Is Metaphysics?', Heidegger provides a topology of the nothing. In the latter the nothing is taken as an entity in itself, that is 'the nothing' is to be distinguished from simply 'not'. In the nothing we find the always present power of 'nihilation': not the potential destruction of all things but the immanent possibility that all things might not have come to be such as they are, a grounding nothing which when experienced through anxiety belies the fact that, on a basic level, there is a difference between something, whatever it may be, and nothing. For, if 'anxious', one's experience of being-in-the-world, one's feeling of the totality of all things (this mode or 'attunement', alongside those of 'boredom' and 'joy', for example, revealing *Dasein's* being in the midst of things as a whole) forces that whole into meaninglessness, insignificance and irrelevance.[73] Then, from the standpoint of the nothing, from the experience of anxiety, beings arise once more: 'In the clear night of the nothing of anxiety the original openness of beings as such arises: that they are beings – and not nothing.'[74] The nothing is conceivable as the limit of the meaning of being, a horizon from which we may turn back and reassess our being-in-the-world. It is also conceivable, however, as the always-present source of the 'light' or openness of being, the shadow that accompanies all disclosure. The topology of the nothing comprises both the fact that it results from a particular mood (rather than being the mood itself), that it is revealed in a certain mode of being of *Dasein*, and its role as ground or source, as always present in and constitutive of being.

Earlier in Heidegger's thought, the nothing is afforded an even more 'fixed' place in the phenomenological ontology developed throughout *Being and Time*. There, 'the nothing' is equated precisely with 'the world': 'What crowds in upon us is not this or that, nor is it everything objectively present together as a sum, but the *possibility* of things, at hand in general, that is, the world itself. [...] ... what anxiety is about exposes nothing, that is, the world as such.'[75] The nothing is a constant grounding source that testifies to the possibility that beings may not have been, and, more radically, to the possibility of future disclosure or change. Insofar as Heidegger's thoughts of being are marked by the limits of specifically human being, then, being itself only able to arise as a question through *Dasein's* seeking it, 'the Nothing' as 'world as such', which 'ontologically belongs essentially to the being of *Dasein* as being-in-the-world', occupies a fundamental position in Heidegger's thought; it is constitutive of the entire plane through which and on which his philosophy is enacted. Moreover, the assertion that 'world as such' is the nothing allows us to forge a stronger link between the poem's isolation and nothingness itself. The 'world' thought in these terms concerns the slipping away of the whole: that is, the dissipation of objectively present, meaningless things, revealing their empty logical 'world', or the nothing from which they come to presence.

The ontological status of the nothing itself demands more investigation. Again, in 'What Is Metaphysics?', Heidegger writes:

> For human existence, the nothing makes possible the openedness of beings as such. The nothing does not merely serve as the counterconcept of beings; rather, it originally belongs to their essential unfolding as such.[76]

The nothing must be considered necessary rather than contingent insofar as it relates to the openedness of beings. The essence of being human, for Heidegger, depends on this openedness, which in turn depends on the nothing. More, the 'essential' unfolding of beings carries this nothing with it: the nothing does not just make the openedness of beings possible; it persists in their unfolding. Heidegger continues: 'The nothing does not remain the indeterminate opposite of beings but reveals itself as belonging to the Being of beings.'[77] In the earlier *Introduction to Metaphysics*, the same idea is expressed in the simplest possible terms: 'for us, even Nothing "belongs" to "Being".'[78] 'Presence', too, is always unfolded in parallel with the nothing, providing the site for Heidegger's destruction of the prevailing, static 'metaphysics of presence' in *Being and Time*, a metaphysics or ontology that fails to take constitutive absence into account, privileging the complacent measurement of already present beings over being itself.

Bearing this constitutive nothing or absence in mind, it is interesting that in his later piece 'Letter on Humanism', originally crafted as a response to questions raised by Jean Beaufret in 1946 concerning Jean-Paul Sartre's assertion that 'existence precedes essence', Heidegger proclaims an exclusive relation between language and thought.[79] Sartre's maxim, intended to think the construction of a human 'essence' following the assertion of the individual, 'free' subject's primacy via the cogito, is rejected by Heidegger. For the latter, 'thinking, in its essence as thinking of Being, is claimed by Being', and 'thinking as such is bound to the advent of Being, to Being as advent'.[80] Particularly pertinent to the discussion here, however, is the concordance of language and being *through* thinking, and this is asserted in the following passage:

> But what 'is' above all is Being. Thinking accomplishes the relation of Being to the essence of man. It does not make or cause the relation. Thinking brings this relation to Being solely as something handed over to it from Being. Such offering consists in the fact that in thinking Being comes to language. Language is the house of Being. In its home man dwells.[81]

Again, being takes primacy here; thought can only relate the essence of man to being insofar as being admits this relation. Crucially, this relation between the essence of man and being takes place through the 'coming' of being to language. As Heidegger claims in *Introduction to Metaphysics*, language offers originary access to being: 'In the word, in language, things first come to be and are.'[82] It is in poetic language specifically, for Heidegger, in which such disclosure can be found, and the source of this disclosure is the nothing.

Richard Polt's analysis of Heidegger's *History of the Concept of Time* bears evidence of the privilege of place afforded to poetic language. Poetic language is offered as a foil to what Heidegger calls 'dead language':

> As 'dead' this language is no longer subject to changes in meaning ... whereas in any 'living' language contexts of meaning change with changes in the interpretation of historical Dasein at the time ... A language has its genuine Being only as long as new correlations of meaning and so – although not necessarily – new words and phrases accrue to it from understanding.[83]

Dead language allows no slippage in meaning, no confusion of referent or ambiguity. As Polt comments, it was dead language, in which word and referent are fixed in a relationship refusing ambiguity of signification, that early twentieth-century Analytic philosophers of language dreamt one day of creating.[84] An assumption concerning language grounds such thinking: everyday language is deemed original in some way, forcing poetic language into a secondary, derivative relation. Poetic language, for Heidegger, however, as *Dichtung*, is the archetypal, living language and should be treated as prior to the everyday communicative languages we speak; it is fundamental, 'the elementary emergence into words, the becoming-uncovered, of existence as Being-in-the-world'.[85] In his later essay 'Language' this primacy is made explicit: 'Poetry proper is never merely a higher mode of everyday language. It is rather the reverse: everyday language is a forgotten and therefore used-up poem, from which there hardly resounds a call any longer.'[86] The 'pure' speaking of the poem calls its objects to a presence 'sheltered in absence' and is therefore capable of a primal showing or revealing of being; as Polt claims, 'it recaptures the illuminating power that secretly resides in our ordinary words, letting us see the world as if for the first time'.[87]

The thesis that everyday language is a forgotten or used-up poem is anticipated in Heidegger's earlier discussion of 'idle talk' in *Being and Time*. For Heidegger, *Dasein* is always already 'thrown' 'there' into a world, and it is from the perspective of this 'being-there', in the world with others, that it must begin its investigation of being.[88] *Dasein* in its everydayness and as something necessarily *in* the world, 'there', is thus 'disclosed' alongside other beings. It is claimed moreover that 'discourse', along with 'attunement' (mood), 'understanding' and 'interpretation', belongs to the 'essential constitution of the being of Dasein' and specifically to 'the existential structures of the disclosedness of being-in-the-world'. 'Idle talk' for Heidegger then is a 'positive phenomenon' which 'constitutes the mode of being of the understanding and interpretation of everyday Dasein'.[89] Specifically, idle talk is something 'discourse' becomes when its primary function as communication, 'bringing the hearer to participate in disclosed being toward what is talked about', is modified by the always already present 'average intelligibility' of what is spoken.[90] This average 'intelligibility', and the understanding in which it results, covers over the being of discourse for the listener in their (incomplete) understanding of what is communicated. This understanding fails to 'come to a being toward' what is talked about, a 'primordial understanding' is forsaken: 'One understands not so much the beings talked about; rather, one already only listens to what is spoken about as such.'[91] Idle talk is the amplification of this 'listening' to the detriment of 'being toward', such that being-in-the-world becomes closed off, 'covering over innerworldly beings'. Further, this is complicated by the proliferation of average understanding via idle talk's 'groundlessness', such that 'everything' can be understood in an indifferent manner: 'Idle talk, which everyone can snatch up, not only divests us of the task of genuine understanding, but develops an indifferent intelligibility for which nothing is closed off any longer.'[92]

Poetic language must be distinguished from this idle talk, akin it seems to something like Badiou's 'language of consensus' (Badiou is thinking of Stéphane Mallarmé's 'universal *reporting*'),[93] in which being is covered over and obscured. In *Introduction to Metaphysics*, idle talk is admonished: 'the misuse of idle talk, in slogans and phrases, destroys our genuine relation to things.'[94] And, in *Letter on Humanism*, this thesis is further developed: 'Language thereby falls into the service of expediting communication along routes where objectification – the uniform accessibility of everything to everyone – branches out and disregards all limits.'[95] Idle talk can be conceived then as both the 'forgotten' poem which covers up innerworldly beings preventing their disclosure and the 'used-up' poem in which, via the primacy of an average understanding, communication saturates language's disclosive potential, opening up the 'entire' world to indifferent intelligibility. As well, for Heidegger, idle talk proliferates as a direct result of the cleansing of language enacted by those whom employ it in the service of logic or metaphysics. Beyond idle talk and the language of consensus, being is still disclosed to us through language, for 'those who create with words are the guardians of this [house of Being]'.[96] Further, the disclosure of being through language requires 'thought', just as Badiou's retrospective claim for poetry's 'thought of being' during the Age of Poets does.

How it is that the nothing and poetic language relate in Heidegger is at this stage obscure, but it is through the conjunction of language and being in *thinking* that poetic language and the nothing are brought into relation. In 'Letter on Humanism', Heidegger writes that 'the nihilating in Being is the essence of what

I call the Nothing. Hence, because it thinks being, thinking thinks the nothing.'[97] And, if it is recalled that 'thinking gathers language into simple saying' it must be concluded that there is an intimate relationship between the arrangement of language into simple saying, in poetry, and the nothing.

Paul Celan's poetry often seems to investigate similar questions, not least in 'Speak, You Also', containing the fiat 'Speak —/But keep yes and no unsplit'. To 'keep yes and no unsplit' requires them to be thought together against the rules of formal logic, which rejects such contradiction; the assertion of one is always to include the other. They are mutually implicating, for one can only speak of the nothing in relation to the being of what is, and in turn, the nothing is the source of being, the source of presence. The final line of the fourth strophe, 'He speaks truly who speaks the shade',[98] demands the poet breach the plane of language from within in order to approach 'truth', that which lies beyond the intelligible light cast by everyday speech. One can begin to understand how Badiou has come to his reading of Celan: the 'real darkness' produced in the twentieth century demands its formalization in the poet's language, demands that poetics shifts to reassess its own relation to being and truth, and by correlation, its relation to the nothing too.[99] The '*Sinn*' – the 'sense', or in one of Felstiner's translations, 'gist' (*HI*, 33) – of the time, which it is poetry's task to present, in this case must be shaded, must pass through the nothing. The poem's speaking, then, is seemingly isolated from the world to which it would 'give meaning'.

The respective philosophies of Heidegger and Badiou clearly diverge at this point. When Badiou refers to the world from which poetic speech must isolate itself, he is not referring to Heidegger's empty 'nothing' but precisely to a world saturated with content, the world of present things, of knowledge, of placement. It is true that his philosophy with regard to poetry shares many parallels with Heidegger's, for both thinkers ally poetic speech with isolation from the world of things, or from the world insofar as it is represented by communication or idle talk, as well as with an orientation towards a sense of being for which the nothing is constitutive. However, the central silence harboured by the modern poem, for Badiou, is not to be conflated with Heidegger's nothing, for the latter is nonetheless of 'the world', it is 'the world as such', its bare structure, its ground.

Language and the world are brought into complete coextension in Heidegger, in which there is nothing beyond the nothing, nothing beyond the world. In Badiou, however, there is a point outside of language, outside of 'the world', and 'the modern poem' must attest to this. Returning to what Badiou writes of the poem in 'Language, Thought, Poetry', poetic language's relation to isolation and the nothing can be made clearer:

> This thing that cannot be spoken of in the language of consensus; I create silence in order to say it. I isolate this speech from the world. (*TW*, 240)

The poem's isolation, its 'simple' saying, is a creation of silence insofar as it escapes the background hum of communication, of discourse becoming idle talk. But the poem also brings us closer to the silent nothing that goes hand in hand with being, the contentless 'world' from which the whole has slipped away. Though such a formulation, on the surface at least, appears to exactly mirror Heidegger's, there are two fundamental aspects in which it is divergent, and these are the preoccupations of the final section of this chapter.

The first point of differentiation concerns ontology. Because for Badiou, being qua being is radically multiple, uncounted and inconsistent prior to its presentation, there must be a point in that presentation which is able to attest to this radical inconsistency. In other words, within 'the world', or within presentation, 'the nothing', or 'the void' as Badiou conceives it, that is, the ground of presentation, the empty nothing upon which presentation depends, points directly outwards to a radical inconsistency ('being qua being') subtracted from our grasp. Not only is there a fixed point beyond 'world' then, the 'whole' itself, in which beings appear, is made to reveal its radical contingency and incompleteness. There is no whole for Badiou, and the poem's central silence attests to this. Secondly, the isolation of poetic speech from 'the world' thus configured requires that the thought produced by poetry be separated from the world, that is, discerned as a thought apart from the realm of sensible things; the 'thought of being' produced by Badiou's modern poem must be, following Stéphane Mallarmé, 'pure'. In the section that follows, I want to give these two difficult ideas as full an elaboration as possible by making clear the precise relation between Badiou's void and the demands he makes of the 'modern poem' especially insofar as they relate to the poem's capacity to produce a 'thought of [subtracted] being'. In what follows, then, I offer the most protracted engagement in this book with the mathematical apparatus at the centre of *Being and Event*. I then turn to Badiou's reading of Celan, attempting to elucidate the often undisclosed theoretical concerns that lead Badiou to Celan's poetry, before moving to Badiou's development of a concept of 'poetic idea' in one his readings of Stéphane Mallarmé in *Handbook of Inaesthetics*.

The void and poetry's idea

In one of Badiou's more fragmentary readings of Celan from *Handbook of Inaesthetics*, he writes that, following Celan's poetry, 'the thinking of our epoch cannot come from an open space, from a grasp of the Whole' (*HI*, 32). Badiou's surreptitious uses of 'open space' and 'Whole' mark departures from Heidegger's conception of poetic language specifically. For Badiou, within the Age of Poets, the 'modern poem' is understood as a truth-procedure producing a thought of its own time, but this is not a thinking of the whole in Heidegger's sense. The poem is claimed to produce a singular affirmation, a thought of itself, and this is an intervention upon, rather than an enigmatic disclosure of, the whole. For Badiou, the thought emitted by the poem separates itself from the whole; poetic thought must be discernible, able to isolate itself from the world of sensible things in which it finds its transmission. In 'What Is Metaphysics?', Heidegger claims both that we 'certainly do find ourselves stationed in the midst of beings that are somehow revealed as a whole', and 'No matter how fragmented our everyday existence appears to be … it always deals with beings in a unity of the "whole".'[100] More, the nothing 'makes itself known with beings and in beings expressly as a slipping away of the whole'.[101] The nothing here is conceived as the ground of the whole, the empty 'world as such' through which presence arises and endures. However, the nothing, in this sense, is merely the plot from which presence grows, it does not lie outside the world of things, but rather grounds them; there is no outside, 'even Nothing "belongs" to "Being"'.[102]

In Heidegger's later essay 'Language', he asks which 'presence' is 'higher', that which is called by the words of the poem or that of the objects towards which the poem 'calls'.[103] For Heidegger, language is not merely an instrument for expression 'produced by men, of their feelings and the world view that guides them'.[104] Acknowledging the 'fact' that language is expression fails to adequately account for what Heidegger refers to as the 'nature' of language. For Heidegger, language itself 'speaks', such that in poetic language's disclosure the thinker seeks 'the speaking of language [itself] in the poem'.[105] In 'Language', Heidegger reads Georg Trakl's 'A Winter Evening', whose verses, he claims, 'bring the well-provided house and the ready table into that presence that is turned toward something absent'.[106] Poetic language does not merely 'name' or refer to its objects but 'calls [them] into the word'; it 'brings the presence of what was previously uncalled into a nearness'.[107] Nonetheless, the object remains at a distance from the word; this is a presence in which the object itself remains absent.

Albert Hofstadter's introduction to his translation of Heidegger's collection *Poetry, Language, Thought* offers the following account of Heidegger's line of thought:

> The speech of genuine thinking is by nature *poetic* … The voice of thought must be poetic because poetry is the saying of truth, the saying of the unconcealedness

of beings. It bids all that is – world and things, earth and sky, divinities and mortals – to come, gathering into the simple onefold of their intimate belonging together. It is the topology of being, telling being the whereabouts of its actual presence.[108]

Only in poetic language is truth, the 'saying of the unconcealedness of being', able to come to light. Though in his reading of Trakl, Heidegger's claim that poetic language calls its objects to a presence sheltered in absence anticipates Badiou's later claims for the poem's 'thought of presence upon a background of disappearance', Hofstadter prefigures above the point at which Heidegger and Badiou's respective philosophies radically diverge.

The site of this divergence is the whole: whereas in Heidegger language is invested with the capacity to draw a world into being, gathering earth, sky, mortals and divinities into a 'fourfold', as the fulfilment of its exclusive role as the 'topology of being', Badiou's whole slips away, and it is only at this point, in the singular machinations of the modern poem, in its affirmative thought, separated from the world of sensible things, that poetic truth may emerge. Against Heidegger, the first 'lesson' Badiou learns from Celan in his *Handbook of Inaesthetics* is the following:

> Contrary to the declarations of the modern sophists, there is indeed a fixed point. Not everything is caught in the slippage of language games or the immaterial variability of their occurrences. Being and truth, even if now stripped of any grasp upon the Whole, have not vanished. One will find that they are precariously rooted at the point where the Whole offers up its own nothingness. (*HI*, 33)

Badiou mobilizes Celan's works against those 'modern sophists', from Wittgenstein onwards, who would seek to confine thought to the plane of language, and to deny the existence of philosophical 'truth' beyond the veracity of propositions. One imperative for Badiou is to think how 'truths' are able to impinge upon situations, upon declarations of 'what there is'. That 'not everything' is caught in language and that 'not everything' is immaterially variable together attest to the demand in Badiou's work for the material emergence of that which subtracts itself from language, the unfolding of a truth-procedure within a world.

The 'fixed point' at which the 'Whole offers up its own nothingness', in Badiou's philosophy, is 'the void', a mathematical 'emblem' for the empty set, $\emptyset$. Set-theory requires the empty set to ground each of its presentations of multiplicity, but it is also the point through which mathematical truths must pass: 'The emblem of the unpresented and insensible multiple out of which mathematics makes truth is the void, the empty set' (*HI*, 22). 'The void', then, comes to supplant Heidegger's 'nothing', which testifies to nothing beyond itself. Further engagement with Badiou and Heidegger's respective approaches to ontology is required at this point to lend clarity to how exactly Badiou's concept of the void relates to poetic language and to the poem's 'thought of being'.

Returning to the philosophical project elaborated in *Being and Event* in a little more detail is helpful when thinking through Badiou's decision to oppose his 'subtractive ontology', in which being qua being is foreclosed from presentation, to the 'withdrawal' of being enacted in Heidegger:

> The 'subtractive' is opposed here, as we shall see, to the Heideggerian thesis of a withdrawal of being. It is not in the withdrawal-of-its-presence that being foments the forgetting of its original disposition to the point of assigning us – us at the extreme point of nihilism – to a poetic 'over-turning'. No, the ontological truth is both more restrictive and less prophetic: it is in being foreclosed from presentation that being as such is constrained to be sayable, for humanity, within the imperative effect of a law, the most rigid of all conceivable laws, the law of demonstrative and formalizable inference. (*BE*, 27)

Badiou is adamant that ontologies of 'presence' be discarded. Being is no longer to be disclosed in poetic language, but rigorously conceptualized in set-theoretical discourse. The resources of contemporary set-theory, for Badiou, allows being to be written, rationalized, conceptualized. There is no longer any need for prophecy, the poetic projection of a time in which being may be approached once more. The opening chapters of *Being and Event* argue being qua being to be inconsistent, or uncounted, due to its fundamental multiplicity. In any instance of presentation, a 'situation' in Badiou's terminology, inconsistent being is made consistent through the intra-situational operation of the count-as-one. Multiples 'made one', so to speak, are consistent, instances in which 'being occurs in every presentation', but their initial inconsistency, their multiplicity, can nonetheless be thought retroactively through the void. Being *itself*, then, cannot be grasped, for such inconsistent multiplicity eludes situational presentation, but it remains the 'stuff' of which counted 'ones', or consistent multiplicities, are made.

Badiou's adoption of set-theory results from an axiomatic decision concerning being itself, namely that being is 'multiple', not, as is typical in the history of metaphysics, 'one'. The historical stakes of this decision, and its immediate consequences, are laid out in the first meditation in *Being and Event*, 'The One and the Multiple: *a priori* conditions of any possible ontology':

> Since its Parmenidean organization, ontology has built the portico of its ruined temple out of the following experience: what *presents* itself is essentially multiple; *what* presents itself is essentially one. (*BE*, 23)

That is to say, since the inception of ontology and the thinking of being enacted in Parmenides' poem (Badiou's source is Plato's dialogue, *Parmenides*),[109] what is 'presented' is considered multiple. The 'what' of presentation on the other hand, or being qua being, has hitherto been considered 'essentially one'; for example, in the *Parmenides*: 'what-is is complete, / From every side like the body of a well-rounded sphere, / Everywhere of equal intensity from the centre'.[110] For Badiou, unifying the multiplicity of presentation in a 'one' that precedes it is a conceptual move that enshrines transcendence at the centre of experience. A hierarchy is assigned in which a grounding wholeness, from which multiplicity is then derived, guarantees the multiple presentation of beings. The 'one' thought in this way, then, is the 'portico' to ontology's 'ruined temple' insofar as the latter invokes the transcendence it would seek to overcome. For the history of ontology, being qua being is complete, a unity, and what is presented, 'being-there', is multiple.

Badiou's philosophical decision, 'a decision to break with the arcana of the one and the multiple in which philosophy is born and buried, phoenix of its own sophistic consumption' (*BE*, 23), is to reverse this relation between presentation and ground. Alex Ling is concise in his summary of Badiou's ontological reversal:

> That which is one (or is 'consistent') is not, strictly speaking, what *is*. Rather, what *is per se* is multiple (devoid of any instance of the one, radically withdrawn from all possible unification). Which is finally to say that being, thought in its very being (the 'being-ness' of being, or being *qua* being), is nothing other than inconsistent multiplicity. This is why Badiou holds that ontology is the science of the *pure multiple*.[111]

For Badiou, 'the one *is not*', which is to say there is no originary grounding one, no complete unity of being as Parmenides, and others in his wake, would have it (*BE*, 23). Badiou consequently affirms that being qua being is *multiple*, not 'one'. Being itself then is inconsistent, uncounted, whereas all instances of the one – that which is presented – are only such due to the 'operation' by which they are counted. Operations of this kind are inherent to 'situations', which 'present' multiples. In Badiou's *Manifesto for Philosophy* situations are simply defined: 'In the interests of brevity, let us call "situation", a state of things, any presented multiple whatsoever' (*MP*, 36).

Being itself then, as inconsistent multiplicity, is subtracted from presentation, but once counted by the presenting situation as 'one', multiples are rendered consistent. There is a localized (counted) multiple in every situation then, which, although it is counted as one, testifies to the inconsistent multiple *pre-count*, marks the difference between consistent, counted multiples – 'ones' – and their inconsistent ground, their 'being', so to speak. Badiou puts this point as follows: 'Although there is never anything other – in a situation – *than* the result (everything, in the situation, is counted), what thereby results marks out, before the operation, a must-be-counted. It is the latter which causes the structured presentation to waver towards the phantom of inconsistency' (*BE*, 53). It is 'the void' which allows that retroactive thought of being's inconsistency, and it produces a wavering in presentation reflecting the latter's radical contingency as the result of an operation.

For Badiou, the only thing we can know of being itself *is* the void, that is, nothingness itself. The void, or 'Ø' in set-theory, designates the existence of (the) nothing; in Badiou's words, its positing is in order to '*make* this nothing *be* through the assumption of a proper name. In other words: *verify, via the excedentary choice of a proper name, the unpresentable alone as existent*' (*BE*, 67). One facet of the void, then, is that it is the only thing in each situation that can be known of being; the void is a radical, localized 'nothing'. The main distinction between the void and nothing per se is that the void is local to every situation, each situation containing the void from which its presentation is woven. Badiou's reconfiguration of the Platonic dictum from the *Parmenides* dialogue, 'If the one is not, nothing is' to 'If the one is not, (the) nothing is', illustrates another, more fundamental facet of the void, namely that, in a similar way to Heidegger, 'the nothing' that *is* is foundational (*BE*, 36). Peter Hallward excavates this idea from Badiou's *Court traité d'ontologie transitoire* (published as *Briefings on Existence* in English) in his monograph *Badiou: A Subject to Truth* (2003): 'Set theory "pulls from the sole void a Universe."'[112] Further, in Hallward's correspondence with Badiou, the latter writes, 'I acknowledge only one type of reality: indifferent multiplicity or *multiple de multiple*. For everything else, the void is all I need.'[113]

In accordance with the subtraction of being from presence delineated earlier, the modern poem for Badiou, insofar as it still examines presence, can only testify to a radical 'lack' of being in presence, the void of being. The 'whole' of being cannot be disclosed, and the modern poem, breaking with Heidegger, must orientate itself towards something else: 'Only the poem accumulates the means of thinking outside-place, or beyond all place, "on some vacant or superior surface".'[114] Badiou's primary interlocutor when asserting the singular capacity of poetry to 'accumulate' these means of thinking beyond 'place', from an 'outside', is Stéphane Mallarmé, and he will be of central importance when I examine what Badiou calls 'the poetic idea'. However, Celan is also of understated yet fundamental importance to Badiou's understanding of 'the modern poem', the poem capable of producing a 'thought of being', and staying with Badiou's readings of Celan for now will consolidate the relations in play throughout this chapter between poetic language and divergent accounts of 'the nothing' based on differing approaches to ontology.

Reading Celan in *Handbook of Inaesthetics*, Badiou claims that 'the poem ... must bend itself for a narrow passage' (*HI*, 33). He cites Celan's poem from the posthumously published *Zeitgehöft* (1976), '*Es Kommt*', in John Felstiner's translation:

> From the narrower slit
> a gist is coming too,
> it's broken
> by the deadliest of our
> upstanding liths. (*HI*, 33)[115]

Badiou conflates 'gist' here with 'Idea' in his own language, of which more will be said in dialogue with Badiou's difficult essay, 'What Is a Poem? Or, Philosophy and Poetry at the Point of the Unnameable' (*HI*, 16–27). For now, it is clear that this idea or 'gist' will come from the 'narrower slit', or from an 'impassable' path, in Badiou's words (*TC*, 94). The signification of this 'narrowness' is obscure; it at once connotes the oppressive forcing of movement through constricted space and determines this movement to be outside or beyond whatever lies 'open'. For Badiou, this is distinctly poetry's task, to 'think beyond the open', to think 'the narrowness of the time' (*HI*, 33).

Though such claims can seem like unabashed moments of abstraction from the poem's concrete, textual life, the poem's original German and the decisions determining its rendering in English often lend support, as well as significant nuance, to Badiou's readings. For example, 'slit' in John Felstiner's translation, from 'Schneise', avoids the overtly religious connotations of 'aisle' or the syllabic excess of 'corridor'. In 'Schneise', however, both the noun *Schnee*, or 'snow' in German, and the verb *Schneien*, 'to snow', resonate, which is to say that 'the narrower slit' is a determinately 'poetic one', for 'snow' figures not only as a trope relating to loss across Celan's work[116] but to the practice of poetry itself too. One of many examples of this trope occurs at the outset of Celan's poem 'Homecoming' ('Heimkehr'), which begins 'Schneefall, dichter und dichter'.[117] Michael Hamburger's translation renders the opening line as 'Snowfall, denser and denser'; however, translation into English forecloses the paronomasia on 'Dichter', which means 'poet' in German, from operating beneath the snow's density.[118] Badiou's claim that it is specifically poetry's narrow path is supported via the poem's textual resonances in German.

'It's broken' is Felstiner's fascinating translation of 'Den erbricht'. *Erbricht* is the third-person, present tense of the verb *erbrechen*, or 'to vomit' in English; 'vomits' might be the expected translation. Instead, Felstiner has chosen to read 'erbricht' either as a contraction of 'er bricht', 'it/he breaks' in English, or more likely as an archaic, transitive form of *erbrechen*, in which *Sie erbrach* might mean 'she breaks open', for example.[119] More complications arise in the movement of the German article from 'der' to 'den', which operates, in a non-inflective language, as the means by which the case of the noun in question is shifted from nominative to accusative, so that a sentence's word order may be maintained even if subject and object are switched; 'den' is then used to make 'er' the object of the 'breaking', hence, 'it's broken'. Following 'den', however, the reader is also invited to conceive the verb 'erbricht' as a noun, the object of the sentence. This makes sense only if, beneath 'erbricht', the reader hears the German noun *Erbrecht*, typically 'inheritance' or 'inheritance law' in English. 'den erbricht' then figures both as something like 'the vomiting' and, more distantly, 'the inheritance', as well as a contraction of 'it breaks', or after 'den', 'it's broken'.

The way in which the German original opens a contradiction in its support of 'Sinn', the 'sense' that comes from this narrow, poetic path, or 'gist' in Felstiner's translation, offers Badiou the construction of a fragile, aleatory appearance. The poem sustains in the resonances above a contradictory moment, in which the 'gist' to come from the 'narrow slit' passes through, at the centre of the poem, both the rejection or 'throwing up' of inheritance and the latter's persistence. The German language is at once inherited *as* vomit, *as* broken, but regurgitated in the practice of the poem too. That one of the senses of 'inheritance' is decidedly poetic, like 'narrower slit', is suggested by the source word for 'our', 'unsrer', an archaic, 'literary' form of 'unser', a sense of 'our' then for which the 'we' invoked is embedded within the traditions of a collective experience of language. Poetic inheritance is further suggested in the source word for 'liths', 'Male' (also both 'time' and 'mark' or 'birthmark' in German), by the resonance of the verb 'malen' beneath it, which means to draw or paint, most commonly, but also to write carefully.[120] The narrow path through which the poem must pass is carved through language from within. For Badiou, the poem recognizes that at a particular historical juncture the poem cannot pretend to a grasp of the whole, and that the truth of that whole, its being, cannot be disclosed in the maintenance of a poetic language seeking the originary. Language must be broken, its inheritance vomited, and the poetic 'idea' produced by the modern poem is 'precariously rooted' at this boundary of language. How can these ideas about the capacity of poetic language to produce a 'thought of being', and what that thought of being might be like, relate to the fragment orientating this chapter, however, that 'Celan completes Heidegger'; that, through Celan, Badiou finds the resources to articulate the necessity of moving beyond Heidegger's avowal of the proximity between poetry and philosophy?

In *Manifesto for Philosophy*, Badiou writes that 'the real of [the] epoch', within which Celan wrote, 'was … inconsistency and disorientation'. The Age of Poets – the 'suturing' of philosophy and the poem under the watchful gaze of Heidegger – is closed by Celan's poetry, though the question of what it is about Celan's work specifically that enables Badiou to make this claim remains obscure. During the Age of Poets, each of Badiou's seven poets are said to testify to the *real* inconsistency and disorientation of this epoch: 'Poetry alone, or at least "metaphysical" poetry, the most concentrated poetry, the most intellectually strained poetry, the most obscure also, designated and articulated this essential disorientation.' For Badiou, this poetry testifies to the subtraction of being from presence, firstly, denying the possibility of disclosing once more in poetry an obfuscated or occluded sense of being qua being. But in a roundabout way, Badiou's claim about disorientation in poetry also retrospectively justifies his commitment to being qua being's 'inconsistent multiplicity' against this kind of unifying, transcendent wholeness or 'one' we might associate with ontologies of presence. For Badiou, the Age of Poets coincides with a historical epoch, following the Paris Commune, in which 'disorientation' is 'represented as oriented sense' (*MP*, 71). Badiou reads these 'modern' poems then as uniquely capable of thinking their own time, finding in them the attempt to both undermine consistent representations of 'Progress', 'History' and Utopian prophecying and present the twentieth century's 'real' instead by foregrounding interruptions and undermining static unifications (*MP*, 70–71). To do this the poems need not 'know' or accept of course that ontology equals mathematics, that the discourse of ontology may be written in set-theoretical language, or more broadly that being qua being is inconsistent and multiple, but they can testify in their own way to the fundamental withdrawal of a kind of grounding wholeness beyond the horizon, to the subtraction of being from presence. This is not to say that, with Celan's poems, as the last of the Age of Poets, this intensive examination of disorientation is terminated. Rather, Badiou's claim is that Celan's work testifies to the necessity of conceptualizing and thinking this disorientation in other modes of thought besides the poem: Celan's poems break language apart, deny poetic language's capacity for straightforward representation.

For Badiou, Celan's poems are crushed under the weight of a very particular solitude. Firstly, Celan testifies to the solitude of the poet tasked with being the *sole* producer of 'thoughts of being' in an Age of Poets in which truth is confined (by philosophy) to poetic enterprise. Badiou's claim is that Celan's poems interrupt not poetry per se but poetry insofar as philosophy has handed itself over to it. Badiou argues that Celan's poems demand that poetry's burden, the imperative that it alone must produce a 'thought of being', be rescinded, and this imperative is in direct opposition to the adoption of Celan's poetry to 'pronounce the ineluctable suture of philosophy to its poetic condition', something which Badiou deems Lacoue-Labarthe, for example, to be guilty of.[121] When Badiou writes that 'Celan's drama is to have had to confront sense in the non-sense of the epoch, its disorientation, with nothing but the solitary resource of the poem' (*MP*, 86), he is recognizing both that Celan works within a fundamentally compromised relation between language and meaning in the wake of the Holocaust and that his poetry, and language more broadly, we are to suppose, is overburdened as the sole medium working through the contingency of representation and the fundamental disorientation of the real.

Secondly, Celan's work carries the burden of a specific solitude bound to his relationship with Heidegger. Badiou claims that 'this philosopher referred to the poem, precisely in such a way as to make the poet feel more alone in his presence than ever before' (*MP*, 87). That is, Heidegger's consistent placement of poetic language at the heart of his approach towards being via thought becomes a hugely personal proposition for Celan, driven as he was by a poetic encounter with the horrors of the 1930s and 1940s, and its recapitulation in Heidegger's complicity, of which the latter, of course, remained more or less silent. This troubling intimacy between Heidegger and Celan is consolidated by their encounter in 1966,[122] to which Celan's poem 'Todtnauberg' attests. What is of crucial importance to this meeting, for Badiou at least, is Heidegger's silence concerning the Holocaust: Heidegger, within the suture of philosophy to the poem, remains unable to articulate the ostensibly political valence of his complicity in National Socialism. In Badiou's reading, following Lacoue-Labarthe, this silence proves intolerable to Celan, and his 'hope, today / of a thinking man's / coming / word / in the heart'[123] remains unfulfilled. For Badiou, this silence 'reveals the reductive and nihilating effects of the suture' (*MP*, 87); the exclusivity between philosophy and poem can no longer, in Celan's work, bear such a silence. Poetry's burden then is doubled by Heidegger's withdrawal from speech; the philosopher is unable to speak of history, politics and genocide, nor of complicity, so the responsibility falls on the poet. Badiou's claim is that Celan's poetry marks the end of the Age of Poets because his poems formally disavow the burden placed upon them, refusing to be the exclusive site in which a thought of being must be both produced and reflected upon.

Badiou brings these ideas together in his reading of Celan's 'Anabasis', which I look at far more closely in Chapter 3. The nuances of the solitude Celan's poems bear are gathered in what Badiou calls the 'outer-poem', a poem that moves within a place of exile and works towards the construction of a fragile collectivity: 'When in *Anabasis* he evokes the ascent ("upward and back") toward "the tent-word:/ Together", it is to the outer-poem he aspires, to the sharing of thinking less plunged into metaphoric uniqueness' (*MP*, 86). But there's another important point here. The demand that thought be 'shared' by the poem in this way, within an absence of metaphor, requires that the 'mystery' or 'enigma' of the poem be cut away and that the 'thought of being' that the 'modern poem' produces (its own silence perhaps, with which it confronts, in Celan's case, Heidegger's incapacity to speak) testifies to the fact that, from a philosophical perspective, being qua being can be conceptualized in the wake of mathematical innovations. The philosophical category of the 'Age of poets', then, is not simply closed as an epoch by the historical fact of Heidegger and Celan's meeting. If we recall the intensity with which Celan explores the contemporary condition of language in 'Es Kommt', in which language's broken inheritance must be vomited up, and, if we accept Badiou's gloss, that the 'rooting' of this language at its own conditions of possibility, with no grasp of the whole, we can consolidate our understanding of how Heidegger's sense of poetry's thought of being is radically disfigured in Badiou's work, especially in his reading of Celan's poems, for whom the language itself, having been corrupted by historic violence, is in no fit state to offer a totalizing epic in the manner of Perse testifying to being's return or more broadly to the return of wholeness, redemption, salvation. Celan's poetics crushes that demand: the poem's thought of being must be fragmentary, splintered and truthful to the disintegration of language as a medium of unifying representations.

Uncovering these difficult ideas concerning the sharing of thought beyond poetry's bounds encourages close scrutiny of Badiou's arguments relating the 'matheme' to the poem in his elaboration of 'the poetic idea'. Drawing heavily on Mallarmé, his primary poetic interlocutor, and the source from which he draws his philosophical category of the event,[124] Badiou's elaboration of the poetic idea also helps us to relate his readings of Celan to his readings of Mallarmé to come to a fuller understanding of poetry's 'thought of being' during the 'Age of Poets'.

In his essay 'What Is a Poem?, Or, Philosophy and Poetry at the Point of the Unnameable', collected in *Handbook of Inaesthetics*, Badiou charts the contrast between ancient Greek (Platonic) conceptions of the fraught relationship between poetry and the matheme, and this relationship's 'modern' manifestation. Embarking from a familiar point of departure, Badiou traces from Plato a founding 'quarrel' between philosophy and poetry, which transcends orthodox interpretations of *The Republic* for which the imitative charms of poetry force it into exile from politics, 'the grip of thought upon collective existence' (*HI*, 17). In *The Republic, Book X*, Plato highlights poetry's purely imitative techniques, foreclosing reason (as opposed to '*the lower, less rational part of our nature*') from its purview:

> The poet can use words and phrases as a medium to paint a picture of any craftsman, though he knows nothing except how to represent him, and the metre and rhythm and music will persuade people who are as ignorant as he is ... So great is the magic of poetry.[125]
>
> And this recalcitrant element in us gives us plenty of material for dramatic representation; but the reasonable element and its unvarying calm are difficult to represent.[126]

However, Badiou's intention is to place the question of poetry's relationship with thought in a 'far more radical and far more ancient discord than the one regarding images and imitation'. The heart of the quarrel for Badiou lies in the distinction between *dianoia*, or 'discursive thought', and poetry: '*Dianoia* is the thought that traverses, the thought that links and deduces. The poem itself is affirmation and delectation – it does not traverse, it dwells on the threshold. The poem is not a rule-bound crossing, but rather an offering, a lawless proposition' (*HI*, 17). The poem is an affirmation at the periphery of sense that resists logical reasoning. In fact, the poem reveals the contingency of rules and the law, punctures their movement from the outside – poetic language pitted against the rigorous abstractions of mathematics. As I demonstrated above, Badiou's claim that the modern poem can transmit a thought of being is bound tightly to poetic language's capacity to undermine and rupture false representations of unity or wholeness: the poem interrupts mere representation.

Badiou goes on to examine possible motives for the subversion of poetry by the authority of the matheme, including poetry's yoke 'to the immediate singularity of experience' contra the matheme's progress via deduction from the 'pure idea'. The Platonic distinction between poetic and mathematical thought is expressed by Badiou as follows. If the poem produces a thought, he claims,

> it is a thought *that cannot be discerned or separated as a thought*. We could say that the poem is an unthinkable thought. Mathematics is instead a thought that

is immediately written as thought, a thought that exists precisely inasmuch as it is thinkable. (*HI*, 19)

This distinction forces poetry's exile from philosophy, for Plato seeks to guard philosophy from its corruption by sophistry. In an age in which the poem and mathematics are resolutely opposed, the 'doubtful' status of thought affirmed in poetry forces it out of the 'servant's entrance' for Plato, whence mathematics, as the 'thought that is immediately written as thought', is brought through the 'main door': 'Let no one who is not a geometer enter here' (*HI*, 19). However, Badiou is keen to highlight Plato's own recourse to imagery and poetic language – 'images, like that of the sun … metaphors, like those of "prestige" and "power" … myths, like the myth of Er the Pampylian returning to the kingdom of the dead' (*HI*, 19) – once the limits of *dianoia*, 'a logos subject to a law', of which the paradigm is mathematics, have been reached: 'when thought must be absorbed in the grasp of what establishes it *as* thought', he writes, 'we witness Plato himself submitting language to the power of poetic speech' (*HI*, 18–20). The resolute opposition between poetry and mathematics in Plato, and the subsequent banishing of poetry from philosophy's realm, only serves to smuggle poetry back in via the back door. It is crucial, then, that 'we moderns', in Badiou's words, experience this distinction between poetry and the matheme very differently. How, we might ask, might mathematics inflect the poetry's 'modern' task?

Badiou claims that we have now 'taken the full measure, not just of everything that the poem owes to Number, but of the poem's genuinely intelligible vocation'. Badiou's argument here is that the set-theoretical discourse by which philosophy, from his perspective, is able to apprehend the discourse of ontology clarifies a key site of tension in poetic language concerning its capacity to refer, however indirectly, to objects in the world.[127] For Badiou, the poem in fact is the key site for the exploration of hitherto unaffirmed possibilities beyond the administered realm of the 'given' world due to the peculiarity of poetic signification, its apparent isolation or withdrawal from reference to the social world in which it is nonetheless created. Having passed ontology over to the set-theoretical discourse proper to its multiplicity, philosophy is now capable, for Badiou, of casting aside any lingering 'enigma' or 'mystery' of this 'modern poem' inaugurated by Mallarmé. The poem is rigorous: it organizes the withdrawal of the object from within its own bounds and produces, guided by our new understanding of both being qua being's subtraction from presence and its inconsistent multiplicity, a precise 'thought of being' affirmed without need for verification from the administered world.

Put another way, the thought produced by the poem can now be discerned as a thought separate from the sensible; the poem no longer suffers doubt as to its affirmative capacity. Correspondingly, the role of the matheme in our 'contemporary situation' is precisely to occupy the sophistical role performed by poetry in Plato's *Republic*. Despite his commitment to the Platonic Idea, Badiou divorces poetry from its Platonic imitative function. The poetic idea, for Badiou, stands alone, divorced from representation. There is something of a reversal, then, in the contemporary roles of poetry and mathematics in the wake of Badiou's axiomatic decision concerning being qua being (that it is multiple, inconsistent, conceptualizable, etc.). For Badiou, 'the matheme organizes itself around a vanishing point in which its Real is confronted by the impasse of any straightforward resumption of formalization', which is to say that the development of mathematical theory, especially in the work of Cantor, Gödel and Cohen, does not simply proceed from *itself* but is rather subject to aporias in its foundation, the disjunct between set-theory and category theory, for example, forcing *extra-mathematical* choices to determine the direction of the matheme's course. The modern poem unfolds itself, thinks the thought that it itself is, whereas contemporary mathematics works under the 'constraint of intellectual options the choice of which no purely mathematical prescription can command' (*HI*, 20). Badiou's conclusion at this point is that 'modernity makes the poem ideal and the matheme sophistical', and this lies in stark contrast to the understanding of the poetry/matheme couplet outlined in Plato, for example (*HI*, 21).

Modern poetry, understood as *ideal*, transmits a poetic idea, but crucially this idea is not *sensible*. From Mallarmé's *L'Après-midi d'un faune*, Badiou draws the conclusion that the pure idea of the modern poem surpasses what the sensible is capable of: 'it is because the wind and the water are nothing when compared with the power that art possesses to stir up the idea of water, the idea of wind' (*HI*, 21). The modern poem now 'identifies itself as a form of thought', and, Badiou continues, 'it is not just the effective existence of a thought offered up in the flesh of language, it is the set of operations whereby this thought comes to think itself'. When Badiou speaks of 'great poetic figures' (in Mallarmé: the Constellation, the Tomb or the Swan, for example), he seeks to demote the role of metaphor in poetry; these are not 'blind metaphors', he claims, but examples of organizing principles, creating a 'consistent *dispositif* in which the role of the poem is to engineer the sensory presentation of a regime of thought'. What were once considered metaphors, referring the reader outside the poem's bounds by metaphorical comparison to an object, now serve as integral parts of the poem's isolated machinery and the means via which it affirms the thought particular to it; the world at large barely figures here. In fact, the world of 'objective reality' is precisely what poems, for Badiou, depose.

This perplexing facet of Badiou's reading of Mallarmé is elaborated further in the lecture that gave us Badiou's conception of the 'modern' poem's 'central silence', 'Language, Thought, Poetry'. What Mallarmé's poems present to us, from Badiou's perspective, is an 'ontological affirmation' in a 'subtractive' mode. In other words, these poems present to us an affirmative 'thought of being', external to and poised against 'knowledge' and 'communication', that testifies to the withdrawal or subtraction of the object. Badiou's main point is that the poem organizes the refusal of the object: poetic language 'thinks' for Badiou precisely in its resistance to the object, its organization of the object's withdrawal. In Badiou's words, 'the heart of the poetic experience conceived as an experience of thought' – the matter at the heart of this chapter – 'does not set itself out as the apprehension of an object'. The particular way in which Mallarmé's poems emblematize the object's effacement is named the 'subtractive' mode of the object's deposition. But this subtractive mode is always oriented by the poem's autonomous affirmative potential. In organizing the deposition of the object, the poem presents, for Badiou following Mallarmé, the 'pure notion': 'This is a kind of pure, disobjectified and disenchanted thinking of the object. A thinking that is now *separate* from any givenness of the object' (*TW*, 242). The pure poetic idea is then self-contained, produced within the poem's own limits, and its thought subtracts from and then transcends the holding sway of objects in the sensible world:

> Through the visibility of artifice, which is also the thinking of poetic thought, the poem surpasses in power what the sensible is capable of itself. The modern poem is the opposite of a mimesis. In its operation, it exhibits an Idea of which both the object and objectivity represent nothing but pale copies. (*HI*, 21)

The poem must oppose mimesis, for the latter would only serve to glorify what already exists via representation; mimesis tethers poetic thought to the sensible. Instead, the poem's form, its artifice, consists in the gathering of strictly poetic entities. For Badiou, 'reality', as inconsistent multiplicity, is instead subtracted from experience. The 'modern poem', then, harbours the silence of 'reality' and depositions the object; it is 'a thought of presence upon a background of disappearance' (*HI*, 23).

Badiou's inspiration at this point finds much of its source material in Mallarmé's essay 'Crisis in Verse', in which Mallarmé writes:

What good is the marvel of transposing a fact of nature into its vibratory near-disappearance according to the play of language, however: if it is not, in the absence of the cumbersomeness of a near or concrete reminder, the pure notion.

I say: a flower! And, out of the oblivion where my voice casts every contour, insofar as it is something other than the known bloom, there arises, musically, the very idea in its mellowness; in other words, what is absent from every bouquet.[128]

The play of language in the poem forces the object, presented in nature, to recede. This is a process of purification by which the 'notion' is emptied of its instantiation in the sensible world, so that only the pure concept arises. This 'pure notion' must be discernible as such from the sensible world in order that it be affirmative, in order that is the thought *of itself*, 'what is absent from every bouquet'. This is an affirmation built upon the armature of the object's deposition or, in Badiou, the object's subtraction from poetic language.

For Badiou, through 'the poetic retention of its disappearance', the poem is able to reproduce the Platonic idea of presence, precisely by cutting presence from its ground; this is, in Badiou's words, 'presence itself as Idea' (*HI*, 25). A poetic ontology based on presence depends upon the possible disclosure of the object and its coming into being alongside others in a world. However, in the wake of an ontological decision in which being qua being is both made inconsistent and subtracted from presentation, the promise of such presentation in poetry is foreclosed. At the same time, that being is subtracted from language following the intervention of mathematics upon poetry is precisely what allows Badiou to claim that poetry has only now 'attained the poetic thinking of the thought that it itself is' (*HI*, 20). For, the poem can now offer an authentic 'thought of being', of the object's retreat, exhibiting 'an Idea of which both the object and objectivity represent nothing but pale copies' (*HI*, 21). Returning this conception of the poetic 'idea' or 'the pure notion' to the encounter between Badiou and Heidegger, then, the following illustrates, with specific reference to the modern poem, the former's departure from the latter:

> Every poem brings a power into language, the power of eternally fastening the disappearance of what presents itself. Or, through the poetic retention of its disappearance, the power of producing presence itself as Idea. (*HI*, 24–25)

The thought produced by the poem is a 'thought of being' which operates as testimony, the 'eternal fastening', of being's subtraction from presence. Of what presents *itself*, the unfolding of Heidegger's rose, it is the *itself* that retreats. The object in this case is relegated to a node point of the tension between being and presentation. In Heidegger, both being and presentation anchor each other, being is *phusis* after all. However in Badiou, what is presented is only thus as the result of an operation upon inconsistent multiplicity; in every situation's count-as-one, objects come to be presented. At the level of ontology then, for Badiou, being and presentation are to be radically distinguished, and the in-itself of the object falls away.

This distinction lends nuance to Badiou's subsequent fidelity to the Platonic Idea. The Idea and the subtraction of being are mutually implicating. The power of poetic thought, its capacity to *retain* the subtraction of being, is accomplished in the production of a poetic Idea testifying to the object's lack. And, at the point at which being is dissected from presence or appearance lies the emblem of the void, to which, for Badiou, the sole remaining 'enigma' of the modern poem attests. He writes:

> The mystery is, strictly speaking, that every poetic truth leaves at its own centre what it does not have the power to bring into presence. (*HI*, 23)

At the centre of the modern poem lies the void, its 'central silence', beyond which lies being, subtracted from presentation. The modern poem for Badiou, by testifying to the void of being, to the radical un-counted inconsistency of being qua being, and to this latter's severance from presentation and appearance, also forces poetic thought outside of poetry itself, outside of Celanic solitude, outside the burden of the poem's presence, in order to 'free the poem from its speculative parasites, to restore it to the fraternity of its time, where it will thereafter have to dwell side by side in thought with the matheme, love and political invention' (*MP*, 87). By offering Badiou's readings of Celan both sustained critical attention and their wider theoretical context, I hope to have demonstrated the efficacy of Celan's poems as an interface by which Badiou's philosophy can be placed in dialogue with Heidegger and his legacy. However, further work needs to be done to pursue this chapter's investigations of being, language and truth in the more specific context of the poem's relation to the 'subject'. The following chapter, then, explores Philippe Lacoue-Labarthe's writings on Heidegger, and their presentation of a twentieth-century imbrication of poem and politics, in order to make explicit at its close Badiou's demand for a poetic figure of the political subject capable of transcending the historical strictures of twentieth-century violence.

2

The Poem Becoming-Prose

Desacralization and authenticity

In *Briefings on Existence: A Short Treatise on Transitory Ontology* (1998/2006), conceived as a transitional work between *Being and Event* and *Logics of Worlds*, Alain Badiou opens with a prologue titled, instructively, 'God Is Dead'.[1] There, recapitulating his philosophical opposition to Heidegger, Badiou writes that 'Heidegger makes the Greek gods into the emblem or figure of the God who can return in the German tradition' (*BOE*, 29). Badiou aggressively opposes the lost figure of transcendence invoked here. One way of understanding Badiou's departure from Heidegger's reading of Hölderlin and the poem more broadly is as a process of secularization: What would a secular poem look like when the discourse of ontology forecloses transcendence, and when the infinite is capable of being seized on this earth, here and now? The first chapter's examination of the respective ontologies of Heidegger and Badiou is here pulled into the realm of the poetic in order to reflect on Heidegger's political mobilization of the Hölderlinian imbrication of poetry and the sacred. The 'German tradition' of course marks the other main line of enquiry concerning the relation between philosophy and poem, which is its triangulation by politics. The politics at stake here is related closely to nation building, to the future of Germany, to a people coming into its proper historical being, taking ancient Greece as its model. If the national emergence of a people into their historical being is politically nefarious, what might be the political implications of the 'inaesthetic' relation between philosophy and poem Badiou proposes? This chapter argues that the way into thinking about the political consequences of the relation between philosophy and the poem from Heidegger to Badiou lies in the role of 'myth' in poetry, a topic explored at length by Philippe Lacoue-Labarthe in his writings on Heidegger and Hölderlin. There has not been one study of Badiou's engagement with Lacoue-Labarthe when it comes to the relation between poetry and philosophy, yet Lacoue-Labarthe, across the two elegies written for him by Badiou, has emerged recently as Badiou's most important interlocutor when exploring these questions. This chapter also, then, examines their argument concerning the proximity between poem and philosophy – whether to maintain their intimacy or distance them once more? – and its implications for politics and for philosophy at large. It consolidates this argument by introducing the category of the political subject so prevalent in the book's third chapter. Finally, I argue that the resources Badiou offers to contemporary understandings of the relation between philosophy and the poem are bound to his maintenance of the political subject as an active agent.

Badiou's most pervasive claim about Heidegger's reading of Hölderlin is that he makes poetic language the place for the maintenance and exploration of an idea of transcendence, named the 'God of poets'. The poem's 'putting to work' of being, or its 'thought of being', for the late Heidegger, is wedded to the question of this God's return and is therefore a matter of consolidating, in contrast to Badiou's later commitment to being qua being's subtraction, the 'Oneness' of being, or being's transcendence. Badiou is drawing here on the early texts in Heidegger's in his protracted reading of Friedrich Hölderlin. The publication of his 1934–1935 lecture course in Freiburg on the hymns 'Germania' and 'The Rhine' is prefaced by a 'preliminary remark' in which he writes: 'One treats Hölderlin "historiographically" and fails to recognize the singular, essential point that his work, still without time or space, has already surpassed our historiographical rummagings and has grounded the commencement of another history: that history that starts with the struggle over the decision concerning the arrival or flight of the God.'[2] The poetic word 'grounds' 'Being', inaugurates a new history, surpassing the 'forgetting of Being' enacted in metaphysics. Elucidating these connections between the Gods' possible return, poetry's role as the founding word and the inauguration of a new history, Jennifer Gosetti-Ferencei's important study *Heidegger, Hölderlin and the Subject of Poetic Language* emphasizes the poem's gathering function as it looks to the past and its inaugurative promise in the present: for Heidegger, the poem 'presses on into the danger of metaphysical forgetting in order to gather the traces of remembrance', and he 'affords a supreme power to the poetic word of founding truth'.[3] To become the site of the god's possible return requires the poem mobilize myth, which allows the politically questionable invocation of 'a people' or 'nation', the 'German tradition' for example, whose 'historical vocation' is the 'free use of the national', the 'creating of a space of play within which the national can freely transform itself into history'.[4] Heidegger draws this language from Hölderlin's famous letter to the young poet Casimir Ulrich Böhlendorff, in which he proposes, in Richard Sieburth's words, a 'profoundly dialectical vision of the relation between modern and ancient, northern and southern, German and Greek'.[5] Hölderlin's meditation on an ideal aesthetics here, musing on the alacrity with which Homer transforms the 'innate' Greek quality of possessing 'the fire of the heavens' or 'holy pathos' by 'appropriating the foreign' 'Occidental, *Junonian sobriety*', or clarity of thought and representation, emphasizes reciprocity of cultural exchange: Hölderlin is clear that the relations between these supposed opposites, both during the time of Homer and in Hölderlin's contemporary world in which an ununified Germany in the wake of the French Revolution imaginatively re-engages with the classical world, are generative and reversable. The critic and friend of Celan, Peter Szondi, as Beatrice Hanssen writes in an important study of Walter Benjamin's reading of Hölderlin, explains that 'the interplay between occidental sobriety and Greek pathos didn't merely go beyond the customary cataloguing of antiquity and modernity, typical of classicism, but in fact for Hölderlin became a necessary, constitutive tension'.[6] However, these opposites are given an ostensibly political inflection by Heidegger who emphasizes instead 'the national', the 'Dasein of the Germans', and the necessity of 'struggle' for a people to 'achieve its highest'.[7] 'The hour of our history has struck', writes Heidegger: 'The violence of beyng must first and actually become a question again for our ability to grasp.'[8]

These questions of transcendence and national identity are usefully prefaced by some of Badiou's work in *The Century*. Badiou argues that the main drive behind the twentieth century's artistic and political projects, and the key to understanding their conjunction of innovation and violence, is their attempt to *realize* the utopian dreams of the nineteenth century. Badiou names this desire the 'passion for the real'. Crucially, this passion for the real is in some sense the result of godlessness, of the retreat of the 'meaning' that transcendence affords humankind. Badiou's chosen interlocutor here is Friedrich Nietzsche. In the final chapter of *The Century*, Badiou argues that the content of one of the two 'great hypotheses' produced by the century concerning the relation between God and humankind is Nietzschean, that 'the absenting of God is one of the names for the absenting of man' (*TC*, 171). Anticipating this new era for Badiou, Nietzsche declares the death of God, and in so doing declares the death of humankind too. In the wake of God's death, humankind must reinvent itself in a world from which transcendent guarantees of meaning have fled.

For the first half of the twentieth century, an epoch punctuated by the two world wars, and more importantly for Badiou's purposes by the Russian

Revolution and the Spanish Civil War, Badiou argues that, from the point of view of 'the century' itself (the main conceit at work in *The Century*), 'violence is legitimated by the creation of a new man' in the wake of God's death (*TC*, 32). Humankind is both the subject and the object of this new beginning, and this inauguration is borne by the death of God, the withdrawal of transcendence. It is these two points that allow us to situate Heidegger's reading of Hölderlin as one of many attempts to think through the retreat of the Gods alongside the creation of a new subject. In the Heideggerian stance demands the return in poetic language of being's unconcealedness, and its subsequent restoration for a humanity cut adrift in the midst of technologization.[9] But the Heideggerian motifs of myth and transcendence and their imbrication with the desire for a new beginning are inextricable from nationalist terror and violence.[10] For Badiou, on the other hand, secularization must be a founding tenet of both philosophical and poetic thinking if contemporary thought is to depart from Heidegger.

In *Briefings on Existence*, the directive for poetry specifically is 'to conquer its own atheism', to overcome the assertion of a merely *withdrawn* God by affirming God's death and thus to place the resources for any poetic re-enchantment of the world (by which we might understand any 'new' conception of man too) in the world at large, and not under the auspices of a lost God lying beyond the horizon. 'The poem has only to be devoted', for Badiou, 'to the enchantment of what the world is capable of – as it is' (*BOE*, 29–30); the poem enchants not the 'world' but its infinite possibilities. The 'modern poem' for Badiou must affirm, via the poetic idea, that the infinite can impinge upon the world as it is, without invoking a kind of lost or withdrawn transcendence: '[The poem] has only to discern the infinite "*surrection*" [pertaining to upheaval, uplift, elevation] of invisible possibilities up to the impossible itself' (*BE*, 30). Badiou's desire to kill off the God of poets mirrors a broader directive he imposes on philosophy in his *Manifesto for Philosophy*, namely the imperative to have done with 'nihilism', with the idea that being qua being and truth lie withdrawn elsewhere, beyond the horizon of possible actions.

'Nihilism', of course, is as good a name as any other for what Badiou's philosophical project at large opposes. In Badiou's *Manifesto for Philosophy* we find a relatively rare engagement with Marx, in which Badiou declares, against charges of nihilism, that 'for Marx, and for us, desacralization is not in the least nihilistic, insofar as "nihilism" must signify that which declares that the access to being and truth is impossible. On the contrary, desacralization is a *necessary condition* for the disclosing of such an approach to thought' (*MP*, 56). For Badiou there are three objects of this programme of desacralization, three

'Gods'. In *Briefings on Existence*, Badiou claims the 'God of poets' to be the last remaining God, following the demise of the 'God of religion', or the 'living God', and the 'God of metaphysics'. It is crucial that Badiou retrospectively assigns these two previous Gods to a particular task, that of investing the world with sense or meaning. In the case of the God of religion, Badiou writes, 'There is no question that one of the functions of religion is to give sense to life, and more particularly to the shadow that life bears, death itself, which is anchored to the real' (*BOE*, 24). The 'living' God, for Badiou, both gives meaning to life, but also, more pertinently, provides a palliative to the existential agony produced by mortality; there is a conjunction between the provision of meaning and the soothing of affect.

By contrast, the God of metaphysics is dead: 'As Pascal objected to Descartes', Badiou writes, 'only a dead God is really suitable for metaphysics'. In contrast to the 'living God', by whom we make sense of life, 'metaphysical risk', for Badiou, requires that God be thought only insofar as the 'convincing consistency of a concept' is concerned, according to which we may 'guarantee that truths make sense' (*BOE*, 25). Both the living God of religion and the dead God of metaphysics lend sense to the world. For Badiou, the 'great metaphysical work of the mortification of God' is 'marshalled according to sense'. Yet, in contrast to faith in the living God, this metaphysical work 'holds back on all affects and existential plunging' into the sense thus provided; sense is given to the world, but the palliative for affect is not provided. In the early years of the twentieth century, then, when the death of both the living God of religion and the God of metaphysics are declared following Nietzsche and Heidegger, how are we to appraise this third God, the God of Poets, in terms of both 'sense' (what is the meaning with which this God imbues the world?) and 'affect' (what if anything does the God of poets soothe?). For Heidegger, whose main concern throughout his philosophical writings was to reckon with the withdrawal of being from beings, to claim in his testimonial *Der Speigel* interview that 'only a God can save us' demands God be proposed to thought in a new way (*BOE*, 25).

Before moving on to considering Hölderlin's poetry and the manner in which it engages these ideas about transcendence, I want to consider in a little more detail the 'God of poets' specifically that Badiou draws on in his departure from Heidegger. The most instructive passage from *Briefings on Existence* concerning the God of poets is the following:

> This god, or these gods, or the divine principle do exist. They are the creation of romanticism and distinctly of the poet Hölderlin. This is why I name it the God

of poets. It is neither the living Subject of religion, although it is certainly about living close to Him. Nor is it the Principle of metaphysics, although it is all about finding in His proximity the fleeing sense of Totality. It is that from which, for the poet, there is enchantment of the world. (*BOE*, 28)

The 'God of poets' figures as the assertion in poetry that the gods have withdrawn, and that through poetic language, a proximity to these lost gods may be maintained. Poetic language is the privileged point of access to those gods withdrawn beyond the horizon; it provides a means of transferral, a means of asserting a nearness, potentially bridging the distance. At the level of sense, the world is enchanted via the assertion of this proximity, but the extent to which existential affects are soothed by the God of Poets is altogether more complicated than the cleansing provided by faith in the living God, or the straightforward absence of affective contributions in the work of metaphysics: the God of poets produces proximity, but also longing. Most dispiritingly from Badiou's perspective, one imagines, this maintenance of the God of poets also ensures the lasting primacy of finitude. We are proximate to this withdrawn God insofar as we will surely die. This is an understanding of poetic language that relies distantly on death, towards which 'Totality flees'. Of course, Badiou's 'event' is the alternative way in which the 'Totality' might be punctured, its contingency revealed.

Badiou's process of desacralization, as Christopher Watkin explains in his book *Difficult Atheism: Post-Theological Thinking in Alain Badiou, Jean-Luc Nancy and Quentin Meillassoux*, marks a decisive, constitutive shift away from Heideggerian thinking: '[Heidegger] fails to recognise the originality of the Greek interruption of the poem by the matheme, and so he cannot but restore the sacred authority of poetic speech that locates authenticity in the flesh of language.'[11] Badiou wants to eradicate what Watkin calls the 'sacred authority' afforded to the poem by Heidegger without stripping poetry of its capacity for thought. For Badiou, Hölderlin offers a poetry in which this authority is granted but cannot be fully realized:

> The poet's task – or as Hölderlin wrote, his courage – is to bear in language the thought of the God that has withdrawn as it is also to conceive of the problem of Its return as an open insertion into that of which thought is capable. (*BOE*, 28)

In Badiou's reading of Hölderlin, poetic thought must harbour this withdrawal, must testify to absence, but it must also designate the space of the God's possible return. The poem bears the problem as an opening onto the possible and asks whether the question of the God's return can be maintained in poetic thinking. However, this relationship to the 'poetic God' is one of nostalgia: Hölderlin's poetry 'melancholically envisages a chance to re-enchant the world through the gods' improbable return' (*BOE*, 28). Badiou's directive for philosophy requires this melancholy be dispelled – melancholy, because the wait produces stasis in thought.

One fundamental starting point for Badiou's philosophy then is the desacralization of this 'enchanted world' that finds the source of its enchantment in withdrawn transcendence. But also, in a strict reversal of the philosophical legacy left by the conjunction of Hölderlin and Heidegger, this disenchantment of the world is a 'necessary condition', grounded by the 'Greek interruption of the poem by the matheme', for reclaiming the categories of being and truth. Badiou's conviction is that we can access being and truth now in the wake of Modernist mathematics. Badiou's wager in the opening pages of *Briefings on Existence*, then, is to declare the dissolution of the Gods and their poetic aura in the coldness of the matheme. This dispelling of transcendent aura is the first stage in coming to terms with the political implications, however broad, of Badiou's conception of the relationship between philosophy and the poem, especially insofar as this conception breaks with that of the 'end of the desire for philosophy', Badiou's main point of contention with Philippe Lacoue-Labarthe (*C*, 2). Although there is a move towards the rejection of the hold of transcendence upon philosophy in general here, for Badiou this process of secularization must also take hold in the 'modern poem'. Under the watch of Heidegger throughout the Age of Poets, because poetry is designated as the sole site for philosophical thought, the melancholic loss of the gods and the wait for their return both express a stasis within philosophy itself; philosophy, following the end of metaphysics, is condemned to nostalgia for a lost past or origin, and to a perpetual vigilance with little prospect of forward movement. Badiou's radical secularization is directed towards the demise of all forms of transcendence. But, this is also to invest the world *as it is* with meaning; it is to secularize meaning so that the possibilities of the world itself have the capacity to give sense to life.

The connection between transcendence and myth in the meeting of philosophy and poetry that Badiou opposes is not an obvious one. However, much interpretation of Hölderlin's poetry appears to focus on the connection between myth and the divine. For example, on Norbert von Hellingrath's influence on Hölderlin's reception, Robert Savage writes in his *Hölderlin after the Catastrophe: Heidegger – Adorno – Brecht*:

> Hellingrath's most far-reaching legacy was to discover in Hölderlin a reservoir of divine experience in a godless age [...] Through the force of his experience and the purity of its expression, Hölderlin shattered the categories of historical understanding and literary judgement applied by critics, exposing them to

the deeper truth of myth. Hellingrath's ambition was to recover this mythic dimension in Hölderlin's poetry.[12]

In his appraisal of Hellingrath, Savage forces an intimate connection between the 'divine experience' to which Hölderlin's poetry attests and the 'deeper truth of myth'. Following the enlightenment withdrawal of transcendence, Hellingrath, and Heidegger after him, finds in Hölderlin's work a mythic dimension which allows humanity to begin again, to live in proximity to God once more. The poetic invocation of myth in Hölderlin, then, according to these interpreters, belongs essentially to the realm of transcendence. I want to suggest, however, that it is myth specifically that invites questions of political import.

Savage also traces the interpretation of Hölderlin's poetry by the Hölderlin Society in the mid-twentieth century to the earlier twentieth-century work of both Hölderlin's first modern editor, Norbert von Hellingrath, and the literary scene surrounding the poet Stefan George. Two interrelated motifs dominate this early-twentieth-century reception of Hölderlin's work. The first is his adoption as the poet of the German people, an idea appropriated and amplified under the Third Reich during a period in which Joseph Goebbels was honorary patron of the Hölderlin Society and a hundred thousand copies of a 'field edition' of Hölderlin's work prepared by Friedrich Beißner were sent to German soldiers on the front.[13] Hölderlin's appropriation under National Socialism and the close attention paid to Hölderlin's later works by Heidegger both serve as productive points of departure in assessing the broadly political implications associated with early-twentieth-century approaches to the relationship between philosophy and poetry, and the subsequent rupture marked by Badiou's thought insofar as it concerns this relationship.

Before proceeding to a close reading of Hölderlin's hymn 'The Journey', returning to two key passages from *The Century* helps to clarify how Badiou thinks through the complex relationship between myth and politics. In the first passage Badiou makes the connection between the quest for origin through myth, the Heideggerian concept of authenticity and what is elsewhere in *The Century* deemed a violent attempt at 'purification':

> For a whole host of thinkers, particularly in the area of fascist thought (and without excepting Heidegger), 'the new man' is in part the restitution of the man of old, of the man who had been eradicated, had disappeared, had been corrupted. Purification is actually the more or less violent process of a return of a vanished origin. The new is a production of authenticity. In the final analysis, the task of the century is viewed here as restitution (of the origin) through destruction (of the inauthentic). (*TC*, 65)

In 'Fascist thought' the quest for origin, for 'mythic totalities', is placed under the auspices of a political programme. Man, trapped in inauthentic being, must restore the eradicated man of old. The purification of man requires that authentic 'new' man be created via the restoration of obscured being, via a return to 'vanished origin'. Importantly, it is 'mythic totalities' which provide the resources for thinking this origin – 'race, nation, earth, blood and soil' – and 'the new man' becomes a 'collection' of 'predicates' – 'Nordic, Aryan, warrior, and so on' (*TC*, 66) – on their basis. The relation between inauthenticity and authenticity then is subsumed under identification. That is, the violent production of authenticity depends upon the retrieval and reappraisal of lost identifications. Reality is purified insofar as those identifications which obscure origin are erased, clearing the space for the restoration of 'mythic totalities'.

The second quotation emphasizes the political implications of this return to originary identities, making present their relation to the melancholy 'waiting' that Badiou diagnoses in both the poetry of the Age of Poets and philosophy in the wake of the Holocaust:

> There exists a passion for the real that is obsessed with identity, to unmask copies, to discredit fakes [...] This passion can only be fulfilled as destruction. Herein lies its strength – after all, many things deserve to be destroyed. But this is also its limit, because purification is a process doomed to incompletion, a figure of the bad infinite. (*TC*, 56)

The above quotation conjoins the violent, political programme of purification with the identificatory 'mythic totalities', presented above under the sign of authenticity. The search for the authentic comprises both the violent purification of inauthenticity and the restoration of lost, explicitly mythical, identifications. The passion for the real is here bound to identity, and this is to make the destruction of inauthentic identifications one primary concern, alongside the restoration of identifications bound to myth – 'Aryan', 'warrior', etc. – in order to foster the emergence of a concrete or 'real' hitherto obscured authenticity. It is crucial here that this programme of destruction is 'doomed to incompletion': by subsuming the passion for the real to the destruction and subsequent creation of identity, purification can never be completed. This is because, as Badiou remarks elsewhere in another lecture included in *The Century*, 'The Passion for the Real and the Montage of Semblance', 'semblance' operates as the 'true situating principle of the real' (*TC*, 48). That is, perhaps the 'most real' characteristic of the real is its localization by semblance. Commenting on the Moscow trials in which many members of the Communist Party were 'cleansed', Badiou concludes that 'the real ... is never real enough not to be suspected of semblance'. The 'subjective categories' of revolutionary politics, Badiou continues, 'conviction', 'loyalty', 'virtue', etc., all become suspect (*TC*, 53). By seeking the real in identity, the quest for authenticity is condemned to failure; there is never a way of guaranteeing the requisite level of 'pure' identification has been reached. Put another way, the 'purification' of 'inauthentic' identities to approach 'the real' is always left incomplete by a residue of semblance.

My reading of Friedrich Hölderlin's hymn 'The Journey' below consolidates these ties between transcendence and myth, and examines further how they are mobilized and evolved in Heidegger's reading of Hölderlin. It will also further examine the significance of this thinking with regard to politics, especially insofar as the categories, 'mythic totalities' perhaps, of the 'German' or the 'Greek' people are invoked. Reading Hölderlin will also allow us to draw out the development of important conceptions of the relations between same and other, native and foreign, Germany and Greece, all of which influence the precise nature of the categories of the subject I turn to in Chapters 3 and 4. I want to suggest too that Hölderlin's poem offers us a keener appreciation of what Badiou terms 'a poetics of the wait', and that this theme has important consequences for understanding Badiou's departure from Heidegger insofar as ontology, poetry and thought are concerned.

Hölderlin's 'The Journey'

Hölderlin's hymn 'The Journey' ('*Die Wanderung*', 1807) imagines the dialectical becoming of 'Swabia', the speaker's homeland. The poem's basic movement comprises a departure and a return. From an initial appraisal of homeland, Swabia, the poem departs upon an imaginary journey into the past, following the waters of the Danube towards the Black Sea. The Swabia to which the poem returns is refigured in light of this journey outwith its bounds. Conceived at first in the abstract, 'Swabia' is negated via the assertion of a dream wish, 'But I am bound for the Caucasus!', and is then reappraised following the emergence of a lost, ostensibly Greek origin.[14] Through an imaginary journey into the distant past, 'Swabia' emerges as a homeland imbued with Greek mythology, and the practice of poetry emerges as one inextricably tied to the retrieval of originary transcendence in the form of myth. Pivoting on the speaker's desirous exclamation for the Caucasus, the reader follows the speaker through their utopian (because out of reach) vision of the past, through which the initial address to Swabia is reconfigured.

The structure of 'The Journey' depends on the invocation of two rivers, the Rhine and the Danube, as well as an apparent tension between light and shade. Both of these structuring tropes anchor the question of 'homeland' within the practice of poetry, beyond the auspices of 'The Journey', itself. The hymn begins (in Michael Hamburger's translation): 'Most happy Swabia, my mother, / Whom like the more shining, your sister / Lombarda over there / A hundred rivulets thread!'[15] At first, the speaker presents 'Swabia' and 'Lombarda' in abstract form: summoned in the imagination, the respective landscapes and the Swiss Alps shading them fall across three territories, Swabia, Lombarda and Switzerland. Impossible to view all at the same time, the three regions are dispersed in the imagination. This lack of the 'in itself' is exemplified by the glare, 'more shining', produced by the sun hitting the rivulets of Lombarda: distant Lombarda exists only insofar as it appears, and the concrete apprehension of Lombarda itself is barred by a dazzling light. The poetic invocation of these localities is further abstracted through metaphor: initially, 'Swabia' and 'Lombarda' fall under abstract ideas of the maternal or sororal, 'my mother', 'your sister'.

In the same opening stanza, this invocation of rivulets, which draw the distant landscapes of Swabia and Lombarda together, anticipates an eventual return to the fluvial source from which they 'purl', located in the 'alpine ranges of Switzerland'. This source is designated as a gift from the Gods; the river water emanates from 'silver votive vessels', ' ... poured out / By hands that are pure'. This is the first point in the poem at which the rivers' sources are tied to mythic transcendence. Rivers operate throughout 'The Journey' as sources, providing 'trees enough, white-flowering' and the means of exchange and communication; both of these operations are intimately connected with the invocation of the Gods. Between Swabia and Lombarda lies the source: both the Rhine and the Ticino rivers arise in the Swiss Alps. It is this sharing of origin at the hands of the Gods which allows both landscapes to be invoked at once. This double invocation, born of fluvial source, anticipates the central movement enacted in 'The Journey', the imaginary return to another, more distant, origin by following the waters of the Danube. The 'well-spring' waters figure as the source of both homeland and poetic impulse, inviting a poetic journey downriver in order to consolidate and reconfigure these early invocations of both maternal homeland and the practice of poetry itself.

For Badiou, this fluvial source takes on an even more prominent role because it serves to tie the practice of poetry to homeland. In a meditation on Hölderlin's hymns in *Being and Event*, Badiou declares that, for Hölderlin, homeland is treated as the site via which an event will come.¹⁶ More pertinent to the current discussion, however, is the assertion that the 'fluvial escape' downriver 'is precisely what links one to the homeland', which is to say that 'the very *being* of the homeland is that of escaping' (*BE*, 256). What links all of the distinct territories in the opening stanza is the appearance of rivulets, which, through the glare they emit as the light hits them, actually foreground themselves above the features of the discrete landscapes. Flowing water and its tie to origin is precisely what allows the reimagining of the homeland via an encounter with the other; homeland is coursed through by the fluxive river. Badiou wants to suggest that for the poet to remain faithful to the 'homeland' requires they depart from it, and on their returning, having been 'struck by the god', requires further the poetic restoration of a 'sense of its proximity', 'forever [evaluating] the veritable essence of what is there'. I want to preface what follows concerning the presentation of poetic work in 'The Journey' with Badiou's conclusion on this point, namely that 'fidelity thus designates the poetic capacity to inhabit the site at the point of return' (*BE*, 257). The poet stalks the boundary between abstracted present and distant origin but maintains a privileged point of access to this origin by opening up the possibility of its restoration.

The shade produced by the Swiss Alps at the beginning of the hymn ('And alpine ranges of Swtizerland cast their shade / On you, the neighbouring, too; for close to the hearth of / The house you dwell'), in which the homeland finds its immediate origin, only serves to obscure more distant origins as the poem enters its second stanza:

> [...]
> By hands that are pure, when touched
>
> By warming beams
> The crystalline ice and, tumbled
> By gently quickening light
> The snowy summit drenches the earth
> With purest water.¹⁷

It is the sun's 'warming beams' and 'gently quickening light' which operate as images of transcendence, as correlates of the 'pure hands' from which the 'wellspring purls'. Shaded from the figure of the sun by the Swiss Alps, however, Swabia is placed at a distance from those warming beams which, by melting the snows of the mountains, drench 'the earth / With purest water'. Under the shade of the alps, Swabia benefits from being 'close to the hearth of / The house', yet the real source of its nourishment is out of reach. Shaded by the mountains, Swabia has no access to the sun, and no access therefore to the Gods, to the warming beams. There is a metaphorical exclusion involved here: the poem presents Swabia as a land that benefits from its proximity to the nourishing force of the river, yet Swabia is distanced from the figure of its transcendent origin. Immediate origin, the river's source in the alps, is accessible, but at the cost of a more distant transcendent origin, to light to which the Gods are indexed.

Elsewhere in Hölderlin's hymns, the symbol of the sun attains a constitutive role for the practice of poetry. In 'The Ister', for example, the speaker invokes the sun as a figure of poetic commencement, the symbol of the poetic foundation of a new present. The first three lines read:

> Now come, fire!
> Eager are we
> To see the day.[18]

In Heidegger's reading of this hymn, the 'calling' of the fire marks the poetic inauguration of a new 'Now', a 'Now' to be dissociated from the usual course of things. For Heidegger, the sun's rising each day, and our expectation that it will continue to do so, subtracts its happening from our attentiveness. In the sun's diurnal rising we find the figure of a contemporary timelessness borne by modernity:

> In the succession of night and day, the rising of the sun designates an ever recurring, temporally self-deferring, yet otherwise uniform point in time, a 'now' that has also already been forgotten and fallen into indifference with the breaking of the day.[19]

The 'now' of the rising of the sun forever recurs, always eliding itself in its becoming; it only *is* insofar as it vanishes. This present then is always falling away, is always forgotten. The inauguration of the day has always fallen away from the day itself, there is no 'breaking' of the day, and this is to suggest an experience of timelessness, of indifference with regard to the present. Far from simply 'calling' the sun to come, Heidegger claims that, because it is always already arriving, the sun in fact emits a call to those who would be called by it. 'Which "Now" is meant by the call?', Heidegger continues, 'The "Now" names the time of calling of those who are of a calling, a time of poets.'[20]

The relationship between the light of the sun and the privileged role poetry plays in the quest to uncover source as origin can be read in 'The Journey' too. There, the 'German people' initiate an encounter with the 'children of the Sun'.[21]

> Someone confided to me
> That time out of mind our parents,
> The German people, had quietly
> Departed from the waves of the Danube
> One summer day, and when those
> Were looking for shade, had met
> With children of the Sun
> Not far from the Black Sea's beaches;
> And not for nothing that sea
> Was called the hospitable.[22]

The poet speaker has been tasked with guarding a secret: there was a time now obscured in thought, 'time out of mind', when the German people followed the Danube from its source in the Black Forest towards its mouth in the Black Sea. This was a movement out of the 'shade' of the 'alpine ranges of Switzerland' into light. The poet now takes on the role of envoy. The movement enacted by the German people is towards the warmer climes of the Caucasus, but we also find a metaphorical movement of the poetic consciousness into light; shaded Swabia is negated (becoming light) following the imaginary fulfilment of the speaker's wish, 'But I am bound for the Caucasus.' The journey of the poet and the journey of the German people take place together. The precarity of the situation in which the German people find themselves as well as the poet's assertion of a 'now' force an attempted return, a 'looking for shade'. This is a 'now' determined earlier in the strophe:

> But I am bound for the Caucasus!
> For only today
> I heard it said in the breezes
> That free as swallows the poets are.[23]

The poet is entrusted with his task 'only today', asserting the 'now' of the present, the inauguration of a new time. But also 'only' today, only in this determined present can the poet fulfil the dream wish of travel to the Caucasus. The figure of the swallow operates in a similar fashion. Firstly, poets are as 'free as swallows'. The wish to return to the Caucasus is made actual in its possibility via the freedom afforded to poetic thinking; that is, for the poet to travel towards the 'land of Homer' requires they be free as the migrating swallow. The swallow is invoked further on in the poem too and designated as one of the 'emissaries' of the 'land of Homer':

Your emissaries, in the vineyard for me
The young green peaches cling
And the swallow comes from afar.[24]

Through the figure of the swallow the poem constructs a sense of reciprocity within poetic thinking. Not only can poets travel towards distant origins by virtue of their freedom, they also receive news of these origins via privileged 'emissaries'; the swallow then operates as one of the figures of poetic travel, both towards the pure past and returning from it. Thanks to the images of the sun and the swallow, the poet is to be tasked with inauguration, the creation of a new beginning. In 'The Journey' too, there is a sense in which this beginning depends upon the restoration of the consequences of the German people's encounter with the 'children of the Sun'. The poet must force an encounter with his or her 'worthy forbears' and then travel back, as the swallow does, in order to force through this inauguration.

Robert Savage ties 'inception', or inauguration, explicitly to the transcendent. On Heidegger's interpretation of Hölderlin, Savage writes:

> The leitmotif in the conversation is easy enough to identify: the conviction he announced in 1934, at the beginning of his first lecture course on Hölderlin, that the poet's 'still space-time-less work has already overcome our petty historical affairs and founded the inception of another history, that history that commences with the struggle for the decision about the arrival or flight of the god,' will never waver.[25]

Here, Savage highlights Heidegger's unwavering commitment to a particular idea of Hölderlin as the poet responsible for a new founding of Being, an inception dependent upon both an imaginary turning back towards a distant god and the opening of the poem towards the question of this god's withdrawal or arrival. Hölderlin's work operates as a return from a 'petty' conception of history in which this question of transcendence, as well as the question of 'being' itself, is obscured; the recommencement of an authentic history must take the question of this god as its starting point.

I want to return now to the question of identification in the invocation of both the 'homeland' and 'the German people'. Writing about Stefan George, Savage argues:

> George had addressed Hölderlin from the beginning as the saviour of the *German* people, rather than the people of the Occident or of a fallen modernity more generally. 'We call it a miracle when for generations unheeded or only as

tender dreamer from ages past suddenly the great Prophet of his people steps into the light,' he announced dramatically in 1908.²⁶

Undoubtedly, George's adoption of Hölderlin as the prophet of the German people anticipates Heidegger's own interpretation, but also interprets the problem of 'fallen modernity' as a specifically German one. The causes of the specific localization of this crisis of modernity are manifold and complex; however, in the 'The Journey' it is telling that the German people are deemed to have lost a fundamental relationship with Ancient Greece. Hölderlin provides a narrative of the becoming of Ancient Greece, perhaps a 'genealogical myth' as Sieburth calls it,²⁷ and claims the German people to have had a constitutive role in its emergence. For Hölderlin, the German people and the 'children of the sun' ('Kindern der Sonn'), in Hamburger's translation, encounter each other 'not far from the Black Sea's beaches' and '[barter] the word' in a reciprocal, non-mediated exchange of language. This is the encounter between peoples that gives rise in a mythical origin story to Ancient Greek civilization:

> They bartered weapons and all
> The precious goods of the house,
> And bartered the word, and not in vain
> Did kindly fathers bless there with any wish
> Their children's jubilant nuptials.
> For from the sacredly married
> There sprang a people more beautiful
> Than all who before or since
> Have called themselves human.²⁸

The final two lines of the above strophe remind of Badiou's account of the first half of the twentieth century, an epoch in which the necessity of creating humankind anew and the will to implement this necessity in the form of the collective project drove the century's subjects through experiences of innovation and terror. The conjoining of the German people (the Swabian settlers of the 1770s 'who emigrated toward the lower basin of the Danube',²⁹ Sieburth suggests, made here, we are to suppose, into the support for a genealogical myth) and 'the children of the sun' creates 'a people more beautiful / Than all who before or since / Have called themselves human'. Hölderlin's idealization of Ancient Greek cultural production marks the reference point for the inauguration of a new specifically German culture. More, the emergence of Ancient Greece, and Hölderlin's wish for the restoration of German culture on its basis, is explicitly bound to aesthetics; the Ancient Greeks are *more beautiful*. In his *Heidegger and the Politics of Poetry*, Philippe Lacoue-Labarthe stresses the importance of Heidegger's claims in *The Origin of the Work of Art*, specifically that 'what is really important ... is that the task or the mission of beginning falls henceforth to art and (almost) to art alone'.[30] Finally, the Greek inauguration is bound to transcendence; the migrants and the 'children of the sun' are 'sacredly married'; the product of their encounter emerges upon a plane from which the gods have yet to withdraw.

However, Hölderlin's speaker deems this 'beautiful' people to be lost:

But where,
O where do you dwell, dear kin,
So that we may renew the pact
And remember those worthy forebears?[31]

The assertion is not simply that the German people's 'worthy forebears' are lost to thought; this is not simply a nostalgic, imaginary journey into a pure past of encounter, of exchange, of kinship. The poem demands that the 'pact' may be 'renewed' precisely by finding those 'dear kin' a dwelling place, a homeland. The poem demands that Germany be rejuvenated as the homeland in which these forebears may come to dwell, in which the power of the Greek inauguration may arise once more, interrupting 'petty historical affairs' and 'fallen modernity'.[32] That the poem seeks remembrance here is of course another key Hölderlinian theme taken up by Heidegger, especially when reading Hölderlin's poem 'Andenken', recalling the Heideggerian poem's task to 'gather the traces of rememberance' as it founds a new history.[33]

In 'The Journey', the delimitation of this new Germany comprises two stages. First, the wandering speaker invokes the mythical Greek Gods, and these then imbue the Swabian landscape to which the speaker returns with an originary transcendence. The images produced in the hymn's first two strophes – river, sun, mountain, shade – are all transfigured by the subsequent encounter with the figures of Greek mythology.

There on the shores, beneath the trees of
Ionia, on plains of the Cayster
Where, gladdened by Aether, cranes
Are surrounded by mountains distantly glimmering
There you were also, loveliest ones, or haunted
The islands garlanded with vines
And filled with resonant song; or others dwelled
Beside Taygetus, by widely praised Hymettus,

> These were the last to thrive; but from
> Parnassus' well-spring down to the brooks,
> Gold-glittering, of Tmolus rang
> An everlasting melody; so then did all
> The holy woods and all
> The lyres in unison resound
> When heavenly gentleness touched them.[34]

The speaker's 'dear kin', though lost, are invoked in the retrieval of the landscapes' originary mythic properties. The poem confronts its reader with a journey into the pure past, a past uninhabited by the speaker's 'dear kin', in which the features of the landscape are imbued with their mythic origins and their transcendent personifications; Ionia restores Swabia. The poem invokes the river-God Cayster refiguring the now distant invocations of the Rhine and the Danube at the hymn's opening. Similarly to the Rhine and the Swiss Alps, the Cayster finds its source in Mount Tmolus (both mountain and God), emerging there before flowing towards the Aegean Sea. The earlier 'mountains distantly glimmering' are newly present too, in the ranges of Taygetus and Hymettus. Parnassus, God of the mountains, is also named, and it is his 'well-spring down to the brooks, Gold-glittering', that 'of Tmolus rang / An everlasting melody'. The 'pure hands' of the hymn's first strophe, pouring out the 'well-spring purls', are attributed to a lost God of Greek mythology only named in strophe six. Unlike Swabia, however, this landscape is not shaded by its mountain ranges. The 'plains of the Cayster' are 'gladdened by Aether', or 'light' in Greek. The Greek landscape maintains through its light a connection to source or origin, or alternatively, *in light* this mythical landscape operates as source for both the Greek people and the obscured, distant source for Swabia's shade.

The mythical origins of this landscape envelop it in sound too: 'resonant song' fills the islands, the 'everlasting melody' of Parnassus' 'well-spring' rings out and the subsequent cacophony produced by 'the holy woods and all / The lyres' resounds when touched by 'heavenly gentleness'. The melodiousness of the source, the 'well-spring purls', ties the practice of poetry, of the hymn, with the source of homeland; proximity to origin here is produced by poetic language. As well, throughout this strophe the cacophony increases: the 'resonant song' and 'everlasting melody' build through an encounter with 'heavenly gentleness' until they culminate in the resounding of the 'holy woods' and the 'lyres', and this is to place the practice of poetry, in its form as lyric and song, in a realm 'touched' by the Gods.

The relationship between originary, ostensibly Greek transcendence and poetic practice is consolidated in the exclamation immediately following the above strophe: 'O land of Homer!' The landscape, having been imbued with transcendence, having been personified – the mountains are their gods, the rivers theirs, etc. – is now subsumed under the name of Homer. The ambiguity of the line is crucial: 'Homer' is at once produced by the landscape but also makes an authorial claim for it. There is a dual production of homeland: the landscape produces the poet, but the poet retains a privileged access to homeland and source. In the movement enacted by 'The Journey' we find a similar call: to force Swabia to arise concretely as homeland via the process of poetic inauguration. But Homer also represents, for Hölderlin, successful exchange between 'what is native' – Greek heavenly fire – and the clarity and precision of representations or 'the foreign element' from the perspective of Ancient Greece, in Hölderlin's words.[35]

Swabia is to arise concretely following this imaginary journey to its origins. The main conceit is that the abstract, distanced Swabia 'shaded' by the mountains in the first strophe is negated by the mythical invocation of Ionia and is then actualized once the structure of the poem forces Ionia to arise within Swabia. That is, Swabia arises as homeland once its distant origin is restored. Correlatively, the inauguration of the German people, we are to suppose, can only proceed via this restoration in poetic language. The hymn itself, however, only gestures towards this restoration. The dialectic at play in the poem is not resolved for Swabia remains abstract following the second negation in the poem, the movement away from Ionia back to Swabia. This deferral of reconciliation is largely due to the following, from the penultimate and final strophes:

> You Graces of Hellas, you daughters
> Of Heaven, I went to you,
> So that, if the journey is not too far,
> You may come to us, beloved ones.
>
> When milder the breezes blow
> And morning sends loving arrows
> To us the all too patient,
> And downy clouds like blossom
> Drift over our diffident eyes,
> Then we shall say, how did
> You Charities come to barbarians?[36]

Straddling the empty white of the page, the end of strophe eight and the start of strophe nine look backwards towards a pure past, 'I went to you', and speculate towards an unknown future, 'Then we shall say ...'. The present, however, is effaced in this process and recedes back into the void between the strophes;

the 'Charities' have not yet come to the 'barbarians', revealing only a state of patience, of waiting, characterized by diffidence. The endpoint of 'The Journey' is stasis, and the pursuit of the dream wish to travel to the Caucasus has led only to the wait.

The state of vigilance with which the poem ends anticipates much of what Badiou will come to write of the Age of Poets and the suturing of poetry to philosophy. The Hölderlin of Hellingrath, George and Heidegger persists through this age. There is a sense in which, for Badiou especially, the tethering of thought to the poem, the coupling of poets and thinkers, depends as much on Heidegger's reading of Hölderlin as it does on Heidegger's thought per se. In any case, Heidegger is clear when he writes that his thinking 'stands in an absolutely necessary relation to the poetry of Hölderlin'.[37] Badiou argues that the poetry of the early to mid-twentieth century (up to Celan) constructs a 'poetics of the wait, a poetics of the threshold', whose 'maintenance will have constituted the very power of the poem' (*TC*, 22). Something of the content of 'the wait' is anticipated by 'The Journey': that the concretization of this new German people, the inauguration of a new beginning in poetic language and the becoming of homeland as the site of this beginning are all left unfulfilled; poetry is opened up only to the *possible* return of the gods. For Badiou, the poet of the Age of Poets 'is the protector, in language, of a forgotten opening: he is, as Heidegger says, "the guardian of the Open"' (*TC*, 21). Dedicated to the possibility that what has been lost might be restored, the poet makes poetic language the opening of the possibility of the Gods' return. This 'poetics of the wait' produces a kind of stasis, in which a threshold is 'stalked' or 'guarded'. For Badiou, 'The poetic as such is defined as a guarding of the threshold, marked by the reversibility of crossing and not crossing. To be able to look ahead and behind at the same time.' Poetry 'measures' distant origins and leaves open the possibility of the return of what's lost. 'Crossing' the threshold, the horizon beyond which the infinite lies, and 'not crossing' it become equivalent; the century, for Badiou, then, is 'without a crossing' (*TC*, 24). The poet's looking 'ahead and behind at the same time' returns us to Heidegger and the question of authenticity too, for, as the second division of *Being and Time* attests during the establishment of 'Temporality as the Ontological Meaning of Care' (§65), the authentic being of Dasein requires both a looking back and a looking forward: 'But to take over thrownness means to authentically *be* Dasein in the *way that it always already was*. Taking over thrownness, however, is possible only in such a way that futural Dasein can *be* its ownmost "how it always already was," that is, its "having been."'[38] Philippe Lacoue-Labarthe makes the connection between authentic Dasein and the becoming of the 'German people' explicit in his *Heidegger and the Politics of Poetry*:

> Just as Dasein relates to the abyss of its present only insofar as, thrown toward its future, it is sent back to its past, that is, to the 'invention' of its past; similarly, a possibility of History can be opened in the breach of the present only insofar as a people projects as (its) coming a possibility from its past that has not arrived or has remained concealed.³⁹

This question of authenticity, especially insofar as it is related to the 'poetics of the wait', is inextricable from the political violence borne by what Badiou refers to as 'Fascist thought'. The quest for authenticity, the purification of various identifications and the subsequent retrieval of more originary, mythic or primal identifications to replace them – blood, soil, Aryan, warrior, etc. – is doomed to incompletion, for 'inauthentic' identities can never be purified enough to guarantee their purity against charges of semblance; the real cannot be revealed within an identificatory process. Authenticity, the emergence of the German people into history, founded by poetic language, can never be reached for Badiou without suspicion of the inauthentic. The poetics of the wait, in which the space of a possible opening towards the originary is stalked, reflects the incompletion of this doomed drive for authenticity and opens up the Heideggerian intimacy between philosophy and poem to questions of myth's complicity in the emergence of nefarious political programmes. These questions are explored at length by Badiou's contemporary Philippe Lacoue-Labarthe, and it's in Badiou's engagement with his thought that we find the explicit rendering of myth's relation to politics, against the backdrop of Heidegger's reading of Hölderlin's return to the question of Greece.

Lacoue-Labarthe: The poem becoming-prose

In the first of his elegies⁴⁰ for his friend and interlocutor Philippe Lacoue-Labarthe, Alain Badiou argues that Lacoue-Labarthe's thinking is guided by two lines of enquiry. The first concerns the future of the Western philosophical tradition after Auschwitz – 'the relationship between that monstrosity and the speculative genealogy of the West, Heidegger included' (*PP*, 157) – and the second the capacities of the poem to endure beyond the grand historical project of aesthetic inauguration Heidegger tasks it with and its corresponding violence. These two problematics correspond to what Badiou refers to, with

Heideggerian language, as the 'two poles of our historical site': 'the complicity of a lethal politics and the configuring will of great art, a complicity organized by the work of art's mimetic motif', on the one hand, and 'the poetic possibility of withdrawal, as indicated by an art that escapes any will to contour it and all monumentality', on the other (*PP*, 157). For both Badiou and Lacoue-Labarthe, the 'organization' of the complicity between 'lethal politics' and 'the configuring will of great art' is guaranteed by the imitative impulse central to mythology.[41] This specific conception of mythology is drawn from Lacoue-Labarthe's analysis of Heidegger's reading of Hölderlin and becomes central to Lacoue-Labarthe's attempt to work through the contemporary significance of philosophy's relation to the poem. 'Mythology' here refers specifically to the search for authentic origin and to the political forms of *future* historical emergence grounded by that movement into the past.

Rochelle Tobias highlights Lacoue-Labarthe's engagement with this Heideggerian sense of the mythological in her recent article 'From Mythology to Myth: The Courage of Poetry'.[42] Having pointed to Lacoue-Labarthe's critique of Heidegger's writing on mythology from *Introduction to Metaphysics*, in which he writes of 'knowing a primal history' as a 'mythology', Tobias summarizes Heidegger's position on mythology and its attendant problems: 'The beginning of history is never complete. It has always yet to arrive, and this means it belongs not to the past but to the future as the historical destiny of a people, its mission or vocation, its mythology.'[43] In the first section of this chapter, I outlined the connection between the movement towards mythological origin and its nefarious political effects in Heidegger's reading of Hölderlin's poetry. The stakes for Badiou and Lacoue-Labarthe, then, concern the political ramifications at the heart of the decision between the poem's retention of the mythological at its centre on the one hand and the poem's 'withdrawal' from this Heideggerian sense of the mythological on the other. Both thinkers' writings mark contrasting attempts to force through the possibilities represented by the latter, to tip the balance in favour of a poetry that disassociates itself or interrupts political myth-making, a poetic language whose contours are left unshaped by 'exterior' political geneses, by 'authenticity' or invocations of obscured or distant origin. For Badiou, drawing much from Lacoue-Labarthe's work, this movement away from mythology is harboured in the idea of the poem becoming-prose and more recently by the idea of 'prose' itself.[44]

Badiou sources the concept of the poem becoming-prose in Philippe Lacoue-Labarthe's study of Paul Celan's poetry, *Poetry as Experience*. In Lacoue-Labarthe's influential reading of 'Todtnauberg', Celan's poetic record of his meeting in the Black Forest with Heidegger, he claims that it is 'really barely a poem; a singular nominal phrase, choppy, distended and elliptical, unwilling to take shape, it is not the outline but the remainder – the residue – of an aborted narrative'.[45] Lacoue-Labarthe also writes that Celan's engagement with Heidegger is absolutely fundamental to his poetry: 'I think one can assert that it is, in its entirety, a dialogue with Heidegger's thought. And essentially with the part of this thought that was a dialogue with Hölderlin's poetry.'[46] There is a sense in which by making the German language itself the object of scrutiny, by making that language difficult and unattached to any sense of the 'mother tongue', the Celan of 'Todtnauberg' straightforwardly refuses poetic language in the sense of Heideggerian *Dichtung* that I outlined at the start of this chapter – poetic language as revelation and the founding of a nationally bounded history. Poetic language's capacity to make grand beginnings, to force through the emergence of a people, is radically brought into question in Celan's poetry. However, Badiou also argues that in making this pronouncement about Celan's poetry, Lacoue-Labarthe reveals 'Todtnauberg' to be a poem 'becoming prose, in which the radical disjunction between the experience of poetry and the way the will to configure enframes poetry, transcends all form' (*PP*, 160). A simple gloss of Badiou's reading of Lacoue-Labarthe here is that Celan testifies to poetry's resistance to a philosophy that would seek to 'enframe'[47] it (as, for example, *Dichtung*), and that this 'radical disjunction' between the poem ('barely a poem') and the task given to it by philosophy constitutes 'prose', here referring to the situatedness in history of the poem's writing; the experience of the Holocaust bans in advance any sense of 'poetic' essence (as *Dichtung*) and drags it towards 'prose'. Jeff Fort provides a concordant account of 'prose' in his translator's introduction to *Heidegger and the Politics of Poetry*, arguing that Lacoue-Labarthe, 'wants both to critique – to undo – the philosophical capture of poetry and thus to release poetry into another mode of language (which he calls "prose"), another incision of history into poetry, and vice versa'.[48] 'Prose' as it is used here, then, is something like a conjunction of poem and thought in which the poem testifies to historical destitution, refusing its tethering to myth; what 'prose' signifies, in this passage at least, is a movement away from mythology towards 'the world as it is'. The poem of course can never be completely autonomous in relation to the historical existence from which it separates itself, but at the same time, it must resist the full ingress of the world upon it, must retain its autonomy in the face of 'the will to contour it'. Although Lacoue-Labarthe writes about 'prose' in dialogue with Badiou in *Heidegger and the Politics of Poetry*, in a discussion of the legacy of Heidegger's reading of Hölderlin, he does not actually mention 'prose' in his discussion of 'Todtnauberg' or in *Poetry as Experience* at large. And yet, this peculiar way of framing the distinction between poem and prose comes to be central not only to Badiou's reading of the Heidegger/Hölderlin couple, with Lacoue-Labarthe as his key interlocutor, but also to his reading of Samuel Beckett's late prose, in which a 'latent poem' emerges from 'generic prose'. Coming to some understanding of the relation between prose and poem, then, at least insofar as Badiou understands it, is fundamental to this book's later analyses. Badiou presents his exegete with some difficulties then. He adopts at least the terminology with which Lacoue-Labarthe distinguishes poem and prose, but Lacoue-Labarthe draws his distinction from an extraordinarily difficult early text by Walter Benjamin on two of Hölderlin's poems, 'Two Poems by Friedrich Hölderlin: "The Poet's Courage" and "Timidity"'[49] – a trajectory that Badiou does not disclose, of course, but that we must follow in order to chart the distance between Badiou's seeming approval of the poem's 'becoming-prose' and his source for the term in Lacoue-Labarthe's writing.

The history of philosophical attempts to work through the distinction between poem and prose is extraordinarily complex, ranging from the correspondence between Novalis and Schlegel at the apex of German Romanticism, to Hegel and onwards, to Critical Theory and beyond. Without the space to burrow too deeply into this history, I want to present just a few ideas concerning this important relation in order to lend some grounding to Lacoue-Labarthe's turn to Benjamin's own reading of Jena Romanticism, which is central to Badiou's engagement with Lacoue-Labarthe's work. Friedrich Schlegel's often cited Athenäum fragment 116 seeks to found Romantic poetry as the 'progressive, universal poetry' that should 'mix and fuse poetry and prose, inspiration and criticism, the poetry of art and the poetry of nature, and make poetry lively and sociable, and life and society poetical'. Romantic poetry, for Novalis, further, is 'poetry *itself*, or poetry in its essential form.[50] Yet the burgeoning popularity of the novel at the turn of the nineteenth century comes to inflect this idea of poetry. Prose at the time seems tantalizing because it need not adhere to the formal constraints of epic or lyric,[51] and furthermore, because it need not omit any aspect of historical existence from its scope. The vicissitudes of poem and prose and their respective relations to the philosophical elaborations of the idea of art and the work of art find their pleasingly aphoristic distillation in Walter Benjamin's phrase from 'The Concept of Criticism': 'the idea of poetry is prose', which he claims grounds the philosophy of art of early Romanticism.[52] Jena Romanticism finds the 'idea' of a universal poetry in the emerging prose of the period, in which there are no formal constraints and through which poetry's 'originally elastic nature, its unlimitedness, its omnipotence', as Novalis writes, comes to the fore: 'the reflective medium of poetic forms appears in prose', writes Benjamin reading Novalis's correspondence with A.W. Schlegel.[53] We might also be drawn backwards to Hegel's *Aesthetics* in which poetry, as the 'universal art of the Spirit', is the medium in which art transcends itself 'and passes over from the poetry of the imagination to the prose of thought'.[54] We have on the one hand then an idea of prose as the interruption of poetry qua *Dichtung*, the poem's 'becoming-prose' that Badiou draws from Lacoue-Labarthe, a sense of prose that seems rooted more or less entirely in the their discussion concerning the suture of philosophy and the poem in the wake of Heidegger, and on the other, a deep history of the tension between poem and prose, testifying to prose both as the discourse of the everyday, of 'life' more broadly, and as the paradoxical guarantee of a universal poetry. Poetry as *Dichtung*, emphasizing the supposed originary nature of poetic thinking, so prevalent in Heidegger's reading of Hölderlin, is undercut by previous iterations of the relation between poem and prose in which poetry seeks the universal quality of prose. In Badiou's reading of Beckett's late prose in Chapter 4, this relation is complicated even further, whereby Beckett's 'generic' prose carries a latent poem: prose there is tied to ontology, to the counting of multiplicities, to order and measure, to the state of things as they already are; whereas the 'latent poem' is tied to the encounter, to the event and to the interruption of prose. There is often this oscillation between poem and prose then in Badiou's writing, in which the mythological elements of *Dichtung* recede as the poem (Celan being the main example) becomes prose, but on the other hand, in Beckett, the poem has the capacity to impinge on a blank terrain in which nothing happens, submitting being to the consequences of the event.

It is no surprise that Badiou places himself on the same conceptual terrain as Lacoue-Labarthe when it comes to thinking through the conjunction of 'lethal politics' and 'art'[55]: 'within this marked space', Badiou writes, 'we all reside' (*PP*, 156). We all continue to reside in the space, however, which is to say that the horror of Auschwitz and its impact upon art and upon poetry, under the watch of Heidegger, remains a crucial point of departure for thought today; it 'marks' or taints the space in which we produce thinking. In fact, in Badiou's influential collection *Conditions* which arrived in France in 1992 only four years after his *Being and Event*, and just prior to a crucial point in his dialogue with Lacoue-Labarthe,[56] Badiou begins his essay 'Philosophy and Politics' by lamenting the 'retreat of the political' and the 'impossibility of philosophy' announced by Lacoue-Labarthe and Jean-Luc Nancy, and perhaps counter-intuitively produced, for Badiou, as one result of the continued proximity they maintain between poetry and philosophy, and the corresponding, more general difficulty that philosophy faces when attempting to maintain 'the imperative clarity of theses'.[57] In dialogue with Badiou regarding the relations between philosophy and poetry and their triangulation by politics, Lacoue-Labarthe, in his lectures on Heidegger and politics, written and revised between 1990 and 2002 and collected in *Heidegger, La Politique du poème* in 2002 (and in English as *Heidegger and the Politics of Poetry* in 2007), writes that 'Badiou takes Heidegger seriously enough to claim that it is here, in this unsuturing [of philosophy from poetry], that we encounter the "central question" and the "supreme difficulty still facing us today".'[58] We must ask then how Badiou orientates himself towards this 'historical site', this 'extreme difficulty'. In what follows, I argue that by working through the idea of the poem's withdrawal (Lacoue-Labarthe's 'second question') the themes surrounding poetry in Badiou's thought – the Age of Poets, the suture of poetry and philosophy and poetry's interruption by the matheme, for example – harbour political implications or concerns apposite to the overcoming of this 'central question', the legacy of Heidegger's thought. But Lacoue-Labarthe's own analysis of Heidegger's mobilization of Hölderlin and that encounter's grim political resonance is highly technical and depends in part on following his reading of Benjamin's Hölderlin's essay. This work is fundamental to understanding Lacoue-Labarthe's move from the mythological to the mythical and brings Badiou's interest in the poem's 'becoming-prose' into relief, as well as suggesting interesting routes forward for research into the autonomy of the artwork and the question of aesthetic figuration more broadly in Badiou's work. Little has been written on the relationship between Badiou and Lacoue-Labarthe, and in what follows I want to make clear how important this dialogue is when it comes to giving a full account of the Heideggerian legacy in French philosophy and Badiou's particular place within (or perhaps outside) it, both insofar as it concerns the 'triangulation', as Lacoue-Labarthe writes, of philosophy and the poem by politics, and in the extent to which it bears upon philosophy's capacity to conceive the category of the subject anew.

Anticipating conceptual developments Badiou is currently elaborating, especially his conception of 'prose', which finds its most recent reworking in his second elegy for Lacoue-Labarthe, 'In Search of Lost Prose' (2017), Badiou produces in his earlier elegy a range of qualifications to account for the depth of Lacoue-Labarthe's interest in the poem's 'withdrawal'. Badiou writes that Lacoue-Labarthe's thought is motivated by the following:

The question of the poem and of its own mode of possible innocence, as indicated by the non-poetic interiority of the poem, or its idle essence, which we also call its becoming-prose. (*PP*, 157)

Lacoue-Labarthe's thinking concerns, firstly, then the poem's 'possible innocence', by which Badiou means the possibility of the poem's salvation from Heideggerian thought insofar as the latter ties itself to the becoming of the German people or to the complicity of poetic language in nationalist politics. The poem is also invested with a 'non-poetic interiority', reminiscent perhaps of the modern poem's 'central silence' which I examined in the previous chapter. That is, the poem contains within itself, essentially, something of the non-poetic; the poem has a non-poetic core. This core, subsequently named by Badiou as the poem's 'idle essence', is the site of the poem's 'becoming-prose'. For Badiou, the 'idle' essence of the poem invites us to think this non-poetic interiority as a lacuna within the poem which offers a dual escape from both the poem's mobilization as a force for inauguration and the burden placed upon it by its suture to philosophy: the poem, in its essence, cannot be made to work in the service of myth-making nor must it be, from Badiou's perspective, the sole site of a 'thought of being'.

Badiou adopts these ideas, though subjects them to significant change as I will show, from Lacoue-Labarthe's engagement with Benjamin. The broad problematic at stake concerns the distinct ways in which the poem carries and expresses a relation between 'life' and 'art', but also the history of attempts to think the relation or difference between poetry and prose. In his discussion of this latter, Lacoue-Labarthe evokes the language of Jena Romanticism, and more specifically its drive to think through prose with regard to the seemingly 'generic' character of the burgeoning prose fiction of the late eighteenth century, a relative freedom from formal constraints allowing its nomination perhaps as a general 'idea' of art, alongside the poem as a site of relative detachment from the 'prose of the world'.[59] Hegel's conception of the 'prose of thought' also seems to be at stake, though it remains inferential in Badiou's writing on this subject. For now, Badiou's lacuna or 'becoming-prose', when considered essential to the poem, is mobilized as a critique of what Lacoue-Labarthe names elsewhere the 'mytheme', conceived as the Heideggerian *poetic* and mythological essence of the poem. The conceit at the heart of Lacoue-Labarthe's *Heidegger and the Politics of Poetry*, then, is to ask how we might divest the poem of this poetic essence or 'mytheme', as he calls it, but without foreclosing necessarily the possibility of a rejuvenated intimacy between poem and philosophy.[60] By contrast, the poem's becoming-prose, for Badiou, is, as in Lacoue-Labarthe, formulated against this 'poetic essence' but testifies to the poem's release from philosophy, to the end of the suture between them. The poem's idle essence is a kind of passive assertion of the poem's autonomy as a form of thought, but it also of course reflects the consequences of Badiou's subtractive ontology: if being is subtracted from presence, then the poem's essence, insofar as it relates to being rather than being's appearance, can only designate a kind of absent centre; the poem can't be tasked with beginning a new history, based on a sense of lost or obscured being, and can only testify to being's withdrawal. This divergence of conception between Badiou and Lacoue-Labarthe brings much to bear upon the micro-relations between philosophy, poem and politics woven in the aftermath of Auschwitz, especially with regard to philosophy's possible continuance and the corresponding importance of the category of 'subject' as the epoch in question closes.

Philippe Lacoue-Labarthe approaches the question of the mythological in poem by introducing the concept of the 'mytheme' in *Heidegger and the Politics of Poetry*. Lacoue-Labarthe bisects poetic language into the poem itself on the one hand, and its 'origin and essence' on the other, 'which is to say myth … with all the religious, sacred, and sacralising – but also very broadly "political" – connotations the word implies'.[61] Already here there seems to be a latent argument concerning poetic form and autonomy if we presume 'the poem' to be constituted by its formal appearance, as artifice, on the page; 'the poem itself', against any politicized sense of poetic 'origin and essence' forced upon it. Lacoue-Labarthe writes this in response to Badiou's contention in *Manifesto for Philosophy* that, under the watch of Heidegger, philosophy became 'sutured' to poetry; that there was, during the Age of Poets, a philosophical 'absolutizing' of poetry. The problematic element in Heidegger's thought is the 'suture' of philosophy to the poem for Badiou, whereas for Lacoue-Labarthe the problem is a kind of politics stitching itself to this suture – not the poem per se but the 'mytheme'. The invocation of 'the mytheme' becomes for these two thinkers a point of contention, then. Lacoue-Labarthe desires the privileged role of poetry for philosophy, and for thinking, be retained; he does not wish to 'Platonise' the relationship between philosophy and poetry as Badiou does. Lacoue-Labarthe claims the material for this philosophical 'absolutiziation' of poetry, then, in which poetry is entirely subsumed under philosophy and claimed as the site of our access to being, to lie beyond the auspices of poetic language itself, and sources it instead in the assertion of the poem's 'origin' or 'essence', which he calls the 'mytheme'.

Lacoue-Labarthe offers an important account of the trajectory of thought which produces this mythologization of the poem in an analysis of *Dichtung*. Heidegger's conception of myth as the essence of art is presented as early as his *Introduction to Metaphysics* and is developed, as Lacoue-Labarthe notes, throughout Heidegger's working life, up to and including his later works on Trakl in particular:

> The essence of art is *Dichtung*, the essence of *Dichtung* is *Sprache* (both language and speech indissociably), the essence of *Sprache* is *Sage* – which is *muthos* ... The essence of art then, would be myth.[62]

Drawing on the history of German Romanticism and German Idealist thought, Heidegger claims that the essence of art is the poem, with *Dichtung*'s attendant connotations of revelation, disclosure and nationalism, 'this original and natural language that preceded prose', if we go back to Herder.[63] The essence of the poem is language, the essence of language is saying, which, for Heidegger in Lacoue-Labarthe's reading, is myth. The argument which takes Heidegger from *dichtung* to *muthos* is complex, encompassing the vicissitudes of *phusis* and *technē* as well as the conceptual apparatus of *Being and Time*, the founding of historical *Dasein*, authenticity and so on. However, Lacoue-Labarthe makes the movement from 'saying' to myth explicit. He cites Heidegger's definition of 'saying': 'a projection of the clearing in which it is said how being arrives in the open and as what'.[64] For Lacoue-Labarthe this is to equate language's saying with what he calls 'originary *technē*', that is, knowledge as origin; language's saying reveals how being arrives and as what.[65] Language's saying qua originary *technē* is, in Heidegger, a matter of myth, of the fable. Projective saying, then, as poetry, supersedes the artwork as that which brings the dynamic relation between earth and world, between *phusis* and *technē*, into play[66]:

> Projective saying [*Sagen*] is essentially poetry: the fable [*Sage*] of world and earth, the fable of the arena of their strife and, thereby, of every site of the nearness and distance of the gods. [...] In such saying, the concepts of its essence – its belonging to world-history, in other words – are formed, in advance, for a historial people.[67]

This retrieval of essence is mobilized in an ostensibly political inauguration. Myth, produced in poetry, determines the origin for the historical Dasein of the German people. Poetry and politics are transformed into one another but under the auspices of the theological. For Lacoue-Labarthe, this is to invest a people with the 'type' 'of its mode of being in history'.[68] Poetry is the privileged site of access to the originary, providing a people with its historical inscription: 'The poem is originary, both as language and as poetry, to the extent that it is, in a direct and immediate way, the myth by which a people is "typed" in its historical existence. The origin is properly mythical or, if you prefer, the beginning requires the forceful emergence of a "founding myth".[69] It is important to characterize this 'typing' in terms of the relationship between figure (*Gestalt*) and ground, for it is one of the main sites at which Badiou and Lacoue-Labarthe diverge. Lacoue-Labarthe and Jean-Luc Nancy claim the following relationship between figure (*Gestalt*), 'type' and the politics of myth in a reading of Alfred Rosenberg in their essay 'The Nazi Myth':

> Rosenberg [Fascist author of *The Myth of the Twentieth Century*] declares: 'freedom of the soul ... is always *Gestalt*.' ('Gestalt' means form, figure, configuration, which is to say that this liberty has nothing abstract or general about it; it is the capacity to put-into-figure, to embody.) 'The *gestalt* is always plastically limited.' (Its essence is to have a form, to differentiate itself; the 'limit' here, is the limit that detaches a figure from a background, which isolates and distinguishes a *type*.) 'this limitation is racially conditioned.' (Thus one attains the content of the myth: a race is an identity of *a* formative power, of a singular type; a race is the bearer of myth.)[70]

The essence of *Gestalt* is its form, its negative differentiation, its leaving the ground for the foreground. The figure is thus isolated, 'typed', at once written and bounded by form, its limits determined. The determination of the limit in this case is racial: a *people*, founded by a mythological, historical inscription, take on the role of 'bearing' their myth, and emerging as the concrete figure or embodiment of a previously universal, abstract notion – 'freedom'. Poetry qua myth, then, serves as the vehicle for the aesthetic emergence of this figure, recalling Badiou's diagnosis, following Lacoue-Labarthe, of 'the configuring will of great art'. Myth and type are imbricated, and the *Gestalt* or type is a corollary of forceful political inauguration. It should not be forgotten, then, that the demand that poetic language force through a new historical beginning is also tied to the emergence of a new German *subject* based on this process of typing. Elsewhere in 'The Nazi Myth', Lacoue-Labarthe and Nancy write: 'What Germany lacked, therefore, in practical terms, was its subject (and modern metaphysics, as the metaphysics of the Subject, did not complete itself there by accident).'[71] As well as being made a site of both remembrance and future fulfilment of obscured origin, poetry as *Dichtung* is also the site of the nationalist emergence of a new German subject.

Lacoue-Labarthe's attempt to find a non-poetic essence in poetry in order to avoid what he thinks of as the mythological core invested in poetry by Heidegger is heavily dependent on a critical reading of Walter Benjamin's early essay on Hölderlin and more broadly the legacy of Jena Romanticism's various attempts to conceive the relation between poetry and prose. In his translator's introduction to Lacoue-Labarthe's *Heidegger and the Politics of Poetry*, Jeff Fort writes that beyond assigning poetry the 'task of a thinking that philosophy could no longer accomplish', Heidegger also burdens poetry with a political program, '*a mythopoetic annunciation of the historical destiny of Germany and the German people*', and that Heidegger's discourse on Hölderlin is the 'perfectly legible and explicit articulation of this program'.[72] However, Lacoue-Labarthe finds in Benjamin's earlier reading of Hölderlin the resources to untangle the poem from this bestowed political task. In 'The Courage of Poetry', a revised lecture collected in *Heidegger and the Politics of Poetry*, Lacoue-Labarthe invokes Walter Benjamin's essay "Two Poems by Friedrich Hölderlin: "The Poet's Courage" and "Timidity"' in order to, he writes, 'take the measure of an epoch and the philosophical questioning that subtends it'. By placing Heidegger's work on Hölderlin side by side with Benjamin's earlier interpretation from 1914 to 1915, Lacoue-Labarthe believes he can present two interpretations of Hölderlin which, taken together, plot the coordinates of the early twentieth century's thinking on the poem. Tellingly, 'Our politics,' Lacoue-Labarthe writes, 'and not only our politics, still depend on it'.[73] Philosophy's ability to think the political, for Lacoue-Labarthe, requires we take a stance on the relation between poetry, philosophy and myth. It seems pertinent at this stage that Lacoue-Labarthe is returning to an earlier interpretation of Hölderlin's work here, Heidegger's lectures on the poet taking place some twenty years after Benjamin's: it is as if Heidegger's reading invests Hölderlin's poetry with an undesirable supplement, the mythological.

Lacoue-Labarthe's reading of Benjamin focuses on the development of two concepts. The first is the concept at the centre of Benjamin's essay, the enigmatic '*Gedichtete*' (a neologism deriving from Goethe prevalent in Heidegger too), the poem's essence, or in one of Lacoue-Labarthe's many glosses, 'that element of a poem that the poem *had to say* so that it might be attested to; it is thus, in a sense, the poem's attestation of its own origin and conditions of being'.[74] For Lacoue-Labarthe, there is a decision to be made regarding the efficacy of this 'saying', whether it is, as Heidegger would make out, an example of *muthos* or whether it is, as Lacoue-Labarthe argues, 'resolutely prosaic', in Fort's words.[75] The result of this decision brings much to bear on the question of poetry's relation to ethics. For Lacoue-Labarthe, as we have seen, the poem's *saying* as *muthos* unfolds as a correlate of National Socialism, tainting the relation between poetry and philosophy in the wake of Heidegger. Poetry's *saying* as the 'resolutely prosaic', or, perhaps, as a 'becoming-prose', however, contains its own political and ethical implications. Corresponding to this distinction between *muthos* and 'prose' are two translations of *das Gedichtete*: the 'poetized', on the one hand, or the French translation, *dictamen*, as Lacoue-Labarthe prefers, on the other. Following previous attempts to translate the enigmatic 'das Gedichtete', Lacoue-Labarthe ties the problem of poetry to what he calls the 'archi-ethical'. Lacoue-Labarthe cites one attempt at translation by Maurice de Gandillac who settles on *dictamen* from the Latin *dictare*, understood by Rousseau to refer to something like 'the dictates of conscience'. The problematic concerning poetry then is lent an ethical weight by this translation, concerning as it does conscience or ethical judgement. In order to overcome this ethical inflection, Heidegger's translators, as Lacoue-Labarthe notes, have opted usually for 'the poetized' instead; these translators' 'hesitation', Lacoue-Labarthe claims, 'thus reveals all the more forcefully, if we can keep the two proposed solutions ["dictamen" and "the poetized"] together, the link that unites the problematic of poetry to that of ethics'.[76] 'Dictamen' in Latin is a noun meaning either a dictation or a dictate, suggesting the presence both of writing down what is heard and the assertion of a law or principle. It is important to suggest too that in 'dictamen' Lacoue-Labarthe also seems to be offering a subversion of *Dichtung*, which, it is supposed, is likely to share an etymological root in 'dictare'. Lacoue-Labarthe's decision, following Benjamin, to affirm 'dictamen' as the translation of 'das Gedichtete' enables us to think through poetry's relation to the political in a way that brings Badiou's own, more radical approach to the micro-relations between philosophy, the poem and politics into relief, allowing us to think both his overcoming of the manifold problems associated with the way in which poetry, philosophy and politics intertwine in Heidegger's thought and his rejection of all contemporary Heideggerian thinking aiming to sustain the privileged place of poetry for philosophy, of which Lacoue-Labarthe is one exemplar.

The poem's *gedichtete* or *dictamen* is a notoriously difficult concept to pin down. Benjamin describes it as a 'limit-concept' between 'the poem' and 'the task' or its precondition – what the poem 'had to say'. Benjamin is drawing here on an aphorism from Novalis, 'Every work of art has in and of itself an *a priori* ideal, a necessity for being in the world', invoking Kant's transcendental logic: *das Gedichtete* determines the poem's necessary conditions.[77] Benjamin also writes that 'in the poetized [*das Gedichtete*], life determines itself through the poem, the task through the solution'.[78] Lacoue-Labarthe moves to question the possibility of accessing the *dictamen* or 'poetized', settling on the following interpretation of Benjamin's concept: 'The *dictamen*, which is above all not the cause of the poem or what would allow one to "explicate" it, and which in itself is nothing "poetic" (no more than is the essence of *Dichtung* in Heidegger), is purely and simply the condition of possibility of the poem. Its "precondition," as Benjamin says.[79] And, claims Lacoue-Labarthe: 'The task is also to be understood as the precondition of the poem, as the spiritual-intuitive [*geistig-anschaulich*] structure of the world to which the poem bears witness.'[80] Importantly, the intentions of the poet are rigorously foreclosed in Benjamin's essay[81]: the task of the poem, as the structure of the world it represents has nothing to do with the poet, and everything to do with the poem as a created object in the world among other objects. The poem is at once preconditioned by a 'spiritual-intuitive' structure of the world and tasked with bearing witness to it. The *dictamen* then, poetry's essence, is the 'transcendental schema' of the poem, the necessary conditions for its existence. Those conditions are 'life', or 'existence' broadly construed, the only site from which the poem may emerge.

One way of opening up the *gedichtete*, then, is to focus on its role as the 'sphere of relation' between art and life. Rochelle Tobias's recent work on Lacoue-Labarthe's exegesis of the young Benjamin is especially clarifying on this point. The key distinction between Benjamin and Heidegger's respective readings of Hölderlin, for Tobias, comes down to how the poem distinguishes itself from the historical situation in which it is produced. In Benjamin's essay this is expressed as the distinction between 'art' and 'life', recalling the 'prosaic' nature of 'historical existence':

> For Benjamin, as for Heidegger, what is at stake in Hölderlin's work is nothing less than the truth of poetry. But where they diverge is in their understanding of the relation of poetry to life or historical existence. For Benjamin, poetry *versachlicht*, it makes literal, it submits what it names to it own law, and in this fulfils Novalis's dictum that "Poetry is prose among the arts," which could also function as the motto for Lacoue-Labarthe's theory of poetic language as a literalizing idiom.[82]

The *dictamen* of the poem testifies to the poem itself as the organizing principle of the 'mythic elements' of life that it names, organizing its own 'law'. The *dictamen* offers an interface between 'life' and 'poem', coming to condition both, operating as the membrane via which 'life' and 'poem' become reciprocal despite their separation, a 'dialectical constellation' perhaps, as Hanssen argues.[83] The immediate result of this is that, as well as the *dictamen* as task or condition of the poem being 'life' or 'existence', life itself is to be thought as 'poetic', or in Lacoue-Labarthe's words, 'the *dictamen*, as *Gestalt*, is a figure of existence', and 'life (existence – inasmuch as the task of the poem is to bear witness to it – is itself, in its truth, poetic. A poem can say, in truth, that we live (exist) in truth'.[84] Lacoue-Labarthe finds 'the mythic' in the *dictamen* because the latter testifies to life's truth *now*; we need not evoke, as mythology does, an obscured origin to be revealed in the future.

Perhaps counter-intuitively, the *dictamen* retains a sense of the figural, but it offers Lacoue-Labarthe the subversion of what he understands by Heideggerian figurality – the aesthetic emergence of a type, the mythological inscription of a people. Lacoue-Labarthe emphasizes the fact that, for Benjamin, the greatest works of art, 'in respect of their truth' must 'refer to a sphere' beyond the 'immediate feeling of life'; they must refer to something like life in general, bare existence, common humanity, which is to claim, in other words, with Benjamin, that 'life, in general, is the *dictamen* of poems [*das Gedichtete der Gedichte*]'. The mythological figure with which the 'poetized' supplements poems, the assertion of a transcendent origin or 'type' beyond this world, is subverted by the diffusion of myth across existence or the figuration of life itself: 'The poem, to remain within Benjamin's vocabulary', Lacoue-Labarthe writes, 'is a figure of life. Which amounts to saying that life is poetic. Essentially. Not because it is "poetizable" (that would be the mystification par excellence: mythology) but because the *dictamen* of poems – which is never this or that particular poem from which, however, it is indispensable – dictates life'.[85] The *dictamen* testifies to the fact that life is here, now and formed or constructed, unified by the structure of the poem. Whereas, Tobias argues, Heidegger's mythology 'refers to an essence that has yet to be revealed in its fullness'.[86] In this shift away from the mythological, we find an important subversion of the aesthetic figure or what Lacoue-Labarthe refers to elsewhere as 'the aestheticization of politics'[87]; the figure is supplanted by the *configuration* of life itself or what Lacoue-Labarthe calls 'the mythic'. This is broadly reflective, too, of the distinction between a unified, transcendent, mythological whole distanced from 'the earth' and an increased emphasis on the already-present, 'mythic' relations in existence or in the world as it is. The *dictamen* as an organizing principle bans the figuration of a unified world not-yet, a mythological world to come, for its mode of unification is removed from the life or existence that it nonetheless dictates or gives a figure to, providing a 'unity produced by the force of the mythic elements straining against one another'.[88] Reading Benjamin again, Lacoue-Labarthe asserts that 'the poem is powerless to give figure to a world',[89] that is, in a wholesale disavowal of *Dichtung*, the poem, because its *dictamen* is what unifies or figures life, never *realizes* the world it nonetheless gives form to. 'This is Benjamin's project', concludes Lacoue-

Labarthe, 'It would have the immense merit of recognizing the theological in the figure of its failure, and of turning poetry – whence we came – toward prose, where we are.'[90]

The politicized mission of poetry is rejected, and this engenders 'broadly political' consequences insofar as it negates the ostensibly political supplement forced upon the supposed essence of poetry by Heidegger. But the political consequences for Badiou are more pronounced as I will demonstrate as this chapter moves into the next, because the question of what kind of 'figure' of the subject is able to attach itself, not to poetry as *Dichtung* but to a poem becoming-prose, is of crucial importance to Badiou's engagement with Celan and the poem at large, and is the site, too, of his affirmative departure from Lacoue-Labarthe's thought, despite his willingness to follow it as far as he does.

Poem and subject

Despite their intimacy, Badiou's most frequent reproach of Lacoue-Labarthe's thought is that it too easily forecloses the possibility of philosophy or is too indebted perhaps to Heidegger's declaration of philosophy's end. Badiou often returns to Lacoue-Labarthe's claim that Auschwitz specifically precludes the desire for philosophy:

> Philosophy is possible; philosophy is necessary. And nevertheless, in order for it to be, it must be desired. Philippe Lacoue-Labarthe says that History – he had in mind Nazi barbarity – now forbids any desire for philosophy. I cannot grant him this, since such a conviction immediately places philosophy in a position of weakness with regard to modern sophistry. There is another possible solution and that is to desire philosophy against history, to break with historicism. (C, 21)

From Badiou's perspective, the relationship between philosophy and poetry in Lacoue-Labarthe's thought is tied up with philosophy's rejuvenation from the standpoint of its own failure. Badiou characterizes the tension in Lacoue-Labarthe's thought in 'Philosophy and Politics' as the state of philosophy's oscillation between 'an intolerable mutism – that of Heidegger faced with Paul Celan – and the almost desperate search for a prose of thought that would prepare thought's leave for the poem' (C, 147). Steven Corcoran's translation is of interest here: '[une] prose de la pensée qui organiserait sa migration dans le poem' becomes 'a prose of thought that would prepare thought's leave for the poem'. Though this rendering effectively carries the reticence of the subjunctive 'organiserait', 'prepare thought's leave for the poem' is difficult to parse. Given his reading of Benjamin, it is not difficult to imagine Lacoue-Labarthe seeking a 'prose of thought' by which the poem can aspire, via a route at least proximate to Jena Romanticism's, to be the privileged site in which 'thought' takes place; so 'thought' goes on leave, temporarily we might suppose, to the poem. But Badiou also leaves open a possibility that seems far more in tune with his own thinking. Badiou makes clear that the 'prose of thought', for Lacoue-Labarthe, is carried to the poem, potentially settling within its bounds, 'sa migration dans le poem', where 'dans' potentially becomes 'to'. With this in mind, the suggestion that Badiou himself would wish to exert more pressure on the prose of thought's 'migration' specifically, to emphasize the demand that any prose of thought, from within the poem, must travel *through* it, and seek a new abode outwith the poem's bounds (recalling Celan and the poet's solitary burden), does not seem too reaching.[91] Badiou's 'prose of thought' is to be found in formal mathematics, of course, in, at this stage in his writing, the set-theoretical discourse of the multiple and the subtraction of being it articulates. In Badiou's poem becoming-prose, which denies poetic language as the privileged site of being's disclosure, this discourse of the multiple is indirectly attested to. The ruins of philosophy Lacoue-Labarthe inherits in Heidegger's wake, its incapacity to speak, alongside the 'desperate search for a prose of thought' as Badiou describes it, places philosophy's relation to truths in question, for the 'suture' between the poem and philosophy tethers the latter to the play of language at the price of truth or to what Badiou names 'sophistry'.[92] The impossibility of the desire for philosophy is imbricated with the reassertion of an exclusive intimacy between philosophy and the poem.

Badiou's characterization of the problem from which Lacoue-Labarthe's thinking begins is not entirely unfair. Towards the beginning of *Heidegger and the Politics of Poetry*, Lacoue-Labarthe poses the following question:

> Should poetry cease to be of interest to philosophy? Must we – as a necessity or an imperative – sever the tie that for two centuries in Europe has united philosophy (or at least that philosophy that is astonished at its origin and anxious over its own possibility), and poetry (or at least that poetry that acknowledges a vocation toward thought and is also inhabited by an anxiety over its destination)? Must philosophy – by necessity of imperative – cease its longing for poetry and conversely (for there is indeed a reciprocity here), must poetry finally mourn every hope of proffering the true, and must it renounce?[93]

Thought has reached a historical impasse characterized by anxiousness: philosophy is unable to decide its own stakes, poetry unable to articulate its participation in thought. Philosophy and poetry by this schema are inextricable insofar as the questions they respectively pose require transport through their other; philosophy is astonished at its origin via the poem, poetry 'acknowledges' its participation in 'thought'. This state of anxiety, in which the possible reveals itself, consigns thought to an essential, Heideggerian questioning, noted by Badiou in his writing on Lacoue-Labarthe: 'he had of course retained, not to say transformed, Heidegger's maxim to the effect that the essence of thought is the question' (*PP*, 157). Bound to the clarification of these questions, Lacoue-Labarthe, for Badiou, is unable to offer a path for thinking by which this philosophical/poetical stasis might recede.

For Badiou, the poem must be released from philosophy and is to be recognized as the bearer of its own irreducible thought. In the endnotes to his essay 'Mallarmé's Method: Subtraction and Isolation', collected in *Conditions*, Badiou claims that Lacoue-Labarthe extrapolates a 'programme of thought' for poetry from Mallarmé's prose works, subtending the heterogeneous sites of thought poetry produces; in other words, philosophy appropriates poetry's thought as its own. Badiou's criticism is a response to Lacoue-Labarthe's reading of Mallarmé in *Musica Ficta (Figures of Wagner)*.[94] There, in a manner reminiscent of his critique of 'the mytheme' in Heidegger's reading of Hölderlin, Lacoue-Labarthe claims Mallarmé to effect only the purification of what remains an 'onto-typological' schema for the artwork of the kind, from Lacoue-Labarthe's perspective, exhibited by Wagner. In Lacoue-Labarthe's words, for Mallarmé, 'Verse – art – is the stamp of what is: character or Letter as that from which, in sum, because we add nothing to nature, there is a world. The Letter is the transcendental itself'.[95] For Lacoue-Labarthe, Mallarmé's conception of verse only reaches the status of the essentially literary insofar as it 'figures' the poetic idea.[96] That the poetry presents a purified 'ontological impress' is problematized by its proximity to a kind of 'religion of art'; for Lacoue-Labarthe, Mallarmé's poetic 'ontological impress' depends on a theology in which 'God is the being of man, that is to say language',[97] revealing a proximity between Mallarmé's poetics and the Wagnerian 'onto-typology' Lacoue-Labarthe would seek to avoid. Badiou, however, uses Lacoue-Labarthe's criticisms of Mallarmé to undermine the former's philosophical work elsewhere:

> I fully agree that the historical assemblage that turns on the theme of 'great art' is inherently criticisable. For to the extent that it does touch a real, this real is not of the poem, but *alone* that of a certain philosophical seizing of (German? Romantic?) art. (*C*, 297)

For Badiou, Lacoue-Labarthe's work is essentially a repetition of this seizing, despite the various attempts it makes to escape such a totalizing effect. 'Lacoue-Labarthe constantly ... folds the effectiveness of the (poetic or political) truth-procedure, as a locus of autonomous thinking, back onto the singular operations of philosophical seizing of these procedures', Badiou writes, emphasizing the recapitulation of the 'real' point of 'great art'. The main point of critique for Badiou is that despite maintaining an exclusive proximity between thought and poem, Lacoue-Labarthe has only succeeded in apprehending Mallarmé's prose as a programme to which the poems aspire, which is to claim that 'thought', of the kind produced in disparate fields (of which poetry is one), is only efficacious insofar as it is determined by a preceding thought-programme. Badiou contends that, in Lacoue-Labarthe's reading of Mallarmé, he '*apprehends his prose as that which yields the very essence of poetry in the form of a programme for thought*. Or again, Lacoue-Labarthe proceeds as if the prose renderings yielded the thought-programme of poems' (*C*, 297). The prose is apprehended, by philosophy, as a general programme for thought, and poetry itself is not treated as a discourse capable of producing thought without philosophy's aid.

Badiou can only demand the 'reversal' of this schema, and that the programme of thought's 'field of exercise' comes to be impinged upon by thought itself, whether it is produced by the poem or elsewhere among philosophy's conditions. For Badiou, without this rupture the relation between thought per se and the thinking of that thought by philosophy is exhausted. Thought is to rupture the structure by which a programme of thought constructs itself: 'I shall say it bluntly:', Badiou writes, 'every programme of thought comes after thinking, and works to alter its field of exercise' (*C*, 298). In light of this reversal, the question of Mallarmé's 'purification', which Badiou uses as an exemplar of the poem's 'subtractive' potential across his works, most notably in *The Century*,[98] is modified in order to place a far greater emphasis on the poem's 'real' thought:

> Concerning the pure, purification: I do not think that the stakes here involve releasing the onto-typology of 'great art' from its mythical charge, all the while conserving its schema (in the sense that Mallarmé would be a Wagner devoid of an explicit mythology). I posit instead that the stakes of the pure are to understand how – in the pure chance of a vanished event, of a non-original facticity – the regulated effect of a singular truth can be suspended. The issue is, then, to think 'outside of relations', in the shelter opened up by the cut of chance. (*C*, 298)

Lacoue-Labarthe's commitment to the 'exhaustion' of philosophy, the imperative that we 'let philosophy collapse within ourselves'[99] despite mythology's 'release', maintains a privileged role for poetic thought and subsumes it under the broader, philosophical 'task of thinking' after Heidegger. Lacoue-Labarthe's 'hope', 'fragile, tenuous, and meagre as it is', that poetry offer some 'signs' towards the accomplishment of thought's task, to 're-inaugurate history, reopen the possibility of a world',[100] fails to account for the localized productions of thought emitted via the poem described in Badiou's intervention above. For Badiou, Lacoue-Labarthe's imperative for the poem, that it alone 'provide some signs' for 'the task of thinking', could only serve to re-enshrine the suture between philosophy and poetry. In the above quotation, however, it is the question of 'relations' that offers the most productive grounds for comparison between these two thinkers.

Lacoue-Labarthe's invocation of Walter Benjamin's work on the *dictamen* stresses the fundamental importance of 'relations' rather than mythology to any conception of a continued intimacy between philosophy and poem. Lacoue-Labarthe writes, glossing Benjamin's close reading of Hölderlin's poem 'Timidity', both that 'the poet does not have to fear death; he is a hero because he lives at the centre of all relation' and 'the principle of *dictamen* as such is the supreme sovereignty of relation'.[101] Badiou's insistence on poetic thought's emergence 'outside of relations' offers itself, then, as a crucial point of differentiation. Lacoue-Labarthe's diagnosis of a mythological 'typing' of existence, or the emergence of an aesthetic figure for the 'German people', and his own preference for Benjamin's *configuration* of existence, the 'mythic' maintenance of reciprocal relations, finds their adversary in a Badiouian conception of figure for which there is no ground from which to emerge, only 'the cut of chance'. The language Badiou uses – 'non-original facticity' – again points to a material supplement to a situation that it cannot account for, a poem that separates itself from the context it nonetheless must appear in. Most importantly, this facticity is non-original, testifying to affirmative addition rather than the glance backward towards a point of obscured origin. Poetic language is not a field of openness offering obscured being its possible restoration, but, due in part to being qua being's subtraction from presence, only a 'shelter' opened up in a 'cut' against 'meaning' – we might think of Celan again at this point.

Badiou's phrase 'a figure without figure' is difficult to parse, though he does offer some clues in 'The Age of Poets', tying this concept to the disavowal of 'objectivity' and 'meaning'. 'What is an object?' Badiou asks in a revision of his original essay on the Age of Poets from *Manifesto for Philosophy*[102]:

> It is what disposes the multiple of being in relation to meaning or signification. The Age of Poets animates a polemic against meaning, thus targeting objectivity, which is being as *captive* of meaning, and proposing to us the figure without figure, or the unfigurable figure, of a subject without object. (*AP*, 16)

Against Lacoue-Labarthe's reading of the *dictamen* as the configuration of existence, and the 'supreme sovereignty of relation', Badiou proposes the poem's 'figure without figure', the 'unfigurable figure'. The poetic idea is to exceed any figure of the sensible. That the thought of the object's withdrawal finds its presentation in the poems of the Age of Poets implores philosophy to propose a conception of the subject for which being qua being is essentially inconsistent, for whom the 'ground' or the earth has fallen away. That Lacoue-Labarthe requests that the poem provides 'a sign' for thought's progress outward beyond philosophy's exhaustion is telling in this regard, for the Badiouian poem is posed against such demands for signification in the name of thought. Being in all its inconsistency is no longer captive of meaning, and thought is to operate via 'the cut of pure chance': 'against the supposition of a Great Whole', Badiou argues, 'the poets of the Age of Poets think detotalization, the separate, irreconcilable multiplicity. They impose on themselves the rule of a principle of inconsistency'(*AP*, 14).

Lacoue-Labarthe's reading of Benjamin offers a conception of the poem's becoming-prose that dispels the mythological via the immersion of the poem in the world of relations and the reciprocal dependence of life and poem on the *dictamen*. In light of his demand that poetic thought be 'outside of relations', Badiou adopts the poem's becoming-prose as the imperative by which it renounces its privileged role in 'the task of thinking'. More, the poem's becoming-prose, for Badiou, testifies to the modern necessity[103] that thought arise outwith the whole. That Badiou considers Alberto Caeiro, one of Fernando Pessoa's heteronyms, to be the most 'prosaic' of the poets, due to the rigour of his conceptualization of the epoch's essential disorientation, is instructive in this regard (*AP*, 14). The sense in which we can understand both the *dictamen* as an organizing or structuring principle, alongside certain pronouncements of Jena Romanticism, especially a number of Novalis's aphorisms – 'Truly artistic poetry is remunerable', 'Art … is mechanical', et al.[104] – is pushed in Badiou's writing, then, to its apogee. The remunerable nature of 'true poetry' is affirmed as the rigorous conceptualization of being qua being in its subtraction from presence; mathematical innovations come to ground a kind of modern poem from which the task of opening towards being has, thankfully from Badiou's perspective following Celan, fallen away.

What links these fundamental differences of conception concerning the poem's becoming-prose to the question of the political, however, is the category of the 'subject'. When Badiou testifies to the poem's 'diagonal operation' in 'The Age of the Poets', demanding the poem '[wager] that a nomination may come and interrupt signification, and from the point of this interruption for a *localizable* thought to establish itself, without any pretence to totality' (*AP*, 15), he is marking the site of the rejuvenation of the subject, the 'subject without object', the 'figure without figure' of a subject emerging from a local encounter with the rupture of chance. Any exploration of the 'broadly political' implications bound to re-conceptualizations of the relation between philosophy and poetry is by necessity an exploration of the possibility of the political subject. For Lacoue-Labarthe, however, the very possibility of politics qua emancipatory activity is foreclosed: only philosophical interrogation of the 'essence' of the political is permissible in the wake of what Lacoue-Labarthe and Jean-Luc Nancy call the 'completion of philosophy' and the 'closure of the political'.[105] In Simon Critchley's analysis in his 'Re-tracing the Political: Politics and Community in the Work of Philippe Lacoue-Labarthe and Jean-Luc Nancy', for example, Lacoue-Labarthe and Nancy commit to the distinction between *la politique*, or 'real', active political sequences, and *le politique*, the essence of the political, which is bound to philosophical questioning. These, Critchley argues, effect something of a structural equivalence with the Heideggerian thesis of the 'completion of metaphysics as technology' and his subsequent move to the interrogation of technology's essence.[106] The move from politics to the essence of the political is important here because it mirrors Lacoue-Labarthe's continuing commitment to the proximity between philosophy and poem: in Critchley's words, for Lacoue-Labarthe and Nancy, 'the present is marked by the installation of the philosophical *as* the political and the absolute domination of politics'.[107] Critchley continues: 'In virtue of the fact that Lacoue-Labarthe accepts the description of the contemporary world in terms of the total domination of *la politique*, any move back to politics is necessarily prohibited as being a collapse back into metaphysics'.[108] In Critchley's reading, the saturation of politics, both in its diffusion through everyday life under the subsumption of capital and in the 'failure' of 'revolution', allows 'totalitarianism' as a signifier adequate to politics' collapse into the social. 'Totalitarianism', so conceived, anticipates Badiou's later diagnosis of the nefarious primacy of a particular kind of identification in politics under capital.[109] 'Totalitarianism', and here Critchley believes Lacoue-Labarthe and Nancy to follow the analysis of Claude Lefort,[110] 'is that political form of society governed by the logic of identification, where all areas of social life represent incarnate power: the proletariat is identified with the people, the party with the proletariat, the politburo with the party, the leader with the politburo, and so on'.[111] This comes to effect a 'politics without transcendence' or without a 'beyond', 'without remainder or interruption'.[112] Simply put, this foreclosure of political potential is what drives deconstruction's withdrawal from the realm of politics towards a re-questioning of the latter's essence. The 'failure' of politics represents the philosophical failure to adequately delimit the essence of the political.

Immediately, this imperative for philosophy appears to reflect the target of Badiou's criticisms of Lacoue-Labarthe above, insofar as it seeks the rejuvenation of politics, at least in its possibility, in philosophical enquiry. Just as Mallarmé's prose offers a programme consolidated by the poems, emancipatory politics can only be invoked on the basis of its reconceptualization in thought. Both of these results are inadmissible for Badiou, who seeks to leave these two conditions – politics and the poem – to the production of their respective thinking, 'outside of relations', for which only a new understanding of 'subject', as the material bearer of such localized instances of thought, is adequate.[113] For Badiou, the 'theme of the Subject' suffers a radical deconstruction in the work of both Heidegger and his successors' (*MP*, 43). The extent to which Lacoue-Labarthe's writing follows this demand for deconstruction is made explicit in his essay 'The Echo of the Subject', collected in *Typography: Mimesis, Philosophy, Politics*. There, he expresses the imbrication of the question of 'subject' and the state of philosophy following Heidegger:

> This problematic of the subject implies above all that if one attempts to follow the path opened up by Heidegger and test the resistance of the concept of the subject ... it is necessary to go by way of a deconstruction of the area of greatest resistance. Now, this area of greatest resistance ... is nothing other than theoretical or philosophical discourse itself, beginning (and I'm thinking of Heidegger) with that discourse that takes its orientation from the deconstruction of the concept of subject.[114]

Lacoue-Labarthe's path for thought is not the rejuvenation of the subject but a continued fidelity to the constitutive role the deconstruction of the subject plays in Heidegger's philosophy, in which, in light of the continued objectivation of 'the Earth' under the reign of technology, 'subjectivity is driven towards its completion' (*MP*, 44). Theoretical discourse itself, the remnants of philosophy in the wake of the end of metaphysics, must be deconstructed too. In the same essay, Lacoue-Labarthe offers something of the contemporary experience of the subject, 'on its way to death ... irremediably separated from itself (as "subject") ... it comes to itself only in losing itself'.[115]

Badiou's imperative for thought is to take a further step, to avoid the 'completion' of the subject, to demand the modern condition of philosophy be inextricable from the maintenance of a thinking of the subject, in however modulated or excavated a form, as that which binds itself to 'evental', localized intrusions of truth upon the whole. Far from acquiescing to the 'loss' or withdrawal of the subject, then, Badiou seeks its wholesale rejuvenation. Philosophy, encountering these productions of truth, 'outside of relations', is then able to think their compossibility, or put another way, is able to think its own time. The poem's becoming-prose, for Badiou, demands the withdrawal of the poem from its intimacy with philosophy and claims the impossibility, if philosophy is to 'proceed' beyond its historical closure, of maintaining thought's organization solely within the auspices of philosophy. When Badiou writes of the importance of '[desiring] philosophy against history, to break with historicism' (C, 21), he is affirming the singular thoughts produced following events, not only by the poem but by emancipatory politics, mathematical innovations and love too – local productions of thought that impinge upon the 'historical' situations in which they occur. Subtracted from identity, the procedures which emerge following these events require the intervention of a subject, 'a figure without figure'. The following chapter argues that Badiou finds such a figure of the subject in Celan's poem 'Anabasis', a poem built upon the armature of a negated 'homecoming', the subjective route emphasized throughout the later Heidegger's overtly political writings on the task of the poem.

3

Anabasis

Anabasis and homecoming

Alain Badiou unfolds the concept of 'anabasis' in *The Century* (2005/2007) in a meditation upon poems by Saint-John Perse and Paul Celan. Coming to signify the trajectory or movement comprising the essential moments of subject formation in the wake of twentieth-century violence, the concept of anabasis with which Badiou's chapter ends is intended to take account of the fact that, in Badiou's words, 'the century foundered upon a darkness so real that it was forced to change the *direction* of [its] movement, as well as the words that would articulate it' (*TC*, 90). Crucially, Badiou finds the resources for thinking this change of direction in the poetry of Paul Celan. Though ineluctably grounded in Celan's poetics, however, anabasis also comes to resonate beyond the bounds of poetry's own interrogation of subject formation, and this is illuminated by Justin Clemens when he claims that anabasis is actually fundamental to Badiou's philosophy as a whole, remaining consistent despite its invocation in different contexts: 'Once you recognize this operation, you might begin to discern it everywhere in Badiou – if under a sequence of ever-varying names.'[1] More, Marios Constantino has recently argued that anabasis 'serves as the master signifier of the political condition par excellence', explaining that 'Anabasis as an evental signifier of the egalitarian becoming of freedom proceeds by forcing itself against the imperial logic of sheer necessity'.[2]

However, this particular rendering of an ever-present operation – 'anabasis' in *The Century* – has a very specific target encoded beneath its subtle resonances and allusions: Martin Heidegger. In what follows, I want to read anabasis as a trajectory mobilized specifically against the movement of 'homecoming' we find bound to Heidegger's infamous readings of Friedrich Hölderlin's poems, in the hope that Celan's significance to Badiou's departure from Heidegger be made explicit. This chapter begins by exploring the philosophical concerns –

sameness, otherness, identity, alterity – at the heart of these movements of the subject, before offering two close-readings of Celan intended to elucidate Celan's own engagement with homecoming, as well as its centrality to the development of Badiou's anabasis.

Opening his meditation, Badiou asks how the century itself 'envisages' its 'movement'. The three moments he details in his speculative answer – 'a re-ascent towards the source, an arduous construction of novelty, an exiled experience of beginning' (*TC*, 81) – comprise the essential aspects of anabasis per se. Badiou starts his analysis, however, not with the twentieth century's 'own movement' nor with the more particular variant of this movement he reads from Celan but with a return to Xenophon's narrative *Anabasis*.[3] This return operates as a subtle allusion to Heidegger's focused investigations into the obscured etymologies of *phusis, logos, alētheia*, et al., and his attempt to revivify them as constituents of the myth of a pure Greek *arche*.[4] Badiou's return to Xenophon serves as a surreptitious critique here too, insofar as it privileges the Ancient Greeks' military prowess, their discipline especially, over the aesthetic, cultural and intellectual evolution of their 'refined civilisation'. This subversion is completed when Badiou identifies Greek military discipline as a 'discipline of thought' (*TC*, 81). Thought's proximity to the poem in Heidegger is overturned, replaced by a thinking allied to political necessity; and this critique is lent further weight by a playfully disproportionate analogy with the 'iron discipline' Lenin imposes upon his proletarian party. As well, Badiou's use of 'source' is not arbitrary, and alludes to both Hölderlin's obsession with his two rivers – the Rhine and the Ister – and Heidegger's adoption of the discourse of *Ursprung* and source in his own writings on Hölderlin, especially on 'The Ister' hymn.[5] Alongside explicit reference to Heidegger elsewhere in the chapter – to his meeting with Paul Celan in 1966 and the subsequent publication of Celan's 'Todtnauberg', for example – these allusions invite us to consider the 'trajectory' central to Heidegger's reading of Hölderlin – 'homecoming' – alongside anabasis.

At its most abstract, the movement of homecoming contains three points in sequence: the traveller departs, encounters the other and then returns to home's sanctuary. In this movement's Homeric form, Odysseus departs Ithaca for Troy, the majority of this epic poem then presents the various trials he faces in his attempt to return to Penelope, Telemachus and his estate in Ithaca, where he is ensured a hero's welcome. However, the movement of homecoming with which we are dealing concerns fundamentally the becoming of cultural identity, the moving into proximity with what is 'proper' to one – and in its Heideggerian form, the becoming of the historical destiny of the German people. Reading

Hölderlin's 'The Ister', Heidegger remarks that the poet may only 'learn the free use of what is proper to him' by fulfilling one of the conditions of 'becoming at home in what is proper': 'the voyage into the foreign land'.[6] The following year in 1943, Heidegger commemorates the hundredth anniversary of Hölderlin's death with an address subsequently titled 'Homecoming/To Kindred Ones'.[7] There, a sinister reminder of the sacrifice of those 'sons of the homeland ... far distant from its soil' is followed by the explicit imbrication of poetic task with the violent assertion of national identity: 'Are not these sons of the homeland the poet's closest kin?' The political stakes of homecoming, then, a movement which depends on pre-verified limits and boundaries, on blood and soil, become clear: 'homecoming', Heidegger surmises, 'is the future of the historical being of the German people'.[8] The poetic task of homecoming finds its corollary then in the political attempt to inaugurate a new people through the violent dissolution of the other. In order for the same to arise, it must pass through the other as its adversary.

Charles Bambach's reading of Hölderlin in *Thinking the Poetic Measure of Justice: Hölderlin-Heidegger-Celan* seeks to emphasize the reciprocity between same and other evinced in Hölderlin's poems in order to open his poetry to a thought tradition entirely alien to Heidegger's totalizing narrative. Reading 'The Ister' and 'The Journey', Bambach writes that 'to be German then, for Hölderlin, means to journey forth from the provinces and to leave behind what is familiar; it means to enter into the realm of what is foreign, strange, and other, so that what is one's own can be cultivated in and through an encounter with alterity'.[9] Bambach claims that Heidegger's reading of Hölderlin serves to obscure this fundamental aspect of exchange with the other by emphasizing what he calls 'the narrow myth of autochthony' and later describes as 'the myth of a pure Greek *arche* untouched by foreign influence'.[10] The becoming of a people, for Hölderlin, is a reciprocal process demanding mutual exchange between native and foreign, and his account of the becoming of Ancient Greece, in Bambach's reading, is no different. Far from being a pure *arche*, then, Greece, for Hölderlin, depended on a 'positive appropriation of the foreign'. Hölderlin, in his rejection of the hegemony of self-appropriation, for Bambach holds much in common with what the latter calls 'the Jewish critique of ontology', evinced by the likes Rosenweig, Lévinas, Derrida and Celan. For these thinkers, the mutual exchange between self and other at the heart of Ancient Greece allows 'the metaphysics of totality-identity that dominates the work of Western philosophy', or the privileging of identity over difference, to be critiqued, as a way of overcoming the politicized motifs of authenticity and identity at work in Heidegger's absolutization of the poem.[11]

What Bambach sees in Hölderlin is a sense of poetic dwelling which remains open to alterity, and this is to be distinguished from Heidegger's absolute privileging of 'the same', expressed most forcefully in his lecture on Hölderlin's 'Andenken', in which the other is only thought through the proper: 'The origin can be shown only in one way: ... ', Heidegger writes, ' ... returning back from a journeying which first originated from the origin, the showing moves into a nearness to the origin. Thereby the showing itself is pinned down in the steadfastness of the origin.'[12] The origin is left and endures throughout the journey, and the other, towards which the poet embarks, is only thought insofar as it contributes to the eventual becoming enacted in the subject's return to origin and subsequent 'fulfilment in the German homeland'.[13] Bambach seeks to save Hölderlin from this narrative by highlighting the latter's emphasis on the mutual exchange between native and foreign, claiming that Hölderlin 'brings into play the power of ... Lévinasian ethics of alterity'.[14] Though Bambach is keen to open Hölderlin's poetry up to proponents of the 'Jewish critique of ontology', the latter can hardly be said to present an alternative movement to that of Homeric homecoming, despite going some way in overcoming the privilege afforded to the proper via its focus on alterity for its own sake. What Bambach is keen to present in his study is an entirely other movement, opposed to homecoming, and bound to an overarching critique of the centrality of identity to Western metaphysics. To Homeric homecoming Bambach counterposes the 'Abrahamic myth of exile', and this is a movement in which the same moves into the other but never returns. 'In the Jewish experience of wandering and exodus each finds a way of privileging the alterity of the stranger', Bambach writes.[15] Abrahamic movement *depends* upon the experience of exteriority: wandering, exodus and exile replace the pre-verified homeland. This displacement of homecoming favours 'the ethical legacy of Jerusalem', which avoids 'static principles', in opposition to 'the ontological legacy of Athens'.[16] Crucially, Bambach reads Paul Celan in terms of this ethical legacy, emphasizing the impossibility of dwelling enacted in his poems. Alongside many other scholars, Bambach reads Celan as a poet who, in relentlessly seeking alterity, stands as an exemplar of this Abrahamic movement in exile towards the other, against Heidegger's compulsion to totalize in 'coming home'.

Badiou's anabasis is a third movement. It is couched in the same philosophical terms as Homeric homecoming and Abrahamic exile – same, other, alterity, etc. – however, it is intended to overcome both the totalizing of identity tied with the former and the privileging of the other in the latter. Lévinas's conception of ethics affords primacy to the category of 'the Other', and this is a move attacked vehemently by Badiou in his *Ethics: An Essay on the Understanding of Evil* (1993/2001). There, Badiou modulates Bambach's distinction between 'the ontological legacy of Athens' and the ethical legacy of Jerusalem, by claiming that Lévinas 'devoted his work ... to the deposing of *philosophy* in favour of ethics' (*E*, 18). On Badiou's reading, Lévinas is made to conflate the ontological legacy of Athens with philosophy per se, and this is to surreptitiously exclude Lévinas's writings from the practice of philosophy, as well as to posit the centrality of ontology to philosophy itself. Of course, the cornerstone of Badiou's mature philosophy, *Being and Event*, deems the ontological question the necessary starting point for philosophy today (*BE*, 2).[17] As it stands, Badiou's conception of the movement of the subject is unable to find a place in the schemas identified so far; he at once demands ontology be of founding importance, and that the privilege afforded to the same by Heidegger's conception of homecoming be rejected. In other words, Badiou demands the conjunction of metaphysics and ethics.[18] In *Ethics ...* , Badiou produces a further reading of Lévinas's project which anticipates the former's departure from the two movements – Homeric and Abrahamic – identified above:

> Lévinas maintains that metaphysics, imprisoned by its Greek origins, has subordinated thought to the logic of the Same, to the primacy of substance and identity. But, according to Lévinas, it is impossible to arrive at an authentic thought of the Other (and thus an ethics of the relation to the Other) from the despotism of the Same, which is incapable of recognizing this Other. The dialectic of the Same and the Other, conceived 'ontologically' under the dominance of self-identity ensures the absence of the Other in effective thought, suppresses all genuine experience of the Other, and bars the way to an ethical opening towards alterity. (*E*, 18–19)

Heideggerian homecoming subordinates thought to the logic of the same, harnessing the force of alterity for the benefit of the native, for what is 'proper'. Lévinas on the other hand (and in Bambach's study, Celan) seeks an ethical opening towards alterity divorced from the ontological dominance of self-identity evinced from Parmenides to Hegel, Nietzsche and Heidegger.[19] Badiou's anabasis, by contrast, is a movement desiring both an opening towards alterity and the centrality of ontology. The status of alterity in anabasis, however, is markedly different from its mobilization in Lévinas. What is crucial in Badiou's reading of Lévinas is his assertion that the latter reduces the ethical to the theological, 'anulling' the philosophical in the process. Badiou's point of contention is that in an encounter with alterity, with the finitude of the other, there is nothing to guarantee that such an experience is one of non-identity or of difference per se, rather than one based on resemblance or identity – in which one recognizes oneself in the other, for example. The ethical experience on Lévinas's schema aims to traverse the distance between identity and non-identity, but for Badiou the necessity of this non-identity, and of this 'distance' between same and other, would require a grounding principle of otherness far beyond the finite encounter itself; in Badiou's words, 'The other always resembles me too much for the hypothesis of an originary exposure to his alterity to be *necessarily* true' (*E*, 22). Lévinas's 'Altogether-Other' then, via the individual subject's 'infinite devotion' to it, guarantees the 'finite devotion' ensuring that an encounter with the other be one *with otherness*. Badiou deems this infinite grounding principle another name for God and maintains in his own conception of the ethical, and of the relation between same and other, that such a figure cannot simply be suppressed; that is, the category of 'ethics' cannot persist in its current 'abstract arrangement' – the privileging of the other – by simply masking its dependence on an infinite, unifying or *theological* figure (*E*, 22–23).[20]

The complex relation between same and other enacted in Badiou's philosophy comes to light here then, for what he requires of ethics, in order to escape the theological, is a seemingly counter-intuitive return to sameness or the same, which is another way of saying that ethics cannot produce its own guiding principle (of otherness, for example, as in Lévinas) and instead must be tethered to the production of 'truths'.[21] The philosophical innovations made in *Being and Event* – that being qua being is subtracted from knowledge and inconsistent, that 'the one is not' – allow Badiou to make a return to a logic of sameness without acquiescing to the identity-centric metaphysics with which Lévinas takes issue.[22] For Badiou, 'Infinite alterity is quite simply *what there is*' (*E*, 25). The logic of the same is modulated, referring not to a pre-verified identification but to the intervention of unpresented inconsistency upon presented consistency, sustained in the material unfolding of a truth by a subject in a situation; in Badiou's words, 'since differences are what there is, and since every truth is the coming-to-be of that which is not yet, so differences are then precisely what truths depose, or render insignificant' (*E*, 27). The figure of anabasis is to offer a subjective movement based on the philosophical reconfiguration of what is understood by alterity, by the relation between same and other. The 'alterity' at the centre of this movement is *really other* only insofar as it is borne by an encounter with what is effaced by 'differences' or the prescribed identifications of 'the count'; an encounter with alterity then, for Badiou, is precisely an encounter with sameness. Badiou's reading of 'Anabasis' reconfigures the position of Celan's poetry too, then, in its relation to Heidegger, as well as to its uncertain position in the tradition of Jewish thought, and to the early twentieth century's events as a whole, for the sense of the other interrogated so forcefully by Celan comes to be invested, in Badiou's reading, with the results of his philosophical reformulation of identity and difference, same and other.

Anabasis exists in opposition to Homeric homecoming and to Abrahamic exile, though in Badiou's reading of Xenophon, this opposition is not easily discerned. In his initial invocation of both 're-ascent towards the source' and 'exiled experience of beginning', Badiou invites consonance with the two movements from which his own departs. In Xenophon's narrative, he and his ten thousand Greek mercenary troops are left abandoned in foreign lands following the death of their Persian employer at Cunaxa. Badiou further complicates the status of anabasis in relation to homecoming by insisting that the former names the mercenaries' movement 'homeward': ' ... left alone in the heart of an unknown country, bereft of any local support or pre-established destination. "Anabasis" will be the name for their "homeward" movement, the movement of lost men, out of place and outside the law'. Modulating the initial three meanings comprising anabasis, Badiou proceeds to invest anabasis with, firstly, a 'principle of lostness', in this case determined by the mercenaries' being 'deprived of any reason for being where they are' (their essential foreignness in Persia), secondly, with the necessity of invention – they are 'left to their own devices, forced ... to invent their own destiny' – and finally, with the imperative to find something new, for anabasis 'invents a path' without knowing its destination (*TC*, 82).

However, nothing so far testifies to the core of anabasis, a movement that, embarking into the unknown from an empty space, demands disciplined progression, step by step, carving a trajectory from nothing – the 'free invention of a wandering that *will have been* a return' (*TC*, 82). The essence of anabasis, which sets it apart from both homecoming and exile, is its progression through undecidability.[23] In Badiou's words:

> Anabasis leaves undecided the parts respectively allotted to disciplined invention and uncertain wandering. [...] it constitutes a disjunctive synthesis of will and wandering. After all the Greek word already attests to this undecidability, since the verb αναβαvειv [(*anabanein*)] ('to anabase', as it were) means both 'to embark' and 'to return'. [...] this semantic pairing suits a century that ceaselessly asks itself whether it is an end or a beginning. (*TC*, 83)

Anabasis demands disciplined, formal innovation alongside uncertainty. Discipline ensures the progressive movement through the uncertain and unknown, but also its restraint. Wandering is restrained by will, yet wandering must intervene on restraint producing momentum. Badiou's intention in the passage above is to bring anabasis into dialogue with what he elsewhere calls 'thought'.[24] Like thought, the tension internal to anabasis is what propels its movement: there is no external verification (it is 'outside the law'), no 'homeland' via which it can orientate itself, and no pre-determined, pre-verified space from which to embark. 'Will', the desire of a subject body, is subjected to formal discipline, but this subject must also wander in the unknown, avoiding the Kantian prescription of an a priori 'moral' law determining ethical action. For Peter Hallward, 'nothing is more foreign to [Badiou's] notion of the subject than the idea of a will governed by purely a priori principles' *(E*, xvii). It is precisely in the blank open spaces beyond the reaches of the law, of structure or of rules that the subject must wander in order to win reality or in order to sustain the material unfolding of truth within a world. In the language of Badiou's main influence on the question of ethics – Jacques Lacan – we could say that it is only by subtracting away from the prescriptions of the symbolic order in which we submit to our identification that we might approach the real, and, as Hallward suggests, 'ethics' is what allows the subjective encounter with this real to be sustained – this is the 'disciplined invention' of anabasis (*E*, 52).

The 'infinite alterity' of situations in which being qua being, or inconsistent multiplicity, is subject to the count of presentation and made 'one' or consistent, for Badiou, is 'quite simply *what there is*' (*E*, 25). Far from seeking an ethics privileging the other, then, Badiou's main ethical concern is to think through how an essential encounter with the real, with 'the Same' or with being qua being/inconsistent multiplicity, might be unfolded, sustained and prolonged by a subject, in the face of the prescription of 'infinite alterity'. The subjective unfolding of a truth borne by an encounter with inconsistent mulitiplicity – an event – hinges on the undecidability that Badiou claims to persist within 'anabasis', for the material unfolding of a truth is both a process of negation and of affirmation, negating the logic of the situation in which it appears (an eruption of the Same into prescribed difference) as well as affirming a supplement to that situation, a novel truth. Anabasis, in containing this tension between beginning and end, then, harbours this balancing act between affirmation and negation sustained by the material appearance of a truth within a world. Extending far beyond its original bounds, the movement of anabasis that Badiou produces in his reading of Celan concerns the subjective process via which truths are unfolded, the ethical imperatives surrounding that process and the relations they propose between same and other, and the internal dynamics of truths as examples of thought punching holes in knowledge.

But Celan's anabasis is a far more specific and situated one too. For Badiou, it is a movement that supplants Saint John Perse's, responding to the events of the 1930s and 1940s specifically – Celan's 'black consuming fire', in Badiou's words (*TC*, 87). Before investigating the dynamics of the same and alterity in Celan's anabasis, I want to explore how Celan himself engages with the movement of homecoming, how that movement becomes supplanted in the trajectories enacted within his poems, anticipating the investigations of alterity in 'Anabasis' itself. Providing a close reading of Celan's '*Heimkehr*' – 'Homecoming' – serves to consolidate our understanding of why it is that Celan, in Badiou's philosophy, is read as a figure who demands from within poetry an end to the exclusive intimacy between poetry and philosophy evinced by the later Heidegger. However, it also seeks to explore Celan's own well-documented engagements with Heidegger and Hölderlin particularly on the veracity of the movement of homecoming following the Holocaust.

Before investigating Badiou's treatment of alterity in Celan's 'Anabasis', I want to explore how Celan himself engages with the movement of homecoming by close-reading his poem '*Heimkehr*', 'Homecoming'. In Celan's poem, the efficacy of the poetic word in both inauguration and the return to what is proper – one's 'own' – is placed under strain both by the elision of the homeland itself and by the radical reduction or deletion of the assured wholeness of the poetic voice. The 'I', left floating and empty in the wake of its evacuation, is rendered latent and mute but is charged nonetheless with the poetic imperative to trace an alternative movement. For Celan, famously, 'poems ... are a kind of homecoming', but the trajectory this imperative for the poem demands stands in stark opposition to homecoming in its Hölderlinian and Heideggerian forms. Reading 'Homecoming' also anticipates the close-reading of Celan's 'Anabasis' with which this chapter concludes by encouraging us to think the concept of anabasis as a movement built upon the armature of a negated homecoming.[25]

Reading Celan's 'Homecoming'

Paul Celan's 1955 poem 'Heimkehr' ('Homecoming') is from his third collection *Sprachgitter* (*Language Mesh*). 'Homecoming' also names Michael Hamburger's translation of Hölderlin's poem 'Heimkunft' from the turn of the nineteenth century.[26] In their difference, these titles serve to unfold a fundamental contrast in tone and emphasis between the two poems.

'Heimkehr' is Celan's title. Its meaning in everyday German – homecoming, or the return home – is lent poetic nuance by its suffix's derivation from the verb *kehren* ('to turn' in English) and its distance from the verb *kommen* ('to come').[27] To make 'turning' resonate beneath 'coming' in this way is to offer an understanding of homecoming in which completion is deferred; 'home', whatever or wherever that may be, is turned towards, not found and returned to. Beneath 'Heimkehr', then, operates a privilege afforded to embarking rather than returning itself. In idiomatic German, the verb *kehrer* is also used to evoke an introspective pensiveness – *in sich gekehrt* – or an introspective person more generally – *ein in sich gekehrter Mensch*.[28] Any turning towards home, for this poem, is tethered to a subject in a self-reflexive, interrogative mode, and the choice of *kehrer* in this case also serves to make sure that any questioning of the outside – borders, boundaries, territory, homeland – is imbricated with the internal dynamics of the individual subject. Finally, *kehren* is also the German verb for 'to sweep'. Imbuing Celan's title with a distant sense of clearing, *kehren* evokes both the flattened features of an unidentifiable home or homeland and the historical caesura understood by the signifier 'Auschwitz',[29] but also the promise of marking out a journey upon an empty, pure space.

By contrast, Hölderlin's title, 'Heimkunft', harnesses the verb *kommen* in its suffix *-kunft*. This word-choice changes little of the immediate sense in German, for which *-kunft* operates to denote 'come' in conjunction with other prefixes, for example in *Ankunft* – 'arrivals'.[30] Harnessed poetically, however, it offers consonance with *künftig*, an adjective denoting 'future'. In Hölderlin's title, then, we are invited to think the 'futurehome' to which we shall return, and this is to imbue the homeland with a sense of prior verification or guarantee. Hölderlin's dedication of the poem 'to his relatives' (*an die Verwandten*) only serves to consolidate this construction of homecoming which privileges a return, in the future, to origins, to place of birth, but also to abiding structures of familial support. The contrast with Celan's 'Homecoming' becomes sharply focused here if we accept John Felstiner's reading that the 'you' of Celan's poem is an address to his mother, shot in the Autumn of 1942.[31] Celan's 'Homecoming' begins from a wholesale evacuation of those preconfigured, identifiable structures towards which Hölderlin seeks a return.

If there is a negative encounter with lost home in Celan, however, there is also a positive one, to which the final minutes of Celan's 'The Meridian' speech, made on reception of the Georg Büchner Prize in 1960, attest. Homecoming, its Hölderlinian form subverted and supplanted, is conceived instead as a movement vitalized by an encounter between an 'I' and a 'You', 'encounters, paths from a voice to a listening You, natural paths, outlines for existence perhaps, for projecting ourselves into the search for ourselves ... A kind of homecoming'.[32] But, this is a homecoming in which the given is uncertain and unfixed, in which there is no Swabian motherland, for example, to return to. Celan, in a reply to a bookstore questionnaire two years earlier, describes the relation between 'reality' and poetic language as follows:

> This language, notwithstanding its inalienable complexity of expression, is concerned with precision. It does not transfigure or render 'poetical'; it names, it posits, it tries to measure the area of the given and the possible. True, this is never the working of language itself, language as such, but always of an 'I' who speaks from the particular angle of reflection which is his existence and who is concerned with outlines and orientation. Reality is not simply there, it must be searched and won.[33]

Against mythical poetic rendering or transfiguration (*muthos*), Celan's poetics compels the poem to *measure* with precision, to carve out a path through a featureless terrain in which nothing is given.[34] The poet is charged with the painstaking construction and measurement of a reality which resists language. This is a feature of Celan's poetics which helps us to understand not only the subversion of Hölderlinian homecoming in his work but also, in this subversion, the constitution of an entirely new trajectory within and without the realms of the poem, a movement which corresponds to Badiou's 'anabasis'.

That reality must be sought and won, as Celan says, is a demand to which his 'Homecoming' remains faithful. Its taut, self-sufficient strophes restrain and encapsulate dynamic, often contradictory, movements between speaker and 'home' which develop across the poem's five steps. In Michael Hamburger's translation, the poem reads as follows:

HOMECOMING

Snowfall, denser and denser,
dove-coloured as yesterday,
snowfall, as if even now you were sleeping.

White, stacked into distance.
Above it, endless,
the sleigh track of the lost.

Below, hidden,
presses up
what so hurts the eyes,
hill upon hill,
invisible.

On each
fetched home into its today,
an I slipped away into dumbness:
wooden, a post.

There a feeling,
blown across by the ice wind
attaching its dove – its snow –
coloured cloth as a flag.

HEIMKEHR

Schneefall, dichter und dichter,
taubenfarben, wie gestern,
Schneefall, als schliefst du auch jetzt noch.

Weithin, gelagertes Weiß.
Drüberhin, endlos,
die Schlittenspur des Verlornen.

Darunter, geborgen,
stülpt sich empor,
was den Augen so weh tut,
Hügel um Hügel,
unsichtbar.

Auf jedem,
heimgeholt in sein Heute,
ein ins Stumme entglittenes Ich:
hölzern, ein Pflock.

Dort: ein Gefühl,
vom Eiswind herübergeweht,
das sein tauben-, sein schnee-
farbenes Fahnentuch festmacht.[35]

Snow effaces history and asserts a boundless, empty present – 'now'. Both 'as yesterday' and 'stacked into distance', snow homogenizes memory and destination. Subtle communication with Hölderlin's poem 'Heimkunft' is present here too, for 'Snowfall' is a mark of resistance against Hölderlin's naming of 'the Alps' ('Drinn in den Alpen ... ') in the first line of his own 'Homecoming'.[36] This lack of coordinates in Celan's poem is lent sense and further evolved in prosody: the promise in the break between strophes is crushed by a terse reassertion of the snow's hegemony – 'White, stacked into distance'. This is the only point in the poem at which a sentence intervenes on a strophe, although the chiastic contribution of the line in German – 'Weithin gelagertes Weiß', where 'Weiß' completes and recapitulates 'Schneefall' – is lost in the English; 'distance'. fails to reproduce the closed quality of the first four lines and the break between them, inviting us to roll through the full stop into 'Above' without sufficient pause. Regardless, the endless whiteness of the snow does not connote the freedom of boundlessness, so much as entrapment, the difficulty of movement forwards or backwards, in a time and space whose coordinates have been effaced.

However, the very density of the 'stacked' snow also harbours a positive assertion of poetic task. As a poem in communication with Heidegger's mobilization of Hölderlin's homecoming, this is precisely a demand for movement. John Felstiner is keen to emphasize the pun which operates beneath 'denser': '*dichter und dichter*', he writes, 'suggests the concentrate of poems, since *Dichter* also means "poet"'.[37] The first strophe makes 'Snowfall' the surface on which the poet must embark and extends this featureless terrain into both past and future; it becomes the only space from which movement, in poetry, may begin. However, this imperative for poetry is nuanced by the elevation of 'snow' as a metaphor for the medium in which poetic thought is produced; 'dichter und dichter' falls the snow, muffling eloquence, but not mute. 'Homecoming' begins then from a site of contradiction. 'Snowfall' indexes both negative ground and the poetic capacity to explore routes forward, but the first strophe alone is not enough to allow us to separate one from the other; they remain indiscernible. The imperative for 'Homecoming' is to submit this indiscernibility to direction, to carve out a path, but without the benefit of external verification.

For Celan, 'poems are *en route*: they are headed toward'.[38] 'Homecoming' is a poem which asks what this '*en route*' consists of, what it is headed toward, and it does this by elaborating a principle of measurement that steadily submits an empty landscape to orientation. At first, an open, empty surface is only measured by the 'sleigh track of the lost' which extends above the drifts 'as yesterday', its 'endless' extension reaching beyond the horizon. This sleigh track submits the terrain to measure insofar as it produces a point of orientation with which to navigate. 'Drüberhin' – 'Above it' – offers little scope for conceiving the sleigh-track as inscribed in the snow, measuring the terrain with its furrow. The trace is far more distant, a constellation in a dim night sky perhaps, for the setting of Celan's poem, following Hölderlin, is surely perpetual twilight.

The first strophe of Hölderlin's 'Homecoming' invokes a landscape, a 'Chaos trembling with pleasure' in ecstatic anticipation for the coming dawn – 'a gleaming night still delays ... [...] ... For more bacchantically now morning approaches within'.[39] The snow of the Alps is divinely blessed. In Hölderlin's second strophe, dawn, 'rosy-fingered' as in Homer's epithet, brings the light of the sun – 'Full of roses up there, flushed with dawn's rays, lies the snow.'[40] Above the snow for Hölderlin, not the trace of loss but the dwelling of a God made glad by the play of 'holy' sun beams on snow-capped mountains below: 'so now does life bud anew' in a tumult of 'well-allotted fortune', tumbling over fifteen lines of unbroken dactylic hexameter. But in Celan's poem, this dawn never arrives. The 'sleigh track of the lost', inscribed on the abyss of the sky above the snow, supplants Hölderlin's God and the warming sun, and the 'joyful zest' and abundance of hexameter are evacuated and pared down into isolated, one-sentence strophes like stepping stones.[41] Enjambment is conspicuous by its near-complete absence in Celan's poem: often utilized by Celan as a key constituent of a prosody that carves and cuts, its absence here suggests a reduction not a fragmentation of Hölderlin's lines, a withdrawal from eloquent excess which is recognizable finally in the reduction of Hölderlin's six strophe 'Homecoming' to Celan's five. In turn, each compact, pared-down strophe in Celan's poem testifies to a principle of poetic measurement which proceeds point by point through difficulty.

The measure of boundlessness in the second strophe – the sleigh track 'Above' – is supplemented in the third once 'hill upon hill' become features of the terrain. The endlessness of the trace in the sky is concretized and made particular in the features of the landscape below. Eyes strain in an effort to discern the emergence of mounds of snow on a backdrop of 'White'. These hills make the minute transition from being 'hidden' 'below' to pressing up, 'invisible', inscribing landmarks on the surface, but marks only present insofar as they are felt in the eye they make blind. 'What so hurts the eyes' is precisely their inability to discern these mounds, these graves. The poem's measurements at this stage allow an empty territory to be discerned through its bifurcation from the sky above, but also through its own inherent, though invisible, features. Each strophe takes a minute step forwards in constructing a 'home', but the features which construct this home – the sleigh track and the hills, so far – are both qualified in a way that makes their appearance ephemeral or fleeting. The sleigh track's endlessness threatens its efficacy as a point of differentiation, and the hills, though they 'press up' and are felt, ultimately resist our grasp in the final line of the strophe – they are 'invisible'.

This fragility in construction reaches its apex in the fourth strophe, which offers the most tautly woven, dialectical image in the poem. The appearance of the 'I' here harbours much of this strophe's ambiguity, by indexing both the representation of each grave's inhabitant and the singular lyric 'I' on the page. The form works hard to ensure that the strophe's original assertion of plurality – 'On each' – is reduced, filtered, through the appearance of the 'I', in order to become singular, transformed following the colon into 'a post'. Both instances of the I are 'fetched home into [their] today'. The lost – or 'other', in a visceral rejection of Heidegger's mobilization of homecoming – find their 'home' in graves, each grave marked by the slipping away of the inhabitant to which it belongs, each metamorphosing into a readable wooden graphic or dead letter at the same time made resolutely singular by its material placement – 'I' – in the text. 'Today' forces a conjunction between a lost other unable to speak and a lyric I struck dumb.

It is not only the inhabitants of each grave who find their representation in wood then. We also find an assertion of the lyric I's 'dumbness' consonant with Celan's preoccupation with silence. The I, falling silent, is emptied and, 'fetched' like the lost, is subjected to a coming home in which it is made dumb. Although the 'reality' of homecoming is the extermination of the other – each wooden marker attests to this – the poem also presents the lyric I's falling silent as a figure of fidelity towards the poetic injunction to be en route, to seek 'an other', in Celan's words. That is, if the poem seeks to trace an alternative 'coming home', 'dumbness' must support this alternative's movement. Again, the withdrawal from Hölderlin's poem is palpable here, for the 'I' of his poem, appearing in its third strophe, intervenes as a subject responsible for communication with the divine – 'him' – on behalf of a verifiable homeland:

> Much I said to him; for whatever the poets may ponder,
> Sing, it mostly concerns either the angels or him.
> Much I besought, on my country's behalf.[42]

There is an excess of speech here – 'much' – an excess in lyrical song, opened up towards the divine. Celan's speechless subject stands in complete contrast, measuring its path through a terrain that has no promise of dawn, unable to seek anything on behalf of a 'home'. The very process of passively being 'fetched' or thrown into 'home' demands, in Celan's poem, silence, 'dumbness', but poetry's ability to measure, to seek and win reality, depends precisely on this.

However, the movement from 'wooden' to 'post',[43] the most important transition in the poem, and the apex of its dialectical development, bears evidence of a latent subjectivity able to open up, through silence, a seemingly dead object, or 'mere thing' in Heidegger's words. The wooden marker on each of these hills is transfigured into a 'post'. No longer wooden or dead, as 'posts' the grave markers are able to commemorate the lost. The expression of this minimal transition cut off by a colon – 'wooden, a post.' – is this strophe's principle of measurement. This is the first instance in Celan's poem in which measurement demands human agency, for a wooden 'mere thing' cannot become a 'post' on its own but must be raised and planted. Not only is there a principle of measurement at work here insofar as mere things are made commemoratives, posts also mark boundaries. The space upon which poetry embarks is not the motherland but the silence of loss. The posts serve to measure the boundaries of that territory which the 'I' who speaks, in Celan's words, seeks to bring into relief. But the strophe finishes with only one post: the path dictated by the poem is a laborious one with only fragile results.

The final strophe serves to consolidate the measurement undertaken by the poetic voice, and it reconciles this poetic task with homeland. For, not only does the post serve to mark out a territory determined by loss, affect – 'a feeling' – also consolidates this marking by attaching its flag. What we are left with at the poem's conclusion is a lone post-become-flagpole, serving to mark a territory with no features. The ice wind which attaches this flag also threatens to bring more snowfall with it. The assertion of this territory, arduously constructed, results only in precarity, as the snowfall – poetry's saying – is transported by the same wind attaching the flag, yet also threatens to obscure it, to say too much. By way of contrast, the final strophe of Hölderlin's 'Homecoming' bemoans the silence that often befalls everyday speech, elevating lyrical poetry by ascribing it the task of bringing the transcendent into proximity:

> Silence often behoves us: deficient in names that are holy,
> Hearts may beat high, while the lips hesitate, wary of speech?
> Yet a lyre to each hour lends the right mode, the right music,
> And, it may be, delights heavenly ones who draw near.[44]

Poetry's capacity to name the holy in times of joy is bound by an ostensibly political imperative here. That the lyre provides the 'right music' in the 'right mode' is a direct reference to Plato's *The Republic* in which the political founding of the new state excludes all instruments besides the lyre and the cithara, and forbids music played in modes besides the Dorian and the Phrygian.[45] This dialogue with Plato serves to imbue the inauguration tasked to poetic homecoming in Hölderlin with a principle of political state-forming; the *arrival* home – home's verification – and the winning of the gods' proximity are coterminous with the eventual exclusion of the other. This is the sense of homecoming against which Celan poses his own. In a historical situation that renders poetry qua founding-word obscene, the trajectory his poem charts is one of minimal, precise steps towards something fragile and ephemeral, a movement determined by the cut of language: 'toward something open, inhabitable, an approachable you, perhaps, an approachable reality'.[46]

Reading Celan's 'Anabasis'

The question of 'an approachable you' and its proximity in Celan's speech to 'an approachable reality' is precisely what is at stake in anabasis. In *The Century*, Badiou reads Michael Hamburger's translation of Celan's 'Anabasis' from *Die Niemandsrose* (1963).[47] Taking its point of departure in the difficulty of movement faced by language in its approach towards the other, conceived both as the lost and as 'reality', 'Anabasis', for Badiou, reveals the crucial importance of the *encounter* to how we must conceive any movement of the subject seeking to overcome the nefarious complicities implicit within homecoming.

ANABASIS

This
narrow sign between walls
the impassable-true
Upward and Back
to the heart-bright future.

There.

Syllable-
mole, sea-
coloured, far out
into the unnavigated.

Then:
buoys,
espalier of sorrow-buoys,
with those
breath reflexes leaping and
lovely for seconds only-: light-
bellsounds (dum-,
dun-, un-,
unde suspirat
cor),
re-
leased, re-
deemed, ours.

Visible, audible thing, the
tent-
word growing free:

Together.

ANABASIS

Dieses
schmal zwishhen Mauren geschriebne
unwegsam-wahre
Hinauf und Züruck
in die herzhelle Zukunft.

Dort.

Silben-
mole, meer-
farben, weit
ins Unbefahrne hinaus.

Dann:
Bojen-,
Kummerbojen-Spalier
mit den
sekundenschön hüpfenden
Atemreflexen-: Leucht-
glockentöne (dum-,

dun-, un-,
unde suspirat
cor),
aus-
gelöst, ein-
gelöst, unser.

Sichtbares, Hörbares, das
frei-
werdende Zeltwort:

Mitsammen.[48]

The three initial components of anabasis in Xenophon – 're-ascent towards the source', 'arduous construction of novelty' and 'exiled experience of beginning' (*TC*, 81) – are modulated in Celan's poem, appearing there, for Badiou, in '"narrow sign", "impassable-true"', and '"to the heart-bright future"' (*TC*, 94). Together these connections comprise the 'Upward and Back', the movement of Celan's anabasis. The inner workings of this important first strophe reveal much about the precise nature of these 'connections'. The poem begins with the word *Dieses* – 'This' here and now. Hamburger chooses to elevate the present of the poem itself, casting it as the 'narrow sign', though the German glosses more literally as 'written narrow between walls'. The poem's language is condensed into a single 'sign' constrained by the walls surrounding it. *Zwischen* usually translates as 'between' but also suffixes *Zwischenbemerkung* and *Zwischenruf* to mean 'interruption', a sense which is understandably lost in English. The narrow sign, seemingly constrained and reduced, offers itself nonetheless as an interruption to the limits the walls impose and a route along which the 'heart-bright future' may be sought.

This first strophe hinges on a pun on *weg*, German for path. *Unwegsam* denotes 'rough' in English but Hamburger is alert to the negation of *weg* in *unweg*, glossing *unwegsam-wahre* as something like 'the rough and unpathed true', hence his translation 'impassable-true'. Of course, in the German, the fact that any path in the poem is obscured in paronomasia invites us to consider the difficulty of the path, the fact that the route via which anabasis must proceed is not given to us. For Badiou, 'to the degree that [the path] is true, it is impassable' (*TC*, 94). Language constrained between the walls is impassable insofar as it is true, but is also unpathed by the Shoah; language is the only means of continuing, but it must be a resistant language, a 'narrow sign'.

In *The Century*, Badiou begins his reading of 'Anabasis' by removing questions of the other from the bounds of collectivity, from the dialectic of the 'I' and the 'we'. The ground upon which thinking through the other must take place shifts on 'the other side of the century' – after the Holocaust – from the violent assertion of identity and an adversarial or appropriative treatment of the other towards, instead, a situation in which only the 'imperceptible poverty of the call' of the other may be heard (*TC*, 95). In Celan's poem, silence intervenes on the 'I' and the 'we', denigrating their self-sufficiency; all that is left is an unidentified voice, and the movement of the poem is its trace. 'To the question 'Who speaks?', the poem answers: 'No one', Badiou writes, there is just 'an anonymous voice the poem tunes into' (*TC*, 94).

However, this voice on its own is not enough to journey 'Upwards and Back'. The crucial insight Badiou develops in dialogue with Celan's poem is that the undecidability of wandering and will in any anabasis requires an *encounter* in order to proceed. In Celan's anabasis, this encounter is with the buoys' ephemeral 'bellsounds' – for Badiou, the sounds emitted by beacons heralding the retraction of the tide – this is an image of the 'poverty of the call' of the other. Celan's poem evolves its 'Upward and Back' through this image of the beacons as they leave a trace of a Mozart motet – *unde suspirat cor* – on the air, which Badiou qualifies further as 'the minimal difference of the breath of the other' (*TC*, 95). The 'voice trying to trace a way' in a movement of anabasis requires this breath be met: 'Assuming the call – its enigma –' Badiou writes, 'Celan breaks with the theme of an empty and self-sufficient wandering. Something must be encountered' (*TC*, 94–95). The poem works 'Upward' to the maritime call, before its 'Return' to the walls from which it embarks, for the last word of the fifth strophe 'Zeltwort', 'tent-word', recalls the first's last word 'Zukunft' – 'future' – but supplements it too with the finality of 'Mitsammen' – 'Together'.

It is on this encounter that the word 'Together', the projected future of the journey, depends: 'There is a pure call', Badiou writes, 'an almost imperceptible difference that must be made our own, simply because we have encountered it'. Celan's question, in Badiou's words, is 'How are we to make alterity ours?' (*TC*, 95). This is to ask how we may bear the consequences of an encounter with 'minimal difference' without eliding that difference itself – passing it over – or subsuming it under a pre-verified subjective figure. Badiou expresses this shift from a thinking of the other bound to a pre-existing 'I' and the 'We' as follows:

> In Celan, the 'we' is not subject to the ideal of the 'I', because the difference is included within it, as the almost imperceptible call. The 'we' enjoys an aleatory dependence on an anabasis that reascends – outside of any pre-existing path – towards this 'together' that still harbours alterity. (*TC*, 96)

Because the 'we' can only be posited following an encounter with difference, there can never be an equivocation with the 'I' as in Perse, for the 'we' harbours and maintains difference – this is what Badiou means when he speaks of making alterity 'ours'. The encounter found in Celan's anabasis, for Badiou, arises between those wandering on a terrain from which prior verifications, identities and differences have been subtracted, a situation in which we find the disjunctive synthesis of will and wandering – 'out / into the unnavigated' – and the near imperceptible call of *real* difference (the Same, the inconsistent) – that which stands in opposition to the situation. This difference – the call – is *constitutive* for the subject, but the subject only persists so long as this difference is harboured: 'The "we" enjoys an aleatory dependence on an anabasis that reascends – outside of any pre-existing path – towards this "together" that still harbours alterity' (*TC*, 96). The interaction between same and other does not occur at the level of identity or representation as in homecoming, then, but at the level of precarious presentation, the 'tremulous uncertainty' of alterity, ours and 'together'.

Badiou's reading is intended to dispel the idealist conceit of a pre-existing subjective substance through which difference is encountered and then internalized or appropriated as one's own. Broadly speaking, this is idealist insofar as it reconciles encounters with difference within a pre-existing subject. Badiou's rigorous materialism is grounded in his conviction that the subject is never similarly pre-existing but constructed as the material support in each and every unfolding of a truth within a situation; far from guaranteeing unity, or a way of overcoming what Badiou calls the 'aporias of the One', Badiou's subject is dependent on an encounter with an event – this call of the other.[49] For Badiou's purposes, then, it seems important that the encounter with the fleeting 'breath of the other' is rendered within the image-world of Celan's poem as a material supplement – the 'espalier of sorrow-buoys'. The sorrow-buoys' 'espalier' refigures the walls of the first strophe as climbable trellises, which are then supplemented by the 'tent-/word' becoming visible, 'growing free' up the walls. The espalier serves to ornament the material of the poem too, manifesting itself in the prosody's prunes and cuts, and the ornate punctuation and italics of the strophe in which it appears. Only following the immediate assertion of a *material* difference – no longer walls, but 'espalier' – is the call of the bellsounds itself understood as such, as if the encounter forces an immediate material shift in the possibilities of *this* world, even before a subject is able to coagulate around it in order to make those possibilities real.

Earlier in *The Century*, Badiou makes explicit the nefarious complicities accompanying those movements of the subject – like Heideggerian homecoming – that privilege pre-verified, given ideals, movements that subsume the other under the drive for authenticity, or the "restitution (of the origin) through destruction (of the inauthentic)' (*TC*, 65). Under the sign of 'anabasis', Badiou finds the resources to think through the formation, following an encounter, of an ephemeral subject consistently uncertain of itself – 'a "we" that does not pretend to be a subject' (*TC*, 96). It is the intensity with which Celan's poems respond to the dynamics of identification evinced in Heidegger's reading of Hölderlin which elevates them as conditions for Badiou's philosophy. In the wake of twentieth-century violence, the subject is not to be thought in terms of identification but as something arising only after an encounter – an event. The process that guides the subject's formation then is similarly opposed to the identifications that pre-exist such an encounter.

Though elsewhere in *The Century* Badiou is resolute in his distinction between Fascist and Communist subjectivities and their respective politics, they nonetheless both mobilize 'the production of imaginary macroscopic entities and hyperbolic names', which serves, in the particular case of the 'communisms', to stultify truth's immanence by subsuming it under an objective historical category – 'the proletariat', 'the people' or 'the nation' (*TC*, 103). The contemporary force of Celan's anabasis for Badiou, then, arises not only in its rejection of Heideggerian homecoming – its demythologization of the process of subject formation, the clearance of ideals and pre-verified mythical/cultural categories by which a subject orients itself – but also insofar as it offers a movement of the subject that resists, at a later stage, submission to the inert 'communist' categories of 'proletariat', etc., prevalent in and deemed necessary by the century's emancipatory political projects. For Badiou, Celan overcomes Heideggerian homecoming by presenting a process of subject formation which avoids requiring the other's effacement or extermination, but he also anticipates the necessity of reconfiguring twentieth-century subjective movements so that they are able to both coalesce around an event and sustain its thought via an inner dynamism, refusing the external verification of supposedly universal ideals: in Badiou's words, Celan's anabasis offers 'a "we" that would freely convey its own immanent disparity without thereby dissolving itself'

(*TC*, 97). 'Anabasis' is the trajectory of a subject that sustains this dynamism as an interruption: it seeks the rejection of mythical/cultural ideals in subject formation, a non-adversarial approach to the other (which, for Badiou, must be an encounter with alterity – the event – bound to 'the Same'), and the avoidance of any attempt to *represent* the real movement of event and subject or pass the force of radically discontinuous, material unfoldings of truths over to 'fictional objectivities' (*TC*, 109).

4

Subtraction and Love

Badiou and Adorno

Bruno Bosteels has long argued for the centrality of dialectics to Badiou's thinking. In his recent monograph *Badiou and Politics*, he charts the persistence of Badiou's engagement with the history of dialectical thought, from Badiou's early writings of the mid-1970s and his first mature work, *Theory of the Subject* (1982/2009), through the turn to mathematics presented in *Being and Event* (1988/2005), before the explicit revival of a 'materialist dialectic' in the opening pages of *Being and Event II: Logics of Worlds* (2006/2009). For Bosteels, Badiou's work, *The Century*, is an important participant in this prolonged interrogation of the dialectical tradition, insofar as it diagnoses a twentieth-century primacy of the act, borne by 'the passion for the real'. In Bosteels's words, 'It is precisely the absence of any dialectical sublation that seems to have been compensated for by sheer violence, by the "passion for the real" that characterizes many of [the twentieth century's] artistic and political sequences.'[1] This primacy of action (in all its violence) over the internal overcoming of contradictions points to the necessity of reappraising the dialectical tradition in order to open up, for Bosteels, 'concrete alternatives to the predominance of those tragically unresolved, and most often extremely violent, cases of disjunctive synthesis diagnosed in *The Century*.'[2] Bosteels is keen to read these violent instances of formal innovation, then, not as a testament to the utter exhaustion of the dialectical tradition from Hegel through Marx and onwards but to the failure of the twentieth century to live up to the promise of this tradition.

Badiou's reading of Celan's 'Anabasis' in *The Century* is made all the more potent by its implicit participation in Badiou's interrogation of dialectical thought. In its emphases on the subtractive, on the wavering process of anabasis, on the tremulous encounter with alterity and on the tentative assertion of a 'together', Badiou's reading of Celan is brought to bear not only on the construction and maintenance of political collectivities but also on the necessary reformulation of the promise of dialectical thinking in the face of its seeming exhaustion. The opposition between destruction and subtraction operative throughout much of *The Century*'s chapters, especially in 'The Passion for the Real and the Montage of Semblance', marks this attempt to overcome the antidialectical violence of disjunctive synthesis via the reinvigoration of the promise of dialectical thinking. There, Badiou writes that in *Being and Event* he elaborates a 'subtractive thinking of negativity' in order to overcome what he calls the 'blind imperative' of destruction and purification (*TC*, 55).

In this chapter, I want to explore the continuing centrality of the subjective movement of anabasis by following its development in Badiou's reading of Samuel Beckett's late prose. If Celan's encounter with alterity provides a blueprint for a non-adverserial 'we' and its affirmation in the movement of anabasis, Beckett's, in Badiou's reading, retreats from the ostensibly political overtones of collectivity towards a narrower investigation of the importance of an evental encounter in any affirmation of 'the Two' and their unfolding of 'love' as a truth-procedure within a world. What Badiou's reading of Beckett offers is the consolidation and development of his own contribution to the dialectical tradition: by elevating the centrality of the actual affirmation itself – the truth of love as a supplement to the world in which it appears – Badiou also emphasizes the most radical element of his own dialectical thinking. But the singular importance of affirmation to Badiou's conception of dialectics requires a foil if its radicality is to be made explicit.

This foil must be Theodor W. Adorno. With the recent publication of Badiou's lectures on Wagner, collected in English as *Five Lessons on Wagner* (2010), comes Badiou's first in-depth appraisal of Adorno's thought. That *Negative Dialectics* (1968) is the work with which Badiou engages most thoroughly is indicative of a return in his mature work to the importance afforded to the dialectical tradition in his early writings, but also elects Adorno as a *philosophical* interlocutor whom Badiou deems to have made his own attempt to radically alter the terrain upon which the labour of philosophy embarks. Adorno's *Negative Dialectics*, for example, takes account of the promise of the dialectical tradition, or of philosophy per se, in the wake of the twentieth century's violence; for Adorno, Auschwitz specifically. Throughout his works this project is imbricated with the critique of philosophy's complicity in the colonization of 'life' by the abstractions of exchange value,[3] especially in the primacy philosophy affords to identity – 'identity-thinking' for Adorno – throughout the history of Western metaphysics. Similarly to Badiou, the importance of Beckett to Adorno's wider philosophical project cannot be underestimated. Adorno was keen to dedicate his posthumously published *Aesthetic Theory* (1970/1997) to Beckett, admiring his work for its interrogation of the aporias of twentieth-century art, the loss of art's 'self-evidence' in both its categories and materials, as well as for its solidification of poetry's retreat from some higher, sacred and substantial realm, its wholesale abandonment of language to a rigorous process of disillusionment,[4] these alongside a forceful positioning of Beckett's work in relation to the Holocaust in *Negative Dialectics*: 'Beckett has given us the only fitting reaction to the situation of the concentration camps – a situation he never calls by name, as if it were subject to an image ban.'[5] Adorno mirrors this assertion in 'Trying to Understand Endgame' (1961), claiming history to 'devour' existentialism. Beckett's 1957 play *Endgame*, he claims, reveals a historical moment: the absolute destruction and futility wrought by the Second World War, and the completed reification of the world.[6]

Badiou's sixty-year engagement with Beckett's works finds its sharpest expression in English with the publication of his collection of essays, *On Beckett*, edited by Alberto Toscano and Nina Power. Beckett's works of course appear elsewhere across Badiou's writings too, most notably alongside Stéphane Mallarmé's, as one of the two artistic 'conditions' – one in poetry, one in prose – at the heart of Badiou's wider philosophy and responsible, in Beckett's case specifically, for the philosophical development of Badiou's concept of 'generic truth', 'that is the divestment, in the becoming of the True, of all the predicates and agencies of knowledge'.[7] Besides this process of subtraction or 'divestment', Badiou's philosophy is also forced to take account of 'the encounter' in Beckett: for Badiou, 'Beckett tells of how a larval creature, crawling in the dark with its sack, wrests from another, encountered by chance, the anonymous tale of what it is to live. Then comes the sharing of what Beckett calls "the blessed days of blue"' (*LW*, 548). The claim is that Beckett's later works present in a rigorous, conceptual fashion the way out of the impasse faced by the individual subject, trapped in the interminable solipsism of the imperative to speak. Far from succumbing to the mystical evocation of silence beyond language via aesthetic production, for Badiou Beckett's later prose works nominate themselves as providing, in a 'generic prose', the conceptual coordinates for the becoming of the Two following an encounter. This process figures as one inscription within the fictional set-up of Beckett's works of the rupturing effects of chance upon 'what is'; in Badiou's words, we find in Beckett 'traces of [the] break with the scheme of predestination, of this opening up to the chance possibility that what exists is not all there is'.[8] For Badiou, 'the other' becomes decisive for Beckett with the publication of *Comment c'est* (1961), and this is an exploration that, for Badiou, reaches its most beautiful point of development in the short story *Enough* (1967), this 'prodigious text on love' (*OB*, 103–104).

In what follows two readings of Beckett are pitted against each other, and this is to stage a philosophical encounter between a German Critical Theory indebted above all to Kant, Hegel, Marx and Freud, and a mathematically conditioned systematic philosophy beholden to a determinately French tradition of dialectical thinking.[9] These projects, though irreconcilable at many foundational points as will become clear, are wedded by their commitment to broadly Modernist formal innovations in art – both privileging Beckett, Celan and the music of Anton Webern, among others – as well as by their respective commitments to materialism and a pervasive and rigorous philosophical programme of disenchantment. These commitments are instantiated locally in Badiou and Adorno's readings of Beckett, both of which are mobilized against what they consider the failings of those orthodox interpretations of Beckett's works emphasizing his proximity to the 'Theatre of the Absurd', to Parisian existentialism (most notably Jean-Paul Sartre), as well as to nebulous conceptions of 'nihilism'.[10]

For both Badiou and Adorno, a process of subtraction guides Beckett's formal innovations. As the 'affirmative part of negation', subtraction occupies a central role in Badiou's recent attempts to think through the possibility of a contemporary dialectical project. The process of 'taking away' or 'drawing under' in Badiou's case is guided by the appearance of the new. By contrast, Adorno deems the process of subtraction in Beckett's work to overcome that of abstraction, by which we are to understand the drive throughout the history of Western metaphysics to privilege identity over non-identity or the fetishization of concepts rent from their concrete temporal determinants. Underlying this process is what Adorno calls the 'Western pathos of the universal and the immutable'.[11] In 'Trying to Understand Endgame', Adorno's critique of this drive in philosophy is directed more specifically towards the 'Existentialist ontology' of Søren Kierkegaard, Karl Jaspers and Jean-Paul Sartre, a philosophy that finds its reflection in the social impact of the abstractions of exchange value produced under the capitalist mode of production.

Localized in Badiou's reading of Beckett, 'subtraction' is one of the formal innovations comprising Beckett's creation of a 'generic prose'. In their pursuit of the generic, the prose works of Badiou's Beckett are *affirmative*: they seek the 'invariant functions' of a 'generic humanity'. Crucially, for Badiou, though everything ornamental and circumstantial is negated in Beckett's later prose works, they are not to be read as an image of humanity's destitution or of the melancholy absurdity of reified life. Though Beckett's works stand as exemplars of the subtractive procedure Badiou deems operative in Mallarmé through Malevich and others, and are therefore essentially negative insofar as their path is orientated by the reduction of content towards a 'minimal difference', they also open themselves towards chance, exposing purified, fictional presentations – what Badiou calls 'the night of presentation' – to 'what happens', to the encounter, to the rupture of the multiple. It is of importance then, too, especially vis-à-vis Adorno, that the point of revolt, the moment at which these artworks are able to stand in opposition to the world in which they appear, is not the negative point for Badiou but the affirmative one. Far from claiming, like Hegel and Adorno after him, that the negative moment of thought, or thought's 'labour', is the creative one, Badiou claims affirmation to 'come first'. This rejection of the primacy of the negative is expressed in its clearest possible formulation in his recent essay 'Affirmative Dialectics: From Logic to Anthropology',[12] where he writes, thinking of Adorno, that 'this is the Hegelian framework; you have a relation between affirmation and negation, construction and negation, in which the real principle of movement, and the real principle of creation, is negation'.[13] Following his elaboration of the capacity of the event to provide a point from which being may be ruptured, for Badiou, the negation of the world, as the consequences of the event are borne out, is secondary. Only once the consequences of an affirmation are unfolded in a world is it possible to conceive of that world's negation, sustained as a material supplement. Immediately, Badiou and Adorno's respective approaches to the artwork appear distant from each other.

A crude split emerges here between these thinkers' respective mobilizations of 'subtraction' as a Beckettian formal process: for Adorno the Critical Theorist, subtraction is oriented towards the maintenance of negativity in a reified world that precludes the efficacy of positive identifications; for Badiou the philosopher, subtraction is a process guided by the imperative that truths be affirmed and unfolded by subjects as novel ruptures within situations. Following some initial philosophical distinctions between these thinkers concerning subtraction and the negative capacity of the artwork, an account of Adorno's reading of Beckett's *Endgame* in particular will help to unfold Adorno's primary concerns – catastrophe, history and subject – all of which find their points of density in 'the artwork', before returning to subtraction in Badiou's reading of Beckett's late prose. This exploratory work should allow, finally, a full account of the role of subtraction as an affirmative procedure in Badiou's reading of Beckett, its transport through philosophy's relation to poetry and prose, Badiou's novel conception of subject as 'the Two' of love and the project of 'inaesthetics' more generally.

Adorno's *Endgame*

Almost twenty years prior to 'Trying to Understand Endgame', Adorno offers a diagnosis of the philosophical situation in the aftermath of the Second World War. In the first of *Minima Moralia*'s three parts (from 1944), he writes: '"I have seen the world spirit", not on horseback, but on wings and without a head, and that refutes, at the same stroke, Hegel's philosophy of history.'[14] Adorno upturns Hegel's claim to have witnessed the concretion of world spirit in the image of Napoleon atop his horse.[15] Napoleon is replaced by Hitler's 'robot-bomb', '[careering] without a subject'.[16] Adorno's overarching point here concerns the dissolution of subjectivity, the inability to conceive of the individual subject in the wake of both Auschwitz and the increased technologization and functionalization of society under the rule of exchange value. In the image of the robot-bomb Adorno is met with a symbol of that dissolution, in which 'the utmost technical perfection' and 'total blindness' meet, alongside the arousal of 'mortal terror' and futility. However, the state of the individual subject within history finds itself imbricated here with the possibility of thought, of philosophy. The robot-bomb decapitates Hegel's Owl of Minerva: Adorno's claim is that philosophy is no longer able to reckon with history and is headless, blind to the situation in which it finds itself: the progression of world spirit has been halted and the individual subject of consciousness cut away.

For Adorno, then, philosophy as cultural production is inadequate to the task of thinking its time in the wake of Auschwitz; its categories require wholesale changes. Samuel Beckett's *Endgame*, however, offers something of a palliative to the desuetude of philosophy, though without anything resembling positive, meaningful declaration. Adorno radically historicizes *Endgame*[17]: it produces a thought of its time, and it does so not through the philosophical declaration of categories rendered obsolete by the forces of history but by the persistence of an innovative aesthetic form adequate to the social milieu in which it appears, a form faithful to the withdrawal of meaning from the world. 'The interpretation of *Endgame*', Adorno writes, 'cannot chase the chimera of expressing its meaning with the help of philosophical mediation. Understanding it can mean nothing other than understanding its own incomprehensibility, or concretely restructuring its meaning structure – that it has none'.[18] There is nothing affirmative in Beckett's works for Adorno. They must be read as an essential source of rebellion within art against the '[opposing] of nihilism with ... more and more faded positivities'.[19] In Beckett, Adorno finds a rigorous logic of negation in which negativity is maintained, coherent with his broader demand in *Negative Dialectics* that dialectics fight all attempts to find reconciliation in the positive assertion of concepts: 'To Beckett', Adorno writes, 'the created world is radically evil, and its negation is the chance of another world that is not yet'.[20]

In Adorno's *Aesthetic Theory*, art's role in this negative procedure is further elaborated as follows: 'Art is true only insofar as what speaks out of it – indeed, it itself – is conflicting and unreconciled, but this truth only becomes art's own when it synthesizes what is fractured and thus makes its irreconcilability determinate'.[21] Irreconcilability is made determinate (as a negation)[22] via the formal synthesis, in art, of fractured parts. 'True' art then is able to stand, through innovative form, as the negation of the world in which it appears. For Adorno, Beckett's subtractive process lends *Endgame* this negative power, by which it poses itself against the condition of its own existence – reified life – and the latter's reproduction in the abstractions of Existential ontology.

Positive assertions or identifications are one of Adorno's main targets throughout his philosophical work. *Negative Dialectics* demands that thought be released from the imposition of positivity upon it. Just as labour negates the materials it works on, so thought must be conceived as a negative process: 'As early as Plato', Adorno writes in his preface, 'dialectics meant to achieve something positive by means of negation; the thought figure of a "negation of negation" later became the succinct term. [Negative Dialectics] seeks to free dialectics from such affirmative traits without reducing its determinacy'.[23] For Adorno, *Endgame* makes clownish the speculative will of philosophy, pushing its abstractions and the subject's hope of reconciliation within them 'literally *ad absurdum*, to that Absurd which mere existence becomes as soon as it is consumed in naked self-identity'.[24] As Nina Power and Alberto Toscano remark in their introduction to *On Beckett*, 'Think, pig!', 'Adorno refuses to see in Beckett any concession to the speculative drive and also discounts *a priori* any reading of him as an affirmative or hopeful thinker' (*OB*, xxxii).[25] Not only does Badiou, however, find the affirmation of humanity's generic functions in Beckett, he also produces his reading of Beckett from within, and ultimately for, a systematic philosophical project unapologetic in its commitment to the speculative drive.

Beginning his essay by quietly conceding Beckett's *oeuvre* to demonstrate 'several elements in common' with Parisian existentialism, some existential categories, originally from Aristotle, finding distant resonance in Beckett's work – 'absurdity', 'situation' and 'decision', for example[26] – Adorno immediately proceeds to distinguish the form of Beckett's *Endgame* from those of traditional 'didactic' plays comprising plot, narrative and conclusion or from those plays that would seek to communicate directly and unambiguously a 'message' to their audience. More, for Adorno, when didactic plays saturate what is understood by 'form', they maintain a problematic relationship between representation, or what 'content' appears in them, and the intentions of their author. For Adorno, this is particularly true in the wake of the catastrophe of meaning following Auschwitz: 'The less events can be presumed meaningful in themselves,' he writes, 'the more the idea of an aesthetic *Gestalt* as a unity of appearance and intention becomes illusory.'[27] The abstractions of 'Existential ontology' which Adorno wants to bring into contention are in part reproduced by this traditional form of theatre, and both this philosophical discourse and the form of theatre in which its ideas are presented are ill-equipped to reflect the historical situation in which they arise. Gillian Rose, in her influential study of Adorno, *The Melancholy Science*, writes of this problem with particular reference to Sartre's plays: 'The theme of Sartre's plays is the "absurdity" and "meaninglessness" of existence, but, by making this theme into the clear message of his plays, he confers on it a positive meaning and thereby contradicts his own intention.'[28] By uncritically adopting a form in which events 'make sense', in which 'character' continues as the motive force of the drama, theatre comes to present an abstraction from the real of human suffering under capitalism and after Auschwitz.[29]

The first distinction Adorno makes between Beckett's Modernist form and that of didactic plays is that whereas the latter is 'oriented toward an effect', or serves as the means by which content may be best expressed, in line with its maker's intention, Modernist form is 'audacious' and able to generate possibilities far beyond the simple expression of pre-conceived, abstract ideas in images.[30] These contrasting visions of form find their localization in the concept of 'Absurdity'. For Adorno, Beckett is far from being simply a writer of the absurd: 'Absurdity in Beckett is no longer a state of human existence thinned out to a mere idea and then expressed in images. Poetic procedure surrenders to it without intention.'[31] By way of contrast, Adorno claims Sartre's plays to seek the *demonstration* of the irreducibility of subjective freedom, instead revealing only the complete predetermination of the reality in which the subject finds itself: 'His plays are nevertheless bad models for his existentialism, because they display in their respect for truth the whole administered universe which his philosophy ignores: the lesson we learn from them is one of unfreedom.'[32]

Formal innovation subsumes poetic procedure, surrendering it entirely to the category of the absurd, which is another way of saying that the rejection of the play's declarative potential, the inadequacy of positing the meaning of meaninglessness, requires that the latter be taken up *formally*; metaphysical meaninglessness must be sustained in aesthetic meaning.³³

Lambert Zuidervaart expresses the nuances of this formal procedure, the demands it makes on philosophy, as well as Beckett's importance for Adorno more generally, in his study, *Adorno's Aesthetic Theory: The Redemption of Illusion*: 'The difficulty of interpreting this play', Zuidervaart writes, 'is that it exposes the irrationality of contemporary society while resisting rational exposition.'³⁴ More than this, Zuidervaart isolates *Endgame*'s subtractive form as the motive force behind the play's capacity to reveal this irrationality without succumbing to the temptation to 'name' it: 'Metaphysical meaninglessness acquires meaning as a determinate negation of the dramatic forms that used to *affirm* metaphysical meaning.'³⁵ The metaphysical meaning bolstering the unifying, traditional forms of drama has been rendered obsolete, and *Endgame* is able to reckon with this historical withdrawal.

There is much in Beckett's own writings which supports the notion of an antagonism between his own aesthetic discourse and contemporaneous philosophical productions.³⁶ Clara Locatelli notes that Beckett 'rejected philosophical discourse because of its incapacity to deal with chaos, and because of its non-contradictory language'.³⁷ And, elsewhere, Beckett has expressed a certain incommensurability between the artwork and philosophy: 'It is not a mess you can make sense of. [...] One cannot speak anymore of being, one must speak only of the mess. [...] To find a form that accommodates the mess, that is the task of the artist now.'³⁸ Eschewed by philosophy in its demand for the 'rational', bound to the principle of non-contradiction, the dynamic, concrete experience of living requires a form in art for its transmission, not as the positive assertion of an answer but as a 'statement of the problem itself', as Beckett wrote of Proust far earlier.³⁹ Ironically, this concrete, 'lived' experience is precisely the site of existentialism's opposition to the abstract metaphysics of its precedents, yet, as will become clear, its dependence on 'the human subject' allows Adorno to condemn it as abstraction par excellence, the mere peddling of 'faded positivities'.

Adorno's charge against Existential ontology is that it unknowingly deploys the abstractions it would seek to overcome. Perhaps the main consequence of the process of abstraction and of what Adorno would call 'identity-thinking' more generally is the elision of the temporal from concepts.⁴⁰ This is a familiar reproach against non-dialectical thinking, in which concepts are identified, 'distilled', made immutable and timeless, as if to hover above the dynamics of history. As seemingly universal abstractions, such distillations are deemed to 'blot out' the particular and the non-identical, the concrete content of experience, or that which 'makes existence existence'.[41] For Adorno, *Endgame*'s form is what enables it to dynamically unfold a socially revealing incomprehensibility, as opposed to a blunt meaninglessness, both as a reflection of reified experience and as its determinate negation.[42] Crucially, form, rather than content, is what allows this negativity to be maintained, and though in his *Aesthetic Theory* Adorno writes that 'Günther Anders was right to defend Beckett against those who make his works out to be affirmative',[43] there is nonetheless a form-driven isolation or a self-sameness of the artwork that allows its persistence as a 'source of rebellion'. Adorno opposes nihilism with further negativity: an authentic artwork is able to reveal a utopian hope via the true reflection of the reified world.

The most important passage for understanding the specifics of both the abstractions Adorno deems Beckett to critique and the process of subtraction he utilizes in doing so is the following, worth quoting at length, from the early pages of 'Trying to Understand Endgame':

> Existential ontology asserts the universally valid in a process of abstraction which is not conscious of itself. While it still – according to the old phenomenological doctrine of the intuition of essence – behaves as if it were aware, even in the particular, of its binding determinations, thereby unifying apriority and concreteness, it nonetheless distils out what appears to transcend temporality. It does so by blotting out particularity – what is individualized in time and space, what makes existence existence rather than its mere concept. Ontology appeals to those who are weary of philosophical formalism but who yet cling to what is only accessible formally. To such unacknowledged abstraction, Beckett affixes the caustic antitheses by means of acknowledged subtraction. He does not leave out the temporality of existence – all existence, after all, is temporal – but rather removes from existence what time, the historical tendency, attempts to quash in reality. He lengthens the escape route of the subject's liquidation to the point where it constricts into a "this-here," whose abstractness – the loss of all qualities – extends ontological abstraction literally *ad absurdum*, to that Absurd which mere existence becomes as soon as it is consumed in naked self-identity.[44]

Existential ontology presumes to be conscious of itself, it presumes to be committed to the 'binding determinations' in which thought finds its object. It therefore presumes a broader commitment as well to eschewing rationalisms that would pass over rather than through such entities, those that would ignore the dependence of the movement of thought upon the determination of what is other to it – the concrete, the particular, the temporal. Yet Existential ontology reveals itself, in Adorno's critique, to be wedded to the concept in a way that re-enshrines at its centre the formalism it would seek to overcome: far from expressing a weariness of abstraction, it comes to 'cling' to it.

An earlier comment on Sartre's plays from Adorno's essay 'Commitment' lends nuance to his argument here. Sartre's abstraction is revealed as pushing *subtraction* too far: 'In order to develop his drama and novel beyond sheer declaration – whose recurrent model is the scream of the tortured – Sartre has to seek recourse in a flat objectivity, subtracted from any dialectic of form and expression, that is simply a communication of his own philosophy.'[45] Adorno recognizes the intention in Sartre's plays to present something of humanity's suffering but claims that in seeking more than the simple expression of suffering, Sartre resorts to philosophical categories which stymie the works' formal capacity to harbour the residue of this suffering and sustain it. To subtract away from the 'dialectic of form and expression' is to resort to 'meaningful' positivities, in this case philosophical assertions.

It is not that Adorno wishes to cast out abstraction in its entirety – abstraction, after all, is a necessary part of human experience – but to open it up, to find the residue of the concrete, of the historical, of 'lived experience'. Existentialist ontology for Adorno, however, is incapable of carrying this residue. Existentialism posits the existence of an individual subject invested with autonomy and permanence,[46] and this is to make too little of the relation between individual and history in the wake of what Adorno calls 'catastrophes'. For Adorno, Existential ontology abstracts away from the almost hopeless situation in which the individual finds itself: 'The catastrophes that inspire *Endgame* have exploded the individual whose substantiality and absoluteness was the common element between Kierkegaard, Jaspers, and the Sartrian version of existentialism. Even to the concentration camp victims, existentialism had attributed the freedom either inwardly to accept or reject the inflicted martyrdom. *Endgame* destroys such illusions.'[47] For Adorno, existentialism *posits* a subject able to break out of this realm of abstractions – the irreducible autonomy of the human subject is the site at which the meaninglessness of the world is contested. For Adorno, this is to mistake the concrete, historical situation in which individuals find themselves. To posit the persistence of an individual cut away from its historical moment in which exchange value reduces the human being to a thing among other commodities, and in which Auschwitz ruptures the dialectic by which reason and experience pursue their reconciliation, is precisely to make that individual as abstract as any imposition of reason existentialism would seek to oppose.[48]

Not only has the possibility that human individuals might 'mean something' been 'crushed by the overwhelming power of an apparatus in which individuals are interchangeable and superfluous',[49] but the capacity of language to produce meaning disappears too: for Adorno, *Endgame* is 'constructed on the ground of a proscription of language, and it articulates that in its own structure'.[50]

This problem of 'form' across Sartre and Beckett is addressed here as a question of the transmission of meaning in dramatic works. Adorno's contention is that 'positive metaphysical meaning is no longer possible ... such that dramatic form could have its law in meaning and its epiphany'.[51] When the problem of meaning is imbricated with its 'epiphany', with its positive assertion, meaninglessness is pulled into the latter's sway. Far from charging dramatic works with the task of communicating meaninglessness, Adorno is concerned with how the question of meaning itself is brought into tension via the work's aesthetic form: 'If drama were to strive to survive meaning aesthetically, it would be reduced to inadequate content or to a clattering machinery demonstrating world views, as often happens in existentialist plays.'[52] The task of the artwork is to transpose a meaninglessness borne by historical suffering into aesthetic meaning without its reduction to a flat objectivity.

In *Aesthetic Theory*, the relation of the artwork to meaning was to be evolved alongside further engagement with Beckett's works:

> The dividing line between authentic art that takes on itself the crisis of meaning and a resigned art consisting literally and figuratively of protocol sentences is that in significant works the negation of meaning itself takes shape as a negative, whereas in the others the negation of meaning is stubbornly and positively replicated. Everything depends on this: whether meaning inheres in the negation of meaning in the artwork or if the negation conforms to the status quo; whether the crisis of meaning is reflected in the works or whether it remains immediate and therefore alien to the subject.[53]

An artwork purporting to emerge from a crisis of meaning, in order not to be simply recuperated within that crisis, or by the reified world, must 'take shape', or form itself, as a negative of the society in which it arises. This is a question of how the artwork is able to maintain a negative autonomy in relation to the world while at the same time figuring as the determinate negation of that world insofar as it hinges from it. The 'authentic' artwork, then, must not only negate but ensure through form that its negation persists – a double negation, in a sense, far distant from the affirmative capacity Badiou demands art employ and from the affirmative thought of love as 'the Two' he reads from Beckett's late prose works.

Adorno is claiming here that Beckett's works, alongside the other artists the former privileges, produces a new 'form', yet, as Jean-Michel Rabaté claims, this new form is able to operate precisely as an 'anti-formalist' machine, via which the abstractions into mere form upon which the reified world's effacement of the concrete and the historical depends are subjected to negation: 'Beckett's "subtraction"', Rabaté writes, 'would then oppose the "abstraction" of those who negate concrete life and its historical determination in the name of a reified concept of existence.'[54] To which might be added the abstraction of the commodity form, the chain of equivalence by which exchange value comes to appear as an inherent property of the object.[55] Evolving these thoughts further, Adorno writes in *Aesthetic Theory*:

> Beckett's oeuvre already presupposes this experience of the destruction of meaning as self-evident, yet also pushes it beyond meaning's abstract negation in that his plays force the traditional categories of art to undergo this experience, concretely suspend them, and extrapolate others out of the nothingness ... His work is ruled as much by an obsession with positive nothingness as by the obsession with a meaninglessness that has developed historically and is thus in a sense merited, though this meritedness in no way allows any positive meaning to be reclaimed.[56]

However, the problem of 'abstraction' in Beckett brings much to bear too on the primacy of the question of the subject in Adorno's work, the preface to *Negative Dialectics* famously declaring the desire to 'use the strength of the subject to break through the fallacy of constitutive subjectivity',[57] this alongside his persistent focus on the individual subject's 'lived experience'. The withdrawal of meaning Adorno diagnoses, then, finds its correlate in a paradox at the heart of the subject, a subject whose autonomy, if it has any, must be radically distinguished from the irreducible freedom and permanence afforded it by existentialism. In the contemporary situation of Beckett's post-1944 writing, a situation tainted by the hegemony of exchange value in Auschwitz's aftermath, there exists 'the antimony that autonomous subjectivity is recognized as a semblance produced within a totality which somehow both generates and is the result of this semblance'.[58] This antimony is expressed helpfully elsewhere by Zuidervaart, when he writes, following Peter Dews, of a 'logic of disintegration' 'between the formation of an autonomous self and the loss of genuine autonomy'.[59] This preoccupation with the relationship between subject and world becomes crucial at a later stage in Adorno's reading, though is operative far earlier in his work, not least in *Dialectic of Enlightenment*, written with Max Horkeimer.[60]

For Adorno, the movement of history is expressed by a dialectic of enlightenment, in which the domination of nature, as the trajectory via which the individual subject seeks to guarantee itself freedom, serves only to bind the subject to the unfreedom of rationalization, quantification, function and 'damaged life'.[61] Earlier, in the dedication prefacing *Minima Moralia*, Adorno expresses in plain terms the problematic assertion of autonomy present in existentialist accounts of subjectivity: 'The subject still feels sure of its autonomy, but the nullity demonstrated to subjects by the concentration camp is already overtaking the form of subjectivity itself'.[62] *Endgame* cannot seek to solve this problem, to provide a new thinking of subjectivity by which its freedom might be gained. Teetering on the brink of oblivion, the subject is pushed over the edge in Beckett: the dynamic whole of history, of which the subject is part, and in which it finds its qualities, is opened out, made static in its endlessness, and correlatively, the subject, finding itself divorced from its qualitative instantiation, from its temporal support, from its concrete 'lived experience' as a part of the whole, is made so abstract as to be indistinguishable from the emptiness in which it posits itself. Without the non-identical, the individual is reduced to an 'abstractness which is no longer capable of experience'.[63] Adorno continues: 'Concreteness in Beckett – that shell-like, self-enclosed existence which is no longer capable of universality but rather exhausts itself in pure self-positing – is obviously the same as an abstractness which is no longer capable of experience. Ontology arrives home as the pathogenesis of false life. It is depicted as the state of negative eternity'.[64] The subject is cut from the totality in a way that precludes anything other than its 'self-positing': not only is it unable to define itself against others and against the objects of the world in which it exists, it is also unable to offer anything of itself in a negative capacity; all it can do is posit itself exhaustively. In Adorno's reading, then, Beckett's formal synthesis, the process of subtraction, dynamically extends the abstractions of Existential ontology so that the supposedly autonomous subject is emptied to the point at which it becomes indiscernible from the world in which it is cast: subject and world appear as a single category – 'bare existence' (*OB*, xxxii).

However, for Adorno *Endgame* presents the final *history* of the human subject; it reveals that the absurdity of reason is not ontological but part of a historical process, and as such is open to subversion: 'Blind instrumental reason is a historical fetish that could be superceded',[65] Zuidervaart offers. What remains of hope, for the individual and for the world, is difficult to prise from Beckett's play. The historical dialectic via which rationality proceeds towards freedom is stunted in the play's 'closed space', a space in which time is opened out infinitely, a 'negative eternity' in which reconciliation and the complete reification of the world coincide:

> The imageless image of death is one of indifference. In it, the distinction disappears: the distinction between absolute domination, the hell in which time is banished into space, in which nothing will change any more – and the messianic condition where everything would be in its proper place. The ultimate absurdity is that the repose of nothingness and that of reconciliation cannot be distinguished from each other.[66]

When Adorno writes, in the long passage on 'Existential ontology' quoted earlier, that Beckett's process of subtraction 'extends ontological abstraction literally *ad absurdum*, to that Absurd which mere existence becomes as soon as it is consumed in naked self-identity,'[67] it is this identity of nothingness (the withdrawal of meaning) with reconciliation (everything in its proper place) with no remainder, that figures as the ultimate absurdity: *Endgame* reveals a negative image of a world in which non-identity no longer persists. Hope, then, consists in the gap between the artwork's anticipation of 'what society and its members could become if domination would really turn into reconciliation'[68] and the real state of the world's reification, in which, as a *historical* dialectic, the possibility of freedom must still be present; *Endgame* presents a negative ontology that reveals the real development of reason, of which it is part, to be historical. Opposing Peter Dews's influential study *Logics of Disintegration: Post-Structuralist Thought and the Claims of Critical Theory*, Zuidevaart claims that there must not merely be a 'logic of disintegration' at the culmination of reason's conquest of nature and the human subject, in which the subject wholly adapts, emptily, to the 'world-historical process of reification' in which it finds itself, but a 'genuine dialectic' in which non-identity, or the possibility of freedom, insists. In the final words of 'Trying to Understand Endgame', Adorno invokes Proust, who 'attempted to keep protocol on his own struggle with death, in notes which were to be integrated into the description of Bergotte's death'.[69] In lieu of Proust's real death, the artwork, specifically *The Captive* from *In Search of Lost Time*, presents a negative image of that which is not yet, and in the gap opened between these two deaths resides hope.

Before moving to consider 'subtraction' in Badiou's reading of Beckett, it is worth considering the extent to which Badiou's own writing on theatre anticipates some of the central ways in which 'his' Beckett represents a significant departure from Adorno's. The stakes of such a departure are given by an instructive formulation in Adorno's essay 'Commitment':

> Even the *avant-garde* abstraction which provokes the indignation of philistines, and which has nothing in common with conceptual or logical abstraction, is a reflex response to the abstraction of the law which objectively dominates society. This could be shown in Beckett's works. These enjoy what is today the only humanly respectable fame: everyone shudders at them, and yet no-one can persuade himself that these eccentric plays and novels are not about what everyone knows but no-one will admit. Philosophical apologists may laud his works as sketches for an anthropology. But they deal with a highly concrete historical reality: the abdication of the subject.[70]

The final sentence in the above quotation is of especial interest given Badiou's insistence on a reinvigoration of 'subject' in the wake of its supposed withdrawal or desuetude. That this 'abdication' is a 'highly concrete historical reality' in Adorno is of pertinence too given the Badiouian imperative 'to desire philosophy against history' (C, 21). For Adorno, Beckett's works, in offering a thought of their time, an adequate response to the 'abstraction of the law [of exchange value] which objectively dominates society', draw the whole process of philosophical abstraction into question, a process that, for Adorno, elides historical concretions of human suffering.

There is a way in which Adorno prefigures the discourse of the end of philosophy to which the likes of Lacoue-Labarthe and Jean-Luc Nancy commit,[71] or in Badiou's words, 'Auschwitz is the name for a rupture in history on the basis of which a completely different thinking must be mobilised' (W, 39). With the breakdown of philosophy comes the corresponding importance afforded to aesthetic formal innovations which withhold the simple, positive transmission of content, hence Adorno's enthusiasm for Beckett's *Endgame*, in which a negative image of the world never satisfies itself in declaration. Theatre supplants philosophy in this case, offering a model for thought in which concrete human experience, or non-identity, would find adequate expression, rupturing the supposed hegemony of the concept. For Badiou, however, the primacy of pathos in Adorno's project of negative dialectics, or the imperative to sustain the non-identical without sublation, a 'victimary mode' in Badiou's words, in which 'the appearance of difference comes about in the objective reality of suffering' (W, 39), confines philosophy to the finite or to the human qua suffering animal. It is notable, then, that the 'philosophical apologist' in Adorno's quotation above 'lauds' Beckett's works for their sketch of an anthropology. For Badiou, of course, Beckett 'aims at subtracting the figure of humanity from everything that distracts it, so as to examine the intimate articulation of its functions' (OB, 4), a surely anthropological task – this is Beckett's 'fundamental tendency towards the *generic*' (OB, 3) or towards the affirmation of multiplicity. That such a project bears on the question of 'subject' is all the more pertinent in light of Adorno's insistence on its abdication in the above: whereas for the latter *Endgame* offers the truth of the subject's abdication, Badiou finds in Beckett the affirmation of a subject that subtracts itself from the historical situation of suffering, a situation that this subject, by bearing truth, punctures. It is interesting in this regard that Adorno's privileging of the innovative form of *Endgame* is seemingly to the detriment of spectatorship at the moment of that form's activation. 'Trying to Understand Endgame' treats Beckett's play as a textual object, failing to account for the singularity of its temporal unfolding on stage. It is precisely the play's realization 'at play', however, that allows Badiou to claim a spectator-subject for whom the 'cut' in time introduced in the moment of theatrical performance is constitutive. Badiou proposes not only that 'the art of the stage is before all else the art of the composition of time'[72] but that the moment of the play's performance constitutes an event, around which a spectator-subject may coalesce.[73]

Concluding their introduction to *On Beckett*, Nina Power and Alberto Toscano write:

> At the antipodes of the divine, it would be of interest to consider how the capacity for thought which sustains Badiou's Beckettian venture into philosophical anthropology also signals a *caesura* within man separating him, as rare but Immortal subject of the event, from a 'nihilistic' substrate of corporeality and animality – whence the emblematic nature of Pozzo's exhortation: 'Think, pig!'. (*OB*, p. xxxiv)

Adorno's diagnosis of a historical situation from which meaning and the possibility of its positive communication have withdrawn – 'at the antipodes of the divine', perhaps – and the corresponding 'abdication' of the subject, which it is philosophy's responsibility to sustain in its attention to the non-identical, is supplanted in Badiou's project, and in his reading of Beckett especially, by the insistence that, apart from the 'victimhood' of the suffering human animal, rare, 'immortal subject[s] of the event' may intervene in situations by drawing out the material consequences of transhistorical truths.

In his interview with Peter Hallward and Bruno Bosteels, 'Beyond Formalisation: An Interview with Alain Badiou', Badiou claims a certain ambivalence towards dialectics, expressing the difficulty with which the promise of dialectical thinking might be pursued beyond both the violent disjunctive syntheses proposed by twentieth-century subjectivities – besides those expressed in the (subtractive) work of Celan, Beckett and a few others – and responses to the crisis of the negative, like Adorno's, that would cancel out affirmation in favour of an intensified negativity: 'You could almost say that my entire enterprise is one giant confrontation with the dialectic ... ', Badiou supposes, 'This is why sometimes I declare myself a dialectician and write in defence of other dialecticians (but I mean French dialecticians, which is not exactly the same as the Hegelian dialectic), while at other times I declare myself an anti-dialectician' (*FP*, xxxi). Far earlier, however, in his *Peut-on penser la politique* (1985), Badiou had prefaced his great work *Being and Event* by insisting on the divisive, negative capacity of the concepts that work was to wield: 'I hold that the concepts of event, structure, intervention, and fidelity are the very concepts of the dialectic, insofar as the latter is not reduced to the flat image, which was already inadequate for Hegel himself, of totalization and the labor of the negative' (*FP*, xxxi). The drive by which Badiou's engagement with dialectics continues is to understand how the various referents of these concepts, though they produce a material negation of the situation upon which they intervene, depend on the prior affirmation of novelty as their starting point. Crucially, for the purposes of this book, as it moves into Badiou's reading of Beckett, Badiou has recently, in 'Destruction, Negation, Subtraction: On Pier Paolo Pasolini', defined subtraction as 'the affirmative part of negation'.[74] 'We name subtraction', Badiou continues, 'this part of negation that is oriented by the possibility of something that exists absolutely apart from what exists under the laws of what negation negates' (*AP*, 84). Both Celan and Beckett offer something of a way forward for Badiou out of violent, purely negative or 'destructive' twentieth-century subjective processes towards affirmative constructions by which the situation might be properly opposed.

Celan and Beckett are prophets for Badiou, anticipating for philosophy the subjectivities required at the century's close and beyond: 'That the very essence of negation is destruction has been the fundamental idea of the last century', Badiou argues, concluding that 'the fundamental idea of the beginning century must be that the very essence of negation is subtraction' (*AP*, 85).[75] Against the persistence of the negative in Adorno, Badiou claims the affirmative character of a generic subject, faithful to the consequences of the event. In Theatre, this generic subject is the spectator, called to encounter the 'collective summoning of the Idea'.[76] In Badiou's reading of Beckett's late prose, this generic subject is the Two of love, an affirmative 'insertion' into the situation.

Beckett's generic prose

The contribution of subtraction to a new thinking of 'subject' is central to Badiou's readings of Beckett. Ineluctably philosophical in their points of departure, Badiou claims in 'The Writing of the Generic' that Beckett's late prose works up to *How It Is* (1961/1964) reduce 'character' to the formal intersection of three fundamental questions: 'Until 1960 … the "character" will be – always and everywhere – the man of a trajectory (going), the man of an immobility (being), and the man of a monologue (saying)' (*OB*, 2). Reducing character to the mere formal support for these three questions' investigation, however, is not to be thought as a narrowing of prose's coordinates, but rather as an initial opening of prose, by the divestment of all that obscures its essence, towards what Badiou calls its 'destiny', the 'writing of generic humanity'.[77]

The 'generic' is of central importance to Badiou's philosophical project at large. If we take Badiou at his word, Beckett, as I stated in Chapter 1, is to be considered the primary interlocutor in Badiou's development of the concept of 'generic truth' (*LW*, 548): the 'generic' is subjected to modulation as the consequences of Badiou's 'inaesthetic' reading of Beckett unfold. In *Being and Event*, 'the generic' underpins the subjective unfolding of 'thought', 'truth' and 'truth-procedure', and is to be understood in terms of the relationship between truth and knowledge. It forms the affirmative counterpart to the negative assertion of truth's 'indiscernibility'. Whereas the latter 'indicates … that what is at stake is subtracted from knowledge or from exact nomination', 'the generic' 'positively designates that what does not allow itself to be discerned is in reality the general truth of a situation, the truth of its being'.[78] Truth is deemed indiscernible, but is affirmed too as a generic, predicate-less emergence universally addressed to all. The tie with subtraction is crucial, then, for the generic is the positive assertion of what is *subtracted* from the predicates of identification or 'knowledge'. The set-theoretical underpinning of Badiou's mature philosophy sheds some light on this, for the ontological schema of a 'truth' emergent within a world is precisely a generic set, a set which evades any classification via linguistic predicates. From Badiou's perspective, then, for Beckett's prose to 'write the generic' requires more than simple divestment then: generic writing must be affirmed, accomplished through formal transformation. 'Generic writing' must be evolved through an innovation in what Badiou calls the texts' 'prosodic set-up' (*OB*, 15). This formal evolution is the corollary of a switch of emphasis in Beckett's works following 1960, by which 'the encounter' becomes privileged as a constitutive moment in the becoming of the subject. More, as will become clear, the generic is only accomplished in Beckett's works following the emergence of this subject within the process of love; it depends therefore on the relation of the Two (the subject of love) to generic humanity.

The three initial localizations and designations – being, movement, language – are subsumed under a wider argument, then, concerning the transformation of Beckett's prose works after 1960. For Badiou, the series of prose pieces inaugurated by *How It Is* breaches the speaking I's entrapment in a circuitous 'torture of the cogito' by elevating 'the encounter' to a foundational role in the subject's development; we might think of the evolution from the rigorous and protracted self-interrogation of *The Unnamable* to the formal dependence in *How It Is* on the encounter with Pim. This change of emphasis from the inner machinations of the speaking 'I' to the encounter with the other cannot, however, rely on the prose forms of Beckett's previous works. The exploration of questions of same and other in the works following 1960 requires what Badiou calls a prosodic transformation:

> Beckett treats a set of *problems* in the medium of prose; his work is in no way the *expression* of a spontaneous metaphysics. When these problems turn out to be caught in a prosodic set-up that either does not or no longer allows them to be solved, Beckett displaces, transforms and even destroys this set-up and its corresponding fictions. (*OB*, 15)

That is, the remnants of the traditional means of fictionalization, or the 'functions' of prose – narration, description, et al. – having already been pared back to their most essential constituents, are no longer formally operative in the post-1960 prose works. For Badiou, this formal movement away from prose's traditional focus on fictionalization, or what he calls 'the abdication of the fictive functions of prose' (*OB*, 16), is enough to think through Beckett's 'prosodic transformation' as comprising the emergence of an underlying 'poem', or '*the figural poem of the subject's postures*' (*OB*, 16).

The individual subject is no longer the focalizer of the problems explored in Beckett's prose. The replacement of the fictive function of prose with the 'figural poem' mirrors the movement away from a conception of subjectivity guided by the unity of the individual, however bare or threatened, towards the becoming of the subject in the encounter between same and other. The subjective movement mobilized by the figural poem understands the subject as something that coalesces around such an encounter. The subject that Badiou reads in Beckett, then, follows a remarkably similar trajectory to the subject of anabasis.[79] In the two sections that follow, an in-depth elaboration of what subtraction does in Badiou's reading of Beckett serves to preface a critical exegesis of the Two as the subject of Love. I then investigate this latter's dependence on the prosodic transformation in Beckett's works that allows the appearance in prose of the latent poem, the support for this subject's emergence.

Across his reading of Beckett, Badiou privileges the process of subtraction as the main operator at work in the drive towards a 'generic prose', though it modulates its emphases across the shift between the trilogy and *How It Is*. At the outset of his reading Badiou insists that 'for Beckett, writing is an act governed by a severe principle of economy. It is necessary to subtract – more and more – everything that figures as circumstantial ornament, all peripheral distraction, in order to exhibit or to *detach* those rare functions to which writing can and should restrict itself, if its destiny is to say generic humanity' (*OB*, 3). All ornamental objects, commodities, qualities and circumstantial movements are pared back in order that Beckett's prose touch the essential determinants of humanity – those 'generic' functions that remain following the elision of contingencies. And, this is so that within fictive artifice, such 'rare functions' may be detached and woven, producing a conceptual axiomatic of the (in)human. One way to conceive of this destitution in the workings of fiction is encapsulated in the movement away from representation, of 'characters' in prose, for instance, towards bare presentation. However, this process is also extended towards the fictional spaces in which Beckett's investigation of the invariant functions at the essential core of 'character' or the individual are staged. Crucially, the movement from the 'torture of the cogito' to the foundational importance of the encounter can only be fully understood by following Badiou's analysis of 'the place of being' in Beckett: the tripartite logic at the heart of the individual subject comes to light in all its complexity when worked through alongside the conceptual 'space' in which it finds its localization.

This question of placement is reflective of Badiou's broader concern with the space of fiction presented in Beckett's prose. Investigating the 'triplet' at the heart of Beckett's prose works, 'wandering, immobility, and the voice', or movement, rest, and *logos*, Badiou asks what 'truth' regarding 'what is' may be grasped on this triplet's basis (*OB*, 5). In asking this, Badiou elevates the question of place to a privileged position. For Badiou, it is important that the grey dimness (conceptualized as 'the grey-black' in Badiou's reading) pervasive in many of Beckett's works, from the mud through which Pim crawls in *How It Is* to the 'ash grey' of *Lessness*, be conceived as a localization of being that forecloses any distinction in 'what is'. Through the nomination of 'the grey-black' of being, Badiou is able to ground Beckett's prose works in a fictional world in which determinacy and separation are absent, and in which what is localized (being) by the grey-black can only be thought as void or nothing. Broadly construed, the 'grey-black' comes to signify the conjunction of an open space in which free wandering may occur, the space of the journey in *Molloy*, for instance, with a confined space in which the subject is more explicitly constrained – Malone's bed in *Malone Dies* for example; these are the fictionalized placements of 'wandering' on the one hand and 'immobility' on the other, or 'movement' and 'being' on the tripartite schema of the subject delineated above. The 'grey-black', consistently rendered as *pénombre* in Beckett's French, comes to signify the contorted relation of free wandering to static movement.[80]

Though Badiou finds such a space in Beckett's later works especially, it is also possible to recognize its anticipation in the prose works preceding *How It Is*. Rereading *Malone Dies* in light of the 'grey-black', for example, is instructive, for the narrator's self-interrogation is located within a space at once unbounded and confined, negotiated by compulsive wandering and stumbling, in which 'outstretched arms' fail to meet walls or other points of orientation, but also recedes into circumscribed places of 'hiding' and 'darkness': 'But it was not long before I found myself alone, in the dark. That is why I gave up trying to play and took to myself for ever shapelessness and speechlessness, incurious wondering, darkness, long stumbling with outstretched arms, hiding.'[81] Later, more explicit examples of this localization include, 'Dim light source unknown' from *Worstward Ho*, *Lessness*'s 'Ash grey all sides ... ' (*OB*, 50), the distinction in *How It Is* between the 'mud earth sky', in which its events unfold, and 'above in the light',[82] and *Endgame*'s homogenous grey, and barely distinguishable 'light black'.[83] Together these different names for being's localization testify to the persistent tension between being and non-being within it, both of which slip away from exact nomination. An important point is yielded here, then: for Badiou, this indistinctness must be the condition of any language that seeks the generic and provides the only sense in which language can be said to approach being; the latter must be considered void, or nothing. Badiou fondly returns to Malone's proclamation from *Malone Dies* that '*Nothing is more real than nothing*' (*OB*, 51).[84] For Badiou, the ground of existence is this nothing and language is to scope its plane.

The most important conclusion Badiou attributes to this understanding of the localization of being in Beckett's prose is that being qua being, subtracted from presence in Badiou's philosophy as I explored in Chapter 1, is subtracted from language, it 'inexists' for language. The essence of language will be found then in the 'always possible equivalence between ... *said* and *missaid*'. Badiou concludes that 'the main effect of [the conviction that being inexists in language] is to split being and existence asunder. Existence is that of which it is possible to speak, whereas the being of existence remains subtracted from the network of meanings' (*OB*, 8). Subtraction itself is a process that takes place within the realm of 'existence' on the schema above or within language's purview – the 'network of meanings'. However, what subtraction seeks, what it moves towards, is itself 'subtracted' from the plane of language, as Badiou made clear in the opening address of his 1991 paper 'On Subtraction', delivered at the invitation of the *École de la Cause freudienne*: 'Invited here before you for whom silence and speech are the chief concerns to honour that which subtracts itself from their alternation, it is to Mallarmé that I turn to shelter my solitude' (*C*, 113). The space of a possible affirmation is subtracted from the oscillation between speech and silence, though Beckett's works, for Badiou, remain on the plane of silence and speech until 1960. Beckett's imperative to speak on is operative precisely at the gap introduced between existence and the being of existence. This space is maintained via the process of subtraction, by which existence – identification, contingency, ornament – is pared back towards sameness, or towards the being of existence, being qua being.

In *On Beckett*, the space within existence towards which one subtracts is conceptualized as existence's 'ground'. A familiar Badiouian schema is rendered apparent here: we have being qua being radically subtracted from language, meaning and knowledge, or from the realm of 'existence'. Nestled within existence, however, at its most empty point, is existence's ground, the closest we can get to being qua being itself. Badiou asks: 'Which is the most appropriate colour for the empty place that constitutes the *ground* of all existence? Beckett replies: dark grey, or light black, or black marked by an uncertain colour. This metaphor designates being in its localization, which is empty of any event' (*OB*, 50). The 'grey black' in Beckett then is a localization of being in which existence per se is barely distinguishable from its being, a neutrality in which the difference between night and light is rendered inoperative. And, this is a localization of being, a prepping of the ground, so to speak, intended to capture in fiction a state of being/existence prior to any 'taking place' or happening; the grey black is the localization of being prior to the event.

The three ideas comprising the efficacy of the grey black – the subtraction of being from language and existence, the grey black's neutrality and its emptiness ('of any event') – were to be nuanced further in Badiou's reading of Kazimir Malevich's painting *White on White* (1918) in *The Century* (*TC*, 55–57). Malevich's painting is harnessed as an exemplar of 'the subtractive path', an alternative to 'destructive' manifestations of the twentieth century's 'passion for the real'. Translating the terms of Badiou's Malevich reading into those of his engagement with Beckett, the lesson drawn from Malevich is that 'the real', or being qua being in all its inconsistency, is to be sought not by attempting to annihilate existence's identifications so as to *reveal* the real lying obscured beneath, or by what Badiou calls the process of 'destruction', but by subtracting from these identifications, so that existence, in its empty ground, is *barely* distinguishable from the real or from the being of existence. A 'minimal difference' is to be asserted between what in Beckett is to be thought as the 'grey black', or the localization of being, and the being of existence itself. What Malevich teaches philosophy is that the relation between the real and semblance 'will not be resolved by a purification that would isolate the real, but by understanding that the gap itself is real' (*TC*, 56). That is, existence cannot be simply destroyed or purified entirely in order to reveal being itself. Any approach to being must recognize the fact that being, in itself, is unable to maintain its own question. Put another way, language in poetry or prose cannot eradicate itself; the imperative to speak is always operative. The important question, then, is how this speech may be interrupted.

Just as utterance, reduced to its barest concept, its most essential rendering, for Badiou maintains a wavering between the said and the missaid, so movement is at its most essential in the uncertain tension emitted between mobility and immobility. Again, the process of subtraction in Beckett's works is crucial in realizing the essential core of the three concepts comprising the logic of the individual subject. Initially, for Badiou, the realization of 'the fiction of generic writing' is accomplished by the 'inner metaphor' of Beckett's novels, the fact that his characters are steadily divested of all accoutrements, ornaments, possessions, means of orientating themselves, phrases, destination and so on (*OB*, 3). Malone, confined to his death bed, is released from all such contingencies over the course of *Malone Dies*, losing his stick as well as his pencil. When asserting pressure on the former it slips and he impulsively releases it to prevent falling from his bed. He is rendered immobile there: 'My body is what is called, unadvisedly perhaps, impotent. There is virtually nothing it can do. Sometimes I miss not being able to crawl around any more.'[85] Here, the stakes of divestment in Beckett are brought to the fore. Malone himself questions the efficacy of the 'potent' body, bathetically confining its power to the capacity to 'crawl around', and this is to elevate his own predicament above the presentation of a destitute figure of infirmity and weakness. Malone's 'perhaps' invites us to ask which is the more impotent: his inert body, or the body that crawls? Malone's immobile body is what subsists beneath the body on the move; it is the reduction of circumstantial and contingent destination, purpose and so on, to the essential body. In seeking the bare essence of movement, as Badiou writes in his 'Tireless Desire', 'not only wandering must be detached ... from all apparent sense' but also 'the movement *in* movement'. 'In this dispossession', Badiou continues, 'the "character" reaches a pure moment in which movement becomes externally indiscernible from immobility' (*OB*, 45). Movement is subtracted towards its own 'ideal mobility', which is marked by nothing more than the persistent tension between mobility and immobility.

But, ultimate immobility, in *Malone Dies* at least, is constantly deferred in Badiou's reading, for the process of dying, as an 'irreducible function', never actually becomes death. Were this not the case, were all movement to be subsumed under 'permanent rest', the tension Badiou diagnoses between mobility and immobility would find reconciliation in utter stasis, 'would find its complete metaphor in the corpse' (*OB*, 45). Put another way, the invariant function of mobility, the ideal mobility, would escape presentation. The tension persists in a modulated form between Malone's enclosure alone within his room and the dissolution of all boundaries that would serve to place his situation within the larger schema of identified 'places' constituting the world in which he finds himself. 'All hangs together', Malone permits, but 'I am in chains. Unfortunately I do not know quite what floor I am on, perhaps I am only on the mezzanine. […] All I know is that the living are there, above me and beneath me.'[86] Malone and his room are subtracted from the regime of placement, from the determination of space. Experiencing an interminable 'dying', he is divorced from the 'living' above and below, inhabiting an in-between space between floors, free from placement but nonetheless enclosed. It is not only mobility that is subtracted from in this instance, then, but the identifications ensuring 'one's place' as a 'living' being within a world. To return to the question of being's localization in the 'grey-black', the minute tension between mobility and immobility found in *Malone Dies* above becomes the principle grounding the space upon which Beckett's investigations take place. Malone is seemingly confined to his room but at the same time opened out into a boundlessness apart from all designation; he is between floors. Badiou characterizes this as a fusion between closed spaces in Beckett's works, in which '"what is seen" is coextensive with "what is said" under the sign of the closed' (*OB*, 5) and open 'spaces of wandering' or 'transit'. It is the subtraction from all 'descriptive ornamentation' that serves to bring these closed and open spaces into a fusion, '[resulting] in a filtered image of the earth and sky: a place of wandering for sure, but a place that is itself akin to a motionless simplicity' (*OB*, 6).

This tension is similarly explored in Beckett's later piece *Lessness* (1969/1970): 'All sides endlessness earth sky as one no sound no stir. Grey face two pale blue little body heart beating only upright. Blacked out fallen open four walls over backwards true refuge issueless.'[87] The earth and sky become indistinguishable in motionless simplicity: the space of wandering is homogenized. The bounds provided by the four walls are dissolved into open space but this boundlessness operates as enclosure, as a 'simple' territory eliding the possibility of purposeful trajectories. *Lessness* continues: 'No sound no stir ash grey sky mirrored earth mirrored sky. Never but this changelessness dream the passing hour.'[88] Greyness is modulated in its repetition, extending from face to sky, then mirrored in the earth and vice versa. What initially held the face in relief against the boundless space in which it finds itself is recapitulated: the grey of the face recedes from its figuration into a muted homogenous ground in which it is no longer distinguishable. The individual is no less subsumed by sameness, retreating into the landscape. Closed and open, wandering and rest: their distinction can no longer be maintained.

However, these binaries are not to be conceived as contradictions in process, and their homogenization is not to be thought as one 'moment' of their dialectical development. Badiou is clear that the 'grey black' is not a site of contradiction but of 'unclear equivalence': 'A black grey enough so that it will not enter into contradiction with the light; a black which is not the opposite of anything, an anti-dialectical black. It is here that the closed and the open become indistinguishable, and that voyage and fixity become the reversible metaphors of that aspect of being which is exposed to language' (*OB*, 51). It is this possible equivocation that presents itself to language as its closest point to being. The terrain on which language embarks then is between being and existence, the empty ground of existence at which a wavering between being and non-being occurs. This is the condition of language upon which the journey of the individual subject, locked in a 'torture of the cogito', embarks. This is not yet a prose capable of fulfilling the 'generic intention' because it is only capable of reaching indiscernibility negatively following a process of divestment. The process is able to go no further when the prose is enclosed in the machinations of a single voice; locked in a never-ending struggle for self-identification, this emptied fiction is unable to posit any thought of the generic.

What the prose can do, however, is reach a minimal difference. For Badiou, Beckett's subtraction within prose is able to act as a measure, opening up the possibility of chance. For Badiou, *How It Is* is instructive in this regard, for it places the 'power of the story' in the hands of the other. It is the encounter with Pim with which the narrator furnishes his existence, and he is able to access those 'past moments old dreams back again or fresh'[89] only from a point antecedent to that encounter and the subsequent abandonment: 'I have journeyed found Pim lost Pim it's over that life.'[90] Badiou claims the narrator to have constructed his imaginative life from Pim's, quoting 'that life then said to have been his invented remembered a little of each no knowing that thing above he gave it to me I made it mine what I fancied skies especially' (*OB*, 70). The material (Pim's) with which the narrator 'fabulates' their own life, to use Badiou's expression, is unreachable, however, exclusive to the unfolding of time above in the light, from which only scraps may be won: 'life life the other above in the light said to have been mine on and off no going back up there no question no one asking that of me never there a few images on and off'.[91] Nonetheless, Badiou concludes the following of prose, guided by *How It Is*, and emphasizes in the process the most immediate function of subtraction in prose, the measurement of a minimal difference between presentation and the real:

> The possibility of asking for the story, of extorting it from the one with whom 'it was good moments good for me we're talking of me for him too we're talking of him too happy too' guarantees prose the function of a measure. This measure concerns the gap between the other life and the real, between the dark and the light, and thus inscribes within being itself the possibility of difference. (*OB*, 70)

The idea of a 'measured gap' presented in this passage is, again, lent nuance by Badiou's writings on Malevich in *The Century*. There, Badiou adds that a minimal difference, in which the gap between the symbolic and the real is 'measured', must not only 'inscribe within being itself the possibility of difference', not only produce 'the invention of an outline, the seal of an advance', as he writes in *The Century*, but also anticipate the 'act of subtraction' itself, which is to 'invent content at the place of the minimal difference' (*TC*, 57). Returning again to Badiou's work on Malevich is instructive here, for the way in which 'difference' works in the earlier text on Beckett quoted above is slightly different. 'Difference' in this case is not to be casually conflated with 'minimal difference', the result of measurement, but with the 'content' to be invented following the latter's determination. The possibility of 'difference', then, anticipating the discussion that follows this one, is to be read as the possibility of a disjunctive Two's persistence as the subject of love; 'we're talking of me for him too for him too we're talking of him too happy too' (*OB*, 70). Prose in Beckett offers a subtraction towards minimal difference, in which the possibility of love, of real difference, of the multiple, may be seized against the solipsistic enclosure of the One and its imperative to speak. For the affirmation of this difference to be sustained, however, requires the transformation of the prose in which it unfolds. The name of this transformation in Badiou's reading of Beckett is 'the latent poem'.

The latent poem and love

For Badiou, the latent poem is the active agent of Beckett's subversion of prose: 'There is a kind of subversion of prose and of its fictional destiny by the poem, without the text itself entering poetry. It is this subversion without transgression that Beckett was to refine after 1960 – with a great many hesitations of course – as the only regime of prose adequate to the generic intention' (*OB*, 17). Badiou diagnoses a persistent tension in Beckett's late prose, in which a pared back and reduced fiction, emptied as far as possible, floats, anchored only by an organizing principle, the latent poem, which refuses to make itself explicit. Badiou's main concern is to determine precisely those formal innovations in these late Beckett works that allow, nonetheless *in prose*, a thinking of subjectivity unbound from the interminable, self-reflexive investigations of the individual 'I', brought to saturation point in *The Unnamable*: 'It will be I, it will be the silence, where I am, I don't know, I'll never know, in the silence you don't know, you must go on, I can't go on, I'll go on.'[92]

How It Is is the first of these late prose texts. For Badiou, it

> breaks with the confrontation that opposed the suffering *cogito* to the grey black of being. It attempts to ground itself in completely different categories: the category of 'what-comes-to-pass' – present from the start but now recast – and, above all, the category of alterity, of the encounter and the figure of the Other, which fissures and displaces the solipsistic internment of the *cogito*. (*OB*, 16)

The latent poem is the innovation in prose's 'prosodic set-up' by which these new categories find their unification and regulation. For Badiou, this increased focus in Beckett's works on encounters with alterity is formally grounded in the latent poem's persistence beneath an empty prose; and this movement from the evacuation of prose's fictional capacities towards the latent poem is the formal correlate of a shift in emphasis from the interrogation of the One, tortured by language, to the emergent Two of love, a generic procedure faithful to the consequences of a chance encounter.

When Badiou writes that 'bar the Platonic inauguration, the genuine things that have been said about love – before psychoanalysis rattled its notion – have been said in the order of art, and more singularly in the art of novelistic prose' (*C*, 179), he privileges psychoanalysis as the discourse conditioning contemporary philosophy's relation to love; psychoanalysis has 'rattled' love's notion. With his reading of Beckett, however, Badiou elevates 'the art of novelistic prose' once again as a discourse in which 'genuine things' about love are said. In what follows, I hope to demonstrate the constitutive role played by Beckett's prose works in Badiou's critical engagement with Lacanian psychoanalysis, and that by passing through love's presentation in Beckett's prose, philosophy is offered the means to account for sexual difference in a manner that sidesteps the phallocentrism associated with Lacan's works and for the intimate relation between love and generic humanity, a relation that reflects Badiou's wider commitment to truths' affirmative universality.

Badiou's provocative theses on love come as a direct consequence of his reading of Jacques Lacan, especially his *Seminar XX: On Feminine Sexuality: The Limits of Love and Knowledge (1972-73)*, and it would be remiss to ignore Badiou's consistent engagement with Lacan's dictums concerning the lack of sexual relation, the phallic function (Φx) or sexual difference in the reading of Beckett that follows.[93] For both Lacan and Badiou the question of sexual difference is divorced from naturalistic or biological definitions of sex. For Lacan, psychical experiences of sexed identity are borne not by anatomical differences but by the respective position each subject takes up within the signifying realm and more specifically in relation to the signifier 'the phallus', 'the signifier intended to designate as a whole the effects of the signified, in that the signifier conditions them by its presence as a signifier'.[94] The subjects psychoanalysis understands as 'man' or 'woman' are at times in direct conflict with their respective biological or genetic make up, for they are sexuated only insofar as they occupy particular positions in relation to this signifier. In Lacanian theory, the phallus is not the organ, the penis, though assuming a sexed position as a subject in relation to the phallus requires their conflation. Elizabeth Grosz explains this problematic conflation as follows: 'Lacan's concept of the phallus explains how men and women rationalise their identities as masculine and feminine with reference to biology, and how biology has been confused by them with signification.'[95] By conflating the phallus with the organ, man mistakenly conceives of his 'having' the phallus, and woman, by conflating her anatomical sex with the absence of the organ, conceives of her 'being' the phallus, the lost object of male desire. Grosz continues: 'The male is constructed as the active possessor of the phallus, and the woman as its passive receiver. She becomes the phallus, the object of his desire, by becoming desirable for him, confirming that he has what she lacks (thus wants).'[96] The phallus is the signifier of the Other's desire, the mediating term by which, through language, desire may be exchanged.[97] Its imposition inaugurates a patriarchal symbolic order: man adopts a phallic speaking position in the symbolic, woman a castrated position.[98]

This division has a curious result, expressed by Lacan in his 'The Signification of the Phallus': 'Let us say that these relations will turn around a "to be" and a "to have", which by referring to a signifier, the phallus, have the opposed effect, on the one hand, of giving reality to the subject in this signifier, and, on the other, of derealizing the relations to be signified.'[99] In other words, sexual difference only arises in relation to the phallus, but its unification under that male term serves to obscure the real difference between the sexes. Badiou would claim that the truth of sexual difference is elided here. The context for Badiou's discussion of sexual difference, then, is the burial of this difference, the real disjunction of the sexes beneath the logic of the phallic signifier.

For Badiou, only love produces the truth of sexual difference. Far from consolidating a pre-existing sexual division, love produces two disjunct sexed positions as its *result*. Following a chance encounter (the event), love, as a process, produces a new experience of the world from the perspective of two absolutely disjunct, strictly logical positions, 'man' and 'woman'. These comprise the Two, the subject body of love, which proceeds through the situation without external verification from a third position. Badiou's emphasis is on love as a *process*, by which he distinguishes it from what he calls 'amorous consciousness', the starting point for phenomenological approaches to love. These, Badiou claims, privilege the vicissitudes of the same and the other in consciousness or the difficulty I might experience in love maintaining my 'consciousness of the other as the other' without appropriating the other to myself or prostrating myself before them (C, 188). By contrast, Badiou conceives love as 'the advent of the Two, the scene of the Two … not a *being* of the Two, since that presupposes the three. This scene of the Two is work, a process' (C, 188). More, the absolute disjunction of the two positions forming the Two forecloses any sense in which we might claim love to exhibit the sharing of knowledge or experience from one position to the other; for Badiou '*nothing* in the experience is the same from the position of man or from that of woman' (C, 183); Lacan's dictum that love makes up for the lack of sexual relationship persists in evolved form here.[100] However, far from claiming love to alleviate the pain of non-relation between the sexes, Badiou argues that the process of love produces the truth of this non-relation, this radical disjunction.

This schematic account of Badiou's logic of love, elaborated upon throughout this section, is already a significant departure from Lacan's presentation of sexual difference. Badiou's claim is that Lacan's formulae for sexuation are unable to approach the truth of the disjunction presented in love: 'It is not possible to account for the difference of the sexes, such as love makes truth out of it, on the sole basis of the phallic function' (C, 227). This is an important point to which I will return having explored Beckett's contribution to Badiou's departure from Lacan. Though, before proceeding to Beckett's late prose and the work of the latent poem, it is necessary to concretize Badiou's understanding of love a little further.

Gillian Rose's philosophical memoir *Love's Work: A Reckoning with Life* (1995) insists, as Badiou does, that love be thought as an internally driven process. However, this contemporaneous account of love offers a useful counterpoint to Badiou's. Rose argues that

> the relationship [of love] has a third partner: the work. The work equalises the emotions, and enables the two submerged to surface in series of unpredictable configurations. Work is the constant carnival; words, the rhythm and pace of two, who mine undeveloped seams of the earth and share the treasure.[101]

Beyond the relationship in which it is instantiated, 'love' itself comes to supervene on its 'two' as a third term. The two are drawn by this third term into a dynamic process, elevating a mere coupling to the exploration, in love, of 'unpredictable configurations'. It is the 'rhythm' and 'pace' of *two*, rather than two ones, that drives love onwards, and this 'constant carnival' attests to love's internal energy by which the two actualize the hitherto undiscovered 'treasure' of love's feldspar. For Badiou, however, there cannot be a third term: the 'Two', in their fidelity to the initial encounter, simply are the process of love – in which case, the extent to which love is *produced*, not by way of a third party unifying and realizing the procedure of the initial two but within the bounds of the Two itself, becomes crucial. For Badiou, love *is* where the Two arises as disjunction following an encounter, the event. A third term, or 'work' in Rose, could only serve to count the Two as another One, which would be, in Badiou's conceptual apparatus, to subordinate the radical potential of love qua truth-procedure to the regime of counting which would claim it as One. Badiou's Two must resist such unification, the fusional, 'ecstatic' One of *Tristan and Isolde* for example, a love bound to finitude by its suppression of the multiple.[102] Encountered by philosophy, such a love could only bolster a 'philosopheme of the One' (*C*, 181). More, collapsing the disjunct Two into a One would elide the truth of their radical disjunction. In Rose's conception of love's work, the truth of sexual difference would be obscured by its prostration before a process not immanent to it.

The Two's status *as truth* is offered a more recent formulation in Badiou's dialogue with Slavoj Žižek in *Philosophy of the Present*. Writing on Kenji Mizoguchi's 1954 film *The Crucified Lovers*, Badiou claims its final images to insist on an anti-romantic, non-fusional conception of love: the lovers, bound back-to-back across a mule, are led to their execution, but their faces though 'enraptured' are 'devoid of pathos': 'The film's thought, embodied in the infinitely nuanced black and white of the faces, has nothing to do with the romantic idea of the fusion of love and death. These "crucified lovers" never desired to die.

The shot says the very opposite: love is what resists death.'[103] As if to consolidate Badiou's reading, an onlooker remarks, 'It is hard to believe they are on their way to the scaffold', as the procession and the mule pass by, the lovers facing away from each other, each clasping the other's hand. Love does not give way in this instance, does not submit to what is already visible, but imposes itself upon the situation in which it occurs, even immediately prior to its participants' certain death. That 'Love *supplements* ... ', for Badiou, then, is offered its corresponding image by Mizoguchi, as the lovers passing by demand, 'The truth that the Two, not only the One, *proceed* in the situation' (*C*, 182, my emphasis).

The avoidance of any simple method by which the subject of love might be understood to supplement a situation is expressed in the complexity of the latent poem itself. Badiou's consistent claim that Beckett 'displaces, transforms and even destroys' the prosodic set-up of his early prose anticipates the problem of designating with any rigour exactly how the latent poem operates. Some clarification is offered by Badiou, however, in a passage unfolding the 'latency', the inapparent nature, of the latent poem beneath Beckett's prose:

> We cannot speak of a poem in the strict sense, since the operations of a poem, which are always affirmative, do not involve fictionalization. Instead, I would say that the prose – segmented into paragraphs – will come to be governed by a *latent* poem. This poem holds together what is given in the texts but is not itself given. The thematic recurrences appear on the surface of the text, characterized by their slow motion. Beneath the surface, however, this movement is regulated or unified by an inapparent poetic matrix. (*OB*, 17)

A sparse and reduced fiction comes to be governed by an underlying non-fiction, a matrix whereby the fictional modes of description and narration, having already been pared back, find their regulation in the affirmative operations of the poem. In more abstract terms, the bare presentation to which Beckett's fiction reduces itself finds its governance and unification in the not-presented, in the 'inapparent'. One of the easier ways of concretizing this sense of the latent poem is to stress its 'affirmative' character. Though previously the fictional work done by prose had found its content pared back and reduced, or subtracted, it is no more appropriate to consider this a simple act of negation as it is to think the material unfolding of a Badiouian truth-procedure solely as the negation of the situation in which it occurs. Affirmation, for Badiou, is not bound to identity but to the generic, so there is a way in which the latent poem, beneath the subtracted presentation effected in the prose, serves as this prose reduction's affirmative counterpart. Whereas the prose reduces its fictionalized content to the oscillation between being and saying, and then measures the gap between dark and light, between being and what-is-not-yet, the latent poem operates affirmatively within this gap.

For Badiou, this distance between what remains of prose and the latent poem underpinning it is subject to varied but persistent exploration throughout Beckett's late works. Badiou writes that 'the distance between the latent poem and the surface of the text varies. For example, the poem is almost entirely exposed in *Lessness*, whereas it is deeply buried in *Imagination Dead Imagine*' (*OB*, 17). It is interesting in this regard that Ruby Cohn, in her monograph *A Beckett Canon*, claims *Lessness* to be 'perhaps Beckett's most difficult piece to read *as narrative*'.[104] On the other hand, *Imagination Dead Imagine* is voiced and has an addressee. More, unlike *Lessness*, *Imagination Dead Imagine* is in generously punctuated, recognizable sentences. The first acts as a preface, reading, 'No trace of life anywhere, you say, pah, no difficulty there, imagination not dead yet, yes, dead, good, imagination dead imagine.'[105] The latent poem is buried beneath the oscillations of a single fictive voice that interrupts and corrects itself – 'pah', 'ah' – and identifies itself, however thinly, in opposition to a 'you'. The narrative and descriptive elements of prose are rendered more concretely in *Imagine Dead Imagine* than in much of Beckett's late prose: the narrator positions itself as the subject of the unfolding narrative and offers an empirical study of the space it occupies, its dimensions, temperature, its lighting, how time is experienced within it, as well as its inhabitants, co-opting the reader into judgements made from a singular narrative viewpoint: 'In this agitated light, its great, white calm now so rare and brief, inspection is not easy.'[106]

By way of contrast, *Lessness*, published in France as *Sans* in 1969 and in English the following year, is perhaps the most transparent example of what Badiou has in mind when he writes of the slow modulation and subsequent displacement of meaning effected in the unfolding of a prose work's 'thematic recurrences'. A work in which the latent poem is almost exposed at the text's surface for Badiou, *Lessness* 'describes a kind of picture through the incessant repetition of the same groups of words, and through minute variations which, little by little, displace the meaning' (*OB*, 40). These minute variations, however, are guided not at the level of the textual surface but by an underlying operation submitting the 'groups of words' to the chance permutations of a mathematical algorithm.[107]

Through their determination by a chance procedure, *Lessness*'s sentences evolve, modulating their sense through recapitulation. Ostensibly the purified presentation of a small, grey, upright body situated amidst the toppled walls of a ruin, surrounded by a silent, infinite expanse of grey, the piece begins:

> Ruins true refuge long last towards which so many false time out of mind. All sides endlessness earth sky as one no sound no stir. Grey face two pale blue little body heart beating only upright. Blacked out fallen open four walls backwards true refuge issueless.[108]

As *Lessness* unfolds, fragments of a past life and a will towards the future both come to light. Initially, movement and immobility are indistinguishable from each other and tethered to an all-encompassing silence, 'no sound no stir', 'heart beating only upright'. However, there is a consistent threat of movement in *Lessness* too. The body desires desire, to stir in the sand, to take 'one more step' in the endlessness, and this is bolstered by a dream of diurnal division ('Never but dream the days and nights made of dreams of other nights better days') in which the experience of time passing, of its measure, of being able to look both forwards and back, comes to supplant the persistence of the 'endless', 'timeless' present in which nothing occurs. This is also to seek the actualization of the 'passing hour' and 'the passing light', each hitherto only a 'figment'.[109] The text consistently claims this future step, 'He will live again the space of a step',[110] 'He will stir in the sand there will be stir in the sky the sand',[111] accompanying it frequently with 'He will make it'.[112] Despite this promise of movement, in which the equivalence of mobility and immobility might be ruptured, in which something might occur, it is only the possibility that persists, for Beckett's chosen sentences foreclose the real moment of rupture. There is a sense in which the text, having been opened up to chance by the latent poem, remains indifferent to it: 'The second half of Beckett's work in effect marks an opening onto chance, indifferently sustaining both success and failure, the encounter and the non-encounter, alterity and solitude' (*OB*, 17). Badiou delineates here the transition in Beckett's later works towards an open scene, coursing with the promise of a chance encounter, though as of yet without event, for the latter requires the subject's intervention.

A different promise is present in the two invocations of the past's 'blue celeste of poesy'.[113] These impinge upon an otherwise monochrome palette with an antique blueness bound to the ornamental 'celeste', invoking all at once a woman's name, the treble sound of the celeste keyboard and its meaning in French, 'heavenly'.[114] The gradual development of the piece's 'picture' on the text's surface – the grey body, the white walls, the blue eyes, the grey earth and its mirror in the sky – is interrupted by the ornate beauty of 'celeste', by its invocation of past love and the possibility of its restoration. However, *Lessness* remains the presentation of a situation prior to any happening, it remains the ultimate purification of what Badiou calls the 'space of being' or the grey-black, and on this basis it becomes difficult to discern how exactly, given its centrality to concretizing Badiou's concept of the latent poem, it serves to figure, affirmatively, a new subjectivity borne by encounter. Despite the absence of anything resembling, for example, the couple walking over hills carpeted with flowers in *Enough* or the encounter with Pim in *How It Is*, there is nonetheless an opening towards chance in *Lessness*, by which 'what is' is subjected to slow scrutiny and the threat of an occurrence – 'the step', for example – from beyond the law of its situation, and this is an idea evolved by the text's organization, its latent poem, which submits the prose's measurement of the gap, its opening towards chance, to the actual displacement of meaning following that opening.

For the latent poem to formally support a novel conception of subject, however, requires it not only organize the unfolding of the prose but arise at localizable points in the prose's fabric too. On the one hand, the latent poem operates as the overall governing measure of the prose; on the other, there are also 'sudden' latent poems. As Badiou's argument in 'The Writing of the Generic' proceeds, the latent poem, as well as governing the prose, becomes quotable. There is a sense in which the latent poem subsists beneath the prose as a kind of poetics, a 'semi-poetic set up', but also punctuates the prose at determinable points. 'One chances upon these sudden poems', Badiou writes, 'where, under the sign of the inaugural figure of the Two, something unfolds within the night of presentation' (*OB*, 29). Badiou continues:

> This something is the multiple as such. Love is, above all, an authorisation granted to the multiple, made under the ever-present threat of the grey black in which the original One undergoes the torture of its own identification. (*OB*, 29)

The multiple is sustained in the bare fact of the Two, so long as it resists its collapse into a 'relationship' between two Ones and their respective processes of identification. The operation of the latent poem beneath the prose in *Lessness* is now supplemented in Badiou's work by the actual interruption of the scene of prose, a sense of the latent poem inextricably bound to the emergence of the multiple, to a new figure of the subject presenting itself in all its difference. These punctums remain 'latent within the prose', though, crucially, they occupy the centre of Badiou's radical reading of Beckett; they offer the point at which 'another Beckett may be heard'. Far from the Beckett associated with the Absurd, with dejection in the face of a meaningless world, with analogies for the concentration camps, Badiou's is 'a Beckett who gives voice to the gift and the happiness of being' (*OB*, 29). The most important example of this sense of the latent poem, the authorization of the multiple, is found in Badiou's reading of Beckett's *Enough*, a text in which, for Badiou, Beckett pushes towards his 'terminal' thought, 'the thought that establishes the power of the two as truth' (*OB*, 27). However, another detour via Badiou's reading of Beckett's *How It Is* and Lacan is required to bring this 'terminal' thought into relief.

The masculine and feminine structures produced by the mediation of the phallus in Lacan come to be modulated in Badiou's reading of Beckett's *How It Is*. Badiou observes a subtraction in *How It Is* towards 'four figural postures' of the subject, 'generic figures which cover everything that can happen to a member of humanity' (*OB*, 26):

> To wander in the dark with a sack.
>
> To encounter someone in the active position, pouncing on them in the dark. This is the so-called 'tormentor's' position.
>
> To be abandoned, immobile in the dark, by the one encountered.
>
> To be encountered by someone in the passive position (someone pounces on you while you are immobile in the dark). (*OB*, 26)

These are divided by Badiou into figures of solitude on the one hand, lone wandering and stasis following abandonment, and figures of the Two on the other, the tormentor and the victim. Perhaps counter-intuitively, the status of the two figures of solitude is initially of most interest here. Badiou claims that the figures, wandering and stasis, 'are the results of a separation', but he also claims that in *How It Is*, these two figures of solitude are sexuated 'in a latent manner', not by the explicit invocation of 'man' or 'woman', that is, but 'in accordance with two great existential theorems' in evidence throughout *How It Is*: that, firstly, 'only a woman travels', and secondly, that 'whoever is immobile in the dark is a man' (*OB*, 27). Though he makes no explicit reference to Lacan here, the figures of solitude Badiou reads from Beckett bear an important resemblance to the particular experience of each of Lacan's sexed positions in relation to the symbolic order and seem to be drawn from them.

In Lacan's notoriously problematic account of the sexed positions and their relation to the symbolic, the imposition of the phallus as the mediating term between lovers produces important effects concerning each sexed position's capacity for 'jouissance'. These are formalized in Lacan's formulas of sexuation.[115] For Lacan, following the mediation of the phallus, and their conflation of the signifier with the organ, 'men' become completely determined by the phallic function, 'wholly alienated within language'. Man is unable to desire beyond 'the incestuous wish', in Bruce Fink's words, forever limited in his desire by the inaugural point of his emergence as a subject in the symbolic order. Man is then conceivable as 'whole' because he is entirely delimited by the symbolic. Correlatively, his pleasure is wholly consigned to the symbolic order, to the play of the signifier; this is 'phallic jouissance'.[116] Immediately, Badiou's sexuated figure of solitude above, 'whoever is immobile in the dark is a man', appears to reflect the position of man in relation to the symbolic order. Entirely governed by the phallic function, man is outside and delimited by the signifying realm to which his jouissance is confined.[117]

On the other hand, 'while men are defined as being wholly hemmed in by the phallic function, wholly under the sway of the signifier', Fink explains, 'women ... are defined as *not* being wholly hemmed in'.[118] For Lacan, woman's jouissance is not wholly confined to the symbolic, for women can take up a different relation to the inauguration of the phallus by which they enter language. Without giving much away, Lacan suggests that 'she has different ways of approaching that phallus and of keeping it for herself', allowing 'a jouissance of the body that is, "beyond the phallus"'.[119] However, because it is beyond the phallus and hence beyond the symbolic order, this jouissance is unspeakable and not given to knowledge. Woman becomes defined negatively against the phallus as the 'not all'; feminine jouissance is not wholly related to the phallic function. By claiming the sexuation of one of the figures of solitude in Beckett's *How It Is* – 'only a woman travels' – Badiou is evoking this 'Other jouissance' experienced, though not known, by those that are subjectivized via Lacan's feminine structure. Woman's jouissance is able to travel beyond the symbolic order.

Elizabeth Grosz argues forcefully that even the advent of this 'non-phallic' jouissance within feminine structure fails to offer woman a way out of the phallic function:

> Lacan accords women the possibility of refusing a pleasure and desire that is not theirs, but not of claiming one that *is* theirs. In attributing a non-phallic sexual pleasure to women, Lacan exceeds the narrow constraints of Freud's understanding of female sexuality as necessarily bound to male sexuality. Yet in claiming that this *jouissance* is also beyond discourse and knowledge, ineffable, he back-handedly repositions women in a dependent position. This is a pleasure, a series of sensations and experiences about which nothing more can be said than that they are *non*-phallic.[120]

For Grosz, sexual difference on Lacan's schema here, even if it harbours a distinction in jouissance, only serves to collapse sexual difference into the dependence of the feminine on the masculine. In other words, the sexes, insofar as they take up their positions in relation to the phallus, are not entirely disjunct.

Sexual difference here collapses under its unification by the phallic function. That the two figures of solitude Badiou reads from Beckett are sexuated with recourse to Lacan's phallic function, then, testifies not only to the inadequacy of the psychoanalytical model for thinking *the truth* of sexual difference but also to the promise with which Badiou endows the Two as the subject body that overcomes the respective isolation experienced by each sex in relation to the signifier mediating their exchange. In simple terms, the truth of sexual difference and its transport via the Two can only arise by forsaking any conception of sexual difference that gives a constitutive role to language, or the symbolic order for Lacan. For both Badiou and Lacan, sex is unsubstantial, but following Beckett, for Badiou, the truth of sex can have very little to do with signification either.[121] What Beckett offers Badiou is the means of formalizing the sexuated positions in a way that punctures the symbolic order.

In his reading of Beckett's *Enough*, Badiou finds these subjective figures inaugurated in a different form by the process of love (*OB*, 31–32). For Badiou, Beckett produces 'the thought that establishes the power of the Two as truth' (*OB*, 27) by recourse to four other 'figural postures' pertaining solely to the Two of love. Put another way, in *Enough* Badiou finds the resources to think the truth of sexual difference from within the process of love following the event or encounter, a process resolutely outside the abiding structures of the psychoanalytical subject's emergence in the symbolic order. The four functions organized by the Two's fidelity to their chance encounter become the following. Firstly, the function of wandering persists in love: it 'establishes the duration of the Two and grounds time under the injunction of chance'. Secondly, the function of immobility 'maintains the fixed point of the first naming ... of the event-encounter', that is, maintains the declaration, 'I love you', for example, which testifies to the event's occurrence. Thirdly, there is the function of imperative, 'always to go on'. This third function offers an important point of contrast with the imperative to go on in *The Unnamable*: 'The Two relays that of the soliloquy (*You must go on ... I'll go on*)', Badiou writes, 'but it subtracts the element of pointless torture from it, thereby imposing the strict law of happiness, whether one is a victim or a tormentor'. Finally, there is the fourth function, that of the story, or narrative, 'which, from the standpoint of the Two, offers up the latent infinity of the world and recounts its unlikely unfolding' (*OB*, 31–32).

Briefly, before a closer look at *Enough*, it is important to note Badiou's insistence that these four functions are sexuated: the 'masculine polarity' is bound to the functions of immobility and the imperative, the 'feminine polarity' to wandering and narrative. Once more, the movement beyond Lacan's sexuated subjects is clear. The positioning of 'man' as the phallic speaking subject is overturned, for, in love as Beckett presents it, man is rendered mute; without the narrative function man becomes 'the silent custodian' of the initial declaration, 'I love you', which names the void of the disjunction, the lack of sexual relation. And, without the function of wandering, man, in Badiou's words, is only able to 'retain, motionless in the dark, love's powerful abstract conviction' (OB, 32–33). On the other hand, 'woman', produced by the functions of narrative and wandering, is tasked with bearing witness to love, with 'the infinity of its unfolding in the world, the narrative of its unending glory'. In the process of love, the unspeakable 'Other jouissance' of the Lacanian feminine subject is supplanted by the necessity that inquiries be made into the world from the standpoint of the Two: the feminine polarity is responsible for 'the consequences of the name [or declaration] within speech' (OB, 33). In simple terms, 'man' is tasked with the maintenance of the Two's inner disjunction and 'woman' with the unfolding of this disjunction outward into the world.

Badiou's reading of *Enough* is focused on those instances, latent poems, in which the Two wandering among the flower-carpeted mountains, throughout the consequences of their initial encounter, reveal the world anew, or more precisely, the points at which the Two opens up towards the infinite: 'This text', Badiou declares, 'establishes the precise connections between love and infinite knowledge' (OB, 30). Badiou argues that love's passage from the One to the infinite assigns the subject of love, throughout its procedure, a specific 'numericality', which brings much to bear upon Badiou's later claim of the appearance of the generic in the Two. For Badiou, the process of love demands the movement from one, to two, to infinity; the 'Two of love', he writes, 'elicits a rupture or severance of the *cogito*'s One; by virtue of this very fact, however, it can hardly stand on its own, opening instead onto the limitless multiple of Being' (OB, 28). Beckett's *Enough* demonstrates a transition in the appearance of the sensible world, from the closed scene of the grey black in which the One is trapped to the unveiling of the infinite potentiality of the world as it is, its 'infinite multiplicity'. That love 'resists death' then is offered a different inflection here: love resists not only death but finitude itself, to which Lacan, in Badiou's sympathetic but critical reading in 'The Subject and Infinity', submits his psychoanalytic theory of subject: 'The Lacanian doctrine of the subject is essentially finite, to the extent that even the infinite has to show that its existence does not exceed that of the finite' (C, 225).

Enough's narrator, occupying the 'feminine polarity', describes how their story's male figure, doubled over in a contorted posture of (further) self-interrogation,[122] supplements the 'torture of the cogito' with an increasing awareness of multiplicity: 'On a gradient of one in one his head swept the ground. To what this taste was due I cannot say. To love of the earth and the flowers' thousand scents and hues.'[123] In love, the multiplicity of the sensible in the flowers' 'thousand scents and hues' indexes itself to 'the earth', refigured as the bearer of the infinity of appearances. The earth here serves as a kind of mirror in which the male figure, inhabiting one of the positions of the Two, opens up his own 'oneness' to the possibility of the multiple. However, this hunched figure then uncovers, on the other side of one of the hills upon which the Two journey throughout *Enough*, a real mirror in which he observes the sky:

> In order from time to time to enjoy the sky he resorted to a little round mirror. Having misted it with his breath and polished it on his calf he looked in it for the constellations. I have it! he exclaimed referring to the Lyre or the Swan. And often he added that the sky seemed much the same.[124]

In this passage, one of Badiou's 'latent poems', the world is experienced anew not by each participant in the narrative but from the standpoint of the Two itself. Having drawn his eyes away from the earth, the 'little round mirror' in which the male figure would gaze at his own face becomes the means instead of accessing the 'infinite knowledge' of the constellations, a knowledge only accessible following the advent of the Two. The English translation above does little to suggest the reconfiguration of the sky from the perspective of the Two of love. Alberto Toscano and Nina Power write in their translation notes that, in English, 'the sky seemed much the same' carries little of the sense of the French, '*Et souvent il ajoutait que le ciel n'avait rien*', for which a more 'heroic', 'confrontational' figure of the Two is operative. The English, they claim, retains 'the ultimate indifference of being (the sky) to the event of love', 'whilst in the French text', they continue, 'love allows us to become indifferent to the indifference of being, by fixing it into a "constellation" that we can possess' (*OB*, 143). The constellation is the marker of the multiplicity of the sensible world, grasped *for the Two*: 'I have it!' is the emphatic declaration of the 'multiple of Constellations' (*OB*, 31) and their possession from the standpoint of the Two; their multiplicity, further, subverts the indifference of the night sky. Figuratively speaking, the night sky's *actual* grey black recedes, allowing the emergence in the constellations of what Badiou calls Love's 'second nocturne': 'Love offers beauty, nuance, colour ... not the grey black of being, but the rustling night, the night of leaves and plants, of stars and water' (*OB*, 29). The Two produces infinite knowledge in a way that moves beyond the asymmetry of knowledge in the Lacanian sexed positions, by which the man's knowledge of his jouissance contrasts with the possibility of woman's unknowable but nonetheless experienced jouissance beyond the phallus.[125]

Badiou's 'infinite knowledge' is borne by a truth procedure, the consequences of which pertain to all. It is because, Badiou suggests, the respective experiences of those inhabiting each position are incommensurable – the figures of 'man' and 'woman' in *Enough* for instance – that their knowledge is able to circulate in a sphere subtracted from a world for which objectivity and the One reign:

> Love is this interval in which a sort of inquiry into the world is pursued to infinity. Because knowledge is proven and transmitted between two irreducible poles of experience, it is subtracted from the tedium of objectivity and charged with desire. Knowledge is the most intimate and most vital thing that we possess. In love, we are not seized by what the world is – it is not the world that takes us prisoner. On the contrary, love is the paradoxical and awe-inspiring circulation – between 'man' and 'woman'– of a knowledge that makes it so that the universe is ours. (*OB*, 66–67)

The Two of love bears the most rigorous fidelity to the absolute disjunction of sexual difference, or in Lacanian terms, the lack of sexual relation, while at the same time moving beyond Lacan in the production of a desirous 'transmission' 'between two irreducible poles of experience'. The paradox of love, the 'paradox of an identical difference' as Badiou conceives it elsewhere,[126] is borne by the fact that the maintenance of real difference in the disjunction produces a single interval by which the world is created anew. This paradox is of course sexuated: the male figure guards the void of the disjunction, the 'ontological principle' of the Two and its founding point, but the female figure through wandering and narrative ensures continuous fidelity to the Two itself as it unfolds its inquiries. Expressed another way, man desires the '*nothing* of the Two' and woman '*nothing but* the Two', or 'scission' versus 'endurance'. Individual experiences of jouissance are replaced in Badiou's reading of Beckett by a shared 'happiness' produced by love's sexuation: 'happiness', he claims, is 'indistinguishably "man" and "woman"; it is, at one and the same time, a separating void and the conjunction that reveals this void' (*OB*, 34). However, though 'happiness' is specific to love, it also brings much to bear on Badiou's nomination of Beckett's late prose as a 'writing of the generic', the meaning of which still remains obscure.

At the end of his essay, Badiou defines the process of writing the generic as 'to present in art the passage from the misfortune of life and of the visible to the happiness of a truthful arousal of the void' (*OB*, 36). That all truth procedures, whether inaugurated by events in science, politics, art or love, affirmatively maintain a 'truthful arousal of the void' is a fact of Badiou's philosophy that ostensibly undermines the privileged role afforded to love in Badiou's reading of Beckett, leaving the reader questioning whether love itself is deserving of its privileged position as the central concept through which 'the writing of the generic' is focused. Nonetheless, for Badiou, Beckett's late prose offers a formulation of love that testifies to the crucial role of creative affirmation in any process capable of subverting the world as it stands, and this latter from the perspective of the smallest possible subject body, the Two, a subject that harbours the void in difference, or in what Badiou calls an 'interval' (*OB*, 33). Throughout Badiou's reading of Beckett, the route out of the administered One of self-reflexive, tortuous identification through the Two is rendered consistently. But what love also accomplishes, despite its 'intrapersonal, microcosmic version of the event that, under other conditions, seems a more extensive rupture',[127] in Sigi Jöttkandt's words, is the guarantee of truths' universality.

Throughout 'The Writing of the Generic', Badiou insists that the four functions of humanity produced in love pertain to all truth procedures. The fidelity of the Two to the encounter, Badiou argues,

> organises four functions in Beckett, which are also four figures of the subject *within* love. It is my conviction (for which I am unable here to adduce proof) that these functions have a general value, in the sense that they are the organising functions of any generic process. They relate to the duration of love, of course, but also to scientific accumulation, artistic innovation, and political tenacity. (*OB*, 31)

But in 'The Writing of the Generic', Badiou only gestures towards how we might move from love as an *example* of a generic procedure, bound in this case to 'happiness', towards an axiomatic theory of love that offers its own particular testimony to the genericity of the other truth procedures, an account of love endowed with a singular power to focus 'the writing of the generic'. Badiou's reading of Beckett offers only the starting point for the singular import of the process of love by emphasizing the role of the feminine position in unfolding the consequences of the loving encounter through a series of infinite enquiries into the world. In his essay 'What Is Love?', however, Badiou supplements this reading of the feminine position by claiming it to, from within the process of love, guarantee the generic humanity at stake in the other three truth procedures, science, politics and art.

In 'What Is Love?' the feminine position is responsible for making the connection between the particular process of love and humanity as a whole, or what Badiou calls 'the humanity function': 'the position woman is singularly conveying of the relation between love and humanity'. This is the point in Badiou's complex elaboration of love at which his departure from the Lacanian phallic function is made explicit. For Badiou the 'woman' position testifies to the fact that 'the function $H(x)$ [the humanity function] can only take on value insofar as the amorous generic procedure exists', and further, that 'for this position, the prescription for humanity has value only to the extent that the existence of love has been attested' (C, 195). Put another way, humanity only exists in its universal form, that is, in a form subtracted from its particular mobilizations in the generic procedures of science, politics, art and love, insofar as woman 'knots' from within love the four 'types' of truths together (C, 196–197). The strong form of this claim is that 'it is only as conditioned by love that H, that is, humanity, exists as a general configuration' (C, 197). Badiou's argument is highly technical, and sparse in its expression, but if we remember that the feminine position, already in Badiou's reading of Beckett, desires '*nothing but* the two', the following statement of Badiou's becomes more concrete: 'the woman-position requires for $H(x)$ a guarantee of universality' (C, 197–198). By insisting on an enduring Two, in contrast to man's desire for scission, woman demands the subtraction of individual identity and its disavowal from the standpoint of the Two, such that the individual, insofar as it persists, is confronted by real difference, becoming impersonal, 'human'.

The Two effaces the One of identity that blocks the universal. It proclaims that administered differences, always bound to identity, and to the insidious battle between self and other, must be fought against in the name of real difference, or as Badiou surmises in *In Praise of Love*, 'If we ... want to open ourselves up to difference and its implications, so the collective can become the whole world, then the defence of love becomes one point individuals have to practice' (PP, 98). By demanding not only the universality of the humanity function from within love but also that '*nothing but*' the Two persist, the 'woman' position undermines the supposedly constitutive role of the One, of '*a* situation', for example, as well as the relations the One imposes through unification. This undermining of the One is twofold: the One of *a* situation through which the Two proceeds is revealed in all its contingency (its 'simple law' is not the count-as-one that draws into relation, but disjunctive non-relation), and any recourse to a transcendent One supposedly grounding administered differences – God or nebulous conceptions of 'human nature', for example – is foreclosed as a possibility. Universality is carried by the truth of the Two in the process of love. Against the phallic function, then, which ascribes the universal quantifier only to men (every man is castrated) and defines woman as not-all, Badiou's humanity function purports to '[return] to women, within the complete range of truth procedures, the universal quantifier' (*C*, 198). For Badiou, the latent poem in Beckett's late prose produces a conception of love standing as the universal guarantor of the other truth procedures: the disjunct Two, the smallest possible subject body, testifies to love's processual unfolding, outside of relations, as the bearer not only of real difference but of humanity's universal functions too.

Conclusion

Concluding his opening chapter of *The Century*, Badiou declares that 'the century will indeed have been the century of the emergence of another humanity, of a radical transformation of what man is' (*TC*, 10). The future perfect tense here points to those figures of the subject that extend their reach beyond the century's bounds, offering modes of subjectivity apposite to our current situation. For Badiou, tied as they are to subtraction rather than destruction, and to affirmation rather than (purely negative) negation, the figures of the subject produced by Celan's poems and Beckett's late prose both participate in 'the emergence of another humanity'. And, though he refrains from bringing them directly into dialogue, Badiou deems them to occupy a similar territory, both exemplifying a fundamental mistrust of language at the end of the Age of Poets. It is not for nothing, then, that Badiou subtly weaves Beckett through his chapter on Celan's anabasis in *The Century*: 'In 1958', Badiou writes, '[Celan] is appointed reader in German at the École Normale Supérieure in Paris (before the war, Samuel Beckett had been reader in English at the same institution)' (*TC*, 87); and of Celan's poem 'Anabasis', Badiou acknowledges that 'almost contemporaneously, Beckett, in *Company*, begins with "A voice comes to one in the dark"' (*TC*, 94). That Beckett and Celan are also thought alongside each other by Adorno is of interest too then, given Badiou's critique of Adorno's 'aesthetics of human rights'.[1] Though they never met while living in Paris, Beckett and Celan were aware of each other's work and their shared preoccupations, and both had correspondence with Adorno.[2] More, Stefan Muller-Doohm insists that Beckett and Celan were the 'two artists [Adorno] had in mind' when he wrote that 'the authentic artists of the present are those in whose works the uttermost horror still quivers'.[3] For Badiou, however, these artists' works are more than the transports for still-quivering horror: both affirm new figures of the subject, the tremulous 'we' of anabasis and the disjunct Two of love, capable of transcending the historical endgame through which they wrote.

Emily Apter and Bruno Bosteels write in their introduction to Badiou's recent collection, *The Age of Poets: And Other Writings on Twentieth-Century Poetry and Prose*, that 'philosophy and poetry ... are secretly triangulated by politics' (*AP*, viii). Badiou ensures the explication of this 'secret' in the final words of his reading of Celan's 'Anabasis', in which his commitment to plotting the coordinates of a new, ostensibly political conception of the subject in dialogue with Celan's poem becomes clear. Badiou insists that 'Anabasis', at the end of the Age of Poets, anticipates future political subjectivities:

> Celan ... holds onto the notion of togetherness. 'Together' ... was the main, strange slogan of the demonstrations of December 1995 in France. There really was no other, or at least none that constituted an invention, that had the power to give a name to the anabasis of the demonstrators [...] a 'we' that would freely convey its own immanent disparity without thereby dissolving itself. (*TC*, 96–97)

For Badiou, anabasis leaves its site in Celan's poem, becoming an 'anabasis of the demonstrators'. Not only does Celan provide the blueprint for a collective subject to come over twenty years later in 1995, a subject able to avoid the 'quasi-military', violent and fraternal 'we', he also insists, for Badiou, that this new subject 'freely convey its own immanent disparity'.[4] This insistence on immanence remains the guiding principle for Badiou's contemporary work on the category of the subject; he continues to 'exist within this question'. Taking Badiou's writing on love in Beckett seriously, we might say that it offers the simplest distillation of this 'immanent disparity', this radical difference that undermines all administered differences, providing a conception of the subject of a similarly resistant strain to the subject of politics in Celan's anabasis, but allowing too the specific rejection of the persistence of the negative in Adorno, or the rejection of a reading of Beckett unable to account for the affirmativity of his late prose works. However, it is also necessary that the subject, while expressing its immanent disparity, persists 'without thereby dissolving itself'. The immanence of Badiou's subject is emphasized in various ways throughout this monograph, from dance's 'restrained intensity', through the 'subject without object' sought in the poetry of the Age of Poets, to anabasis's disjunction between will and wandering and the disjunct Two of the subject of love. But the subject, as well as expressing its 'immanent disparity', must also persist. In *The Century*, Badiou claims dance to be a 'crucial art' because 'it is only act. The paradigm of a vanishing art, dance does not produce works in the ordinary sense of the term'. He goes on to ask how such an act might be traced, however, which is to ask, again, by what form its consequences may be sustained. Badiou conceives 'form' in this case as *'what the artistic act authorizes by way of new thinking*. Form is therefore an Idea as given in its material index, a singularity that can only be activated in the real grip of an act' (*TC*, 159). The respective forms taken by the subjective processes summarized above are of course bound to the event, which is to say that the situations in which they occur offer no prior grounds for their emergence.[5] Only in the 'real grip of an act', against knowledge's administered identifications, can such forms be proposed.[6]

Nonetheless, despite this lack of grounding, Badiou has recently committed to something like the aesthetic figuration of these subjective processes. We find in a reading of Wallace Stevens in his recent book *Philosophy for Militants*, for example, a demand for poetry's continuing role in proposing a new 'active figure' of the political subject. For Badiou, 'poetry ... anticipates and clarifies political subjectivity'.[7] Prefacing his reading of the figure of the soldier in Wallace Stevens's '*Esthétique du Mal*', Badiou demands a new figure by which art and politics may be drawn together:

> We must create a symbolic representation of this humanity that exists beyond itself, in the fearsome and fertile element of the inhuman. I call that sort of representation a heroic figure. 'Figure', because the type of action that is at stake here is essentially a recognisable form. 'Heroism', because heroism is properly the act of the infinite at work in human actions. (*PM*, 25)

Elsewhere, such calls for aesthetic figuration come with significant qualification. Five years prior to the publication of *Philosophy for Militants*, Badiou cites the following statement from Philippe Lacoue-Labarthe as an example of one of the latter's 'true' 'sayings': '[It is incumbent on us to go to] that place where we stubbornly tried to articulate and bind together (or bind together again) art and politics. We still have to destroy the figure as the concept of that binding' (*PP*, 162–163). The myriad ways in which Badiou undermines such a thinking of 'figure' are present throughout this book, not least in Chapter 2 where the poem's becoming-prose is mobilized against Heidegger's demand for the aesthetic figuration of a new German people. However, it is clear that the figure is not submitted to wholesale destruction in Badiou. From the Age of Poets' 'figure without figure, or the unfigurable figure, of a subject without object' (*AP*, 16) to Badiou's call for a new figuration thought in relation to the familiarity of the 'form' of political acts, we find that the possibility of literary figurations of the subject persists in Badiou's work albeit in a peculiar manner. Badiou's reading of Beckett, for example, proposes a further 'figure without figure' by emphasizing the resolutely formal trajectories undertaken by the disjunct formal positions in the subject body of the Two. This is a 'subject without object', a subject for which the only 'ground' from which to emerge as a figure is the void of the disjunction, a figure subtracted from any particularity, offering the universal functions pertaining to the unfolding of generic truth. The figure remains but, bound to process and to rupture, it is offered its privileged transport in the eventual form of the poem; that the thought of the Two for Badiou requires the transformation of Beckett's 'prosodic set up' and the advent of the latent poem testifies to this.

My starting point for this book was Badiou's fragmentary and often reverential readings of Celan's poems. This study, I hope, contributes towards continuing research on Badiou's work in the first instance by offering these small passages on Celan both sustained critical attention and their wider theoretical context. I hope to have demonstrated too the efficacy of Celan's poems as an interface by which Badiou's philosophy can be placed in dialogue with Heidegger and his legacy. Though Chapters 1–3 unfolded Badiou's distance from Heidegger concerning ontology, truth, politics and the poem, it was only with Chapter 3 that the full expression of Badiou's passing through Celan in his rejection of Heidegger came to light; that anabasis can be read against Heidegger's 'homecoming' offers a useful site for further enquiry, then, into both the poem's role in thinking subjectivity following twentieth-century violence and philosophy's capacity to retrospectively engage with poetic thinking of this nature. Badiou and Lacoue-Labarthe have rarely been placed in dialogue, but the subtle distinction in their respective readings of the Heideggerian suture between the poem and philosophy offered its 'broadly political' implications in a way that grounded their more concrete rendering via the category of the subject.

However, Badiou and Lacoue-Labarthe's discussion of the poem's 'becoming-prose' also serves as a fruitful link between the modern poem's 'central silence', in Badiou's words, and his reading of the 'latent poem' in Beckett's late prose. This study's broad conceptual scope is secured and lent focus by the distinctive reciprocity evinced between poem and prose throughout Badiou's writings on Celan and Beckett. Analysing these writings demonstrates that, for Badiou, the emergence of the modern, secular poem depends on its becoming-prose, its refusal of any poetic essence bound to myth, and similarly, that the poem's singular capacity within art to think the event and produce novel conceptions of subject is at its most luminous when rupturing the operations of prose. Staging the confrontation in Chapter 4 between Badiou and Adorno's respective readings of Beckett was my attempt to pursue the relationship between the poem (including the latent poem), philosophy and politics beyond contemporaneous extensions of the Heideggerian legacy – in Philippe Lacoue-Labarthe's work, for example – into broader considerations of the poem's ability to think an affirmative subject for the future in the wake of twentieth-century violence. Reading Badiou's emphasis on affirmation in Beckett in Chapter 4 against the maintenance of negativity in Adorno also elevates Beckett and Celan retrospectively as privileged interlocutors by which we might make sense of Badiou's opposition to Adorno's negative dialectics. Both writers, for Badiou, open up questions of art's relation to history, to abstraction, subtraction and the subject, via which his work radically opposes Adorno's. Any attempt to deal with the question of dialectics in Badiou must surely pass through Adorno, and my hope is that this book is successful in nominating Celan and Beckett as especially productive sites for this passing.[8]

My argument in Chapter 4 that Badiou demonstrates his departure from a Lacanian conception of sexual difference in his development of the 'Two of love' in dialogue with Beckett's late prose also supplements recent work on Badiou that anticipates the emergence of 'love', precisely because of its conjunction of sexual difference and the universal, as perhaps the condition par excellence as Badiou moves into a new period in his thought with the publication in France of the third volume of *Being and Event: L'Être et l'Événement, 3: L'immanence des vérités*,[9] where, it should be noted, there is also a significant further engagement with Paul Celan's poetry. Louise Burchill expresses this shift in Badiou's work on the basis of love as follows, emphasizing the now constitutive role of difference in Badiou's philosophy: 'The universal can no longer be indifferent to difference since, with love's introduction of sexual disjunction/difference into its very core, it is, itself, no longer in-different at all.'[10] In fact, we can anticipate only further interest in love in Badiou's anglophone reception. Burchill, whose work on Badiou, feminism, the feminine and sexual difference has been especially enlightening in this regard, has recently argued that Badiou, having criticized liberal, reformist feminism throughout the 1980s and 1990s as a demand to be included in 'what already exists', favouring instead radical attempts to force change through the lens of the universal, has opened his thought, following, we are to suppose, feminist critiques of his work to the possibility of formally 'sexed universals', elaborated on the back of his account of love.[11] Badiou's disavowal of Lacan's formulae for sexuation and the primacy of the phallic function via Beckett, and his subsequent endeavour to 'return to women the universal quantifier', 'within the complete range of truth procedures', though at risk perhaps of maintaining an exceptional quality of the feminine as Lacan does, certainly seems to be notable as a step towards this important development in his thought, in which the universal, isolated hitherto from mobilizations of 'identity', is indelibly marked by the history of feminist thought. Burchill claims this welcome development, given the frequently dispiriting experience of reading the work of Badiou and his contemporaries from a contemporary feminist perspective, as a 'remarkable' 'turn' in his thought over the last ten years: 'Badiou's thinking on the universal has taken a "turn" whereby the non-neutrality of symbolic thought is no longer denounced as an error entertained by feminists and other postmodernist protagonists of a contemporary sophism, but affirmed as having characterised the history of "humanity" up until today.'[12] Badiou's elaboration of his theories of sexuation, the universal and love in dialogue with Beckett's late prose, however, is a conjunction of philosophy, literature and psychoanalysis that has so far been underexplored, and I hope my attempts to pass through it in Chapter 4 stand as a useful supplement to the inspiring work accomplished by Burchill and others, most notably Sigi Jöttkandt,[13] interrogating Badiou's writing on love.

It would be remiss to ignore Badiou's recent further elaboration of the relations between love and the poem/prose, which stands in closer proximity perhaps to the analyses I have undertaken in this book, and suggests I think fruitful pathways for continuing work on Badiou's philosophy and its engagement not only with literature and love, broadly, but also with the specific difficulties pertaining to philosophy's relations to both poem and prose that I examined with regard to the poem's 'becoming-prose' in Chapter 2 and the 'latent poem' beneath Beckett's late prose in Chapter 4. These recent modulations in his thought are, excitingly, elaborated again in dialogue with Philippe Lacoue-Labarthe, who is emerging as the most important of Badiou's contemporary interlocutors.

In 'In Search of Lost Prose', Badiou elaborates new connections between love, poetry and prose in a close reading of Lacoue-Labarthe's meditations on 'the phrase', from his prose and verse sequence, *Phrase*, written in the twenty-five years before his death.[14] It is intriguing, however, that these strange new connections between love and poetry elaborated in Badiou's elegy draw initially on two consecutive meditations from Lacoue-Labarthe's text on Paul Celan, *Poetry as Experience*. Badiou cites from the first of these, 'Vertigo', Lacoue-Labarthe's examination of a key line from 'The Meridian'. Following example translations from Blanchot, Du Bouchet and Launay, Lacoue-Labarthe settles on 'Poetry, Ladies and Gentlemen –: that infinite speaking of pure mortality and the in-vain'. 'Poetry is thus', Badiou glosses, 'a knotting of speaking, the infinite, and death' (ISLP, 1254). In the wake of God's death, and one presumes in this context the Holocaust, a contemporary poetry, seeking prose, must secure the infinite elsewhere: 'if we can only love on Earth, and only speak on the verge of death, then we are delivered, Lacoue tells us, [...] from prayer' (ISLP, 1255), Badiou writes. But the poem's search for prose, in the wake of God's death and the conjunction of speaking and finitude, can only orient itself negatively. For Badiou, both Celan and Lacoue-Labarthe are 'martyrs' to, using Celan's famous lines from 'The Meridian', a 'wholly other' poetry, an idea of poetry as prose. But, they only 'glimpse' this prose due to, from Badiou's perspective, the proximity they maintain between speaking and death – the supposed site of the infinite, and for Lacoue-Labarthe, the site of the phrase.

Badiou wants to claim that we already have 'the bridge to prose'; the infinite does not lie beyond the horizon but exists here, most obviously, perhaps, in love. Love is, by this account, the guarantee of the poem's 'becoming-prose'. The promise of love, from Badiou's perspective, was recognized by Lacoue-Labarthe in the second of the two meditations from *Poetry as Experience*, 'Blindness', in which he finds a 'definition of love' in the final strophe of Celan's poem 'Les Globes': 'All things, / even the heaviest, were / fledged, nothing / held back' (ISLP, 1254).[15] Badiou composes the following formulation of love and its fundamental role in securing poetry's route to prose on the back of Lacoue-Labarthe's readings of Celan:

> Love: a visionary blindness, a decoding of existence where everything is uprooted for the sake of the invisible, where restraint no longer exists.
>
> I would like to suggest that poetry and love are ultimately fused together under the name of 'prose'. And that 'prose' designates the inscription or emergence of the phrase, contra so-called 'poetry', which we can also call poetry without love.[16]

A full examination of these shifts in emphases between Badiou's elaboration of love and the latent poem, bound to his work in *Being and Event*, and these more recent pronouncements, indebted to the most recent elaboration of his philosophical project, *The Immanence of Truths*, point beyond the limits of this book, but in anticipation of further study I want to specify a few points of interest in this new work. It is only in 'prose', a poem's 'becoming-prose' perhaps (which in this piece at least stands for something like 'real poetry'), that the intervention of 'the phrase', 'which comes from elsewhere' (recalling perhaps Beckett's 'a voice comes to one in the dark'), may be heard, sustained and carried. But for Badiou, Lacoue-Labarthe's quest for a new 'prose' conjoining the poem and love is a melancholy one that seeks the emergence of the 'phrase' from beyond the world's bounds: 'Everything must be thought on the basis of death, where the phrase indeed originates', claims Badiou of Lacoue-Labarthe. Badiou has always claimed Lacoue-Labarthe's work to be too wrapped up in finitude, too concerned with philosophy's 'end', too willing to elevate proximity to death, from which 'the phrase' calls only as a promise without the capacity to be seized, as the site of potential meaning and perhaps reconciliation. 'Of the "phrase" [Lacoue-Labarthe] seeks in this book [*Phrase*]', Christopher Fynsk writes, 'he declares that it will have never been pronounced by him, that it will have remained haunting: "That aborted pronunciation, that haunting, I call, decidedly, literature"' (*P*, 12).[17] When Badiou writes of the 'inscription or emergence of the phrase', then, as that which binds the poem and love under the name of prose, he is testifying to the potential of the poem's secular transmission of the Two of love, an opening towards, recalling Badiou's reading of Beckett's '*Enough*' in Chapter 4, infinite multiplicity. But Badiou's new account of the transition from 'poetry' to 'prose', and the capture of the unutterable 'phrase', intriguingly elevates Badiou's conception of love as a truth procedure in a way that reflects Louise Burchill's recent commentary on the growing role of difference in Badiou's system. Love, as the fundamental experience of difference and as the most local, small example of a subject body unfolding the consequences of an event, is the privileged marker of the world's infinite possibilities. The promise of prose, then, for Badiou, is to 'separate' one's self from the finite world, and love offers the most familiar, local and intense experience of this separation. The poem, in the wake of God's death, becomes prose only if it makes itself compatible with the infinite possibilities prescribed by love as the emergence of difference in the world.

Notes

Introduction

1. Alain Badiou, *Five Lessons on Wagner*, trans. Susan Spitzer (London: Verso, 2010), ix. Hereafter cited parenthetically in the main body of the text using the abbreviation 'W'.
2. Annette Michelson describes Wieland Wagner's restaging of his grandfather's operas in the following terms, emphasizing his commitment to abstraction: 'Wieland Wagner, literally sweeping the stage of the debris of nineteenth-century scenography, shaped the Wagnerian performance as a deliberate, ritualized progress across the naked "disc of the world," enveloping the still, sparse, symbolic groupings of his design with perpetually shifting modulations of light. In so doing, he installed the spatiality of abstraction, its horizon of immensity, its infinite extension of optical depth, thereby confirming and intensifying Wagner's spectacle as apparitional in character.' Annette Michelson, 'Bayreuth: The Centennial "Ring"', *October* 14 (Autumn 1980), 65–70, 66–67.
3. It is interesting in this regard that Michelson claims Wieland Wagner's 'abstractive techniques' to result in 'the de-temporalization of the spectacle, or rather the reenforcement of the apparitional as atemporal'. Michelson, 'Bayreuth', 67.
4. Two such figures, Philippe Lacoue-Labarthe and Theodor W. Adorno, are explored at length in Chapters 2 and 4 of this book, respectively.
5. Alain Badiou, *Theory of the Subject*, trans. Bruno Bosteels (London: Continuum, 2009), xl.
6. Badiou draws his understanding of thought's 'diagonality' from Cantor's diagonal theory, which, in Christopher Norris's words, 'enables thought to conceive and then work with multiple orders or "sizes" of infinity'. Norris explains further that, with Cantor, the paradoxes of the infinite in play throughout the history of mathematics find their conceptual articulation in a way that alters the field of their concern: 'What Cantor's discovery made it possible to think was the concept (not merely the idea) that there existed multiple orders of the infinite … that these could be reckoned with or subject to calculation in rigorous and perfectly intelligible ways.' Christopher Norris, 'Diagonals: Truth-Procedures in Derrida and Badiou', in *Speculations, A Journal of Speculative Realism, Speculations III* (New York: Punctum Books, 2012), 150–188, 155–164.

7. See Oliver Feltham's translator's preface in *Being and Event*: 'Badiou champions ... the orientation which states that there is no unique response but a plurality of responses to the gap between representation and presentation, and the only place they are to be found is in practice.' Oliver Feltham, 'Translator's Preface', in Alain Badiou, *Being and Event*, trans. Oliver Feltham (London: Continuum, 2005), xvii–xxxiii, xxii.

8. Again, see Oliver Feltham's translator's preface to *Being and Event*: 'In Lacanian terms, it subjects philosophy to the *real* of mathematics, and in two forms: first, in that of the impasses – such as Russell's paradox – which forced the axiomatization of set theory and determined its shape; and second, in the form of unpredictable future events in the field of mathematics that may have implications for the metaontological apparatus set out in *Being and Event*.' Ibid., xx.

9. Peter Hallward, *Badiou: A Subject to Truth* (London: University of Minnesota Press, 2003), xxx.

10. Badiou claims at the outset of *Being and Event* that his 'debate with Heidegger will ... bear simultaneously on ontology and on the essence of mathematics, then consequently on what is signified by the site of philosophy being "originally Greek"'. Concerning ontology specifically, Badiou writes that, against Heidegger, 'whatever the subjective price may be, philosophy must designate, insofar as it is a matter of being qua being, the genealogy of the discourse on being – and the reflection on its possible essence – in Cantor, Gödel, and Cohen rather than in Hölderlin, Trakl and Celan'. Badiou, *Being and Event*, 9–10.

11. Alain Badiou, *Handbook of Inaesthetics*, trans. Alberto Toscano (Stanford, CA: Stanford University Press, 2005), 1. Hereafter cited parenthetically in the body of the text using the abbreviation 'HI'.

12. Alain Badiou, *The Adventure of French Philosophy*, ed. and trans. Bruno Bosteels (London: Verso, 2012), li–lxiii. Hereafter cited parenthetically in the body of the text using the abbreviation 'FP'.

13. Badiou would claim Plato, Descartes and Hegel among the philosophers who have most influenced his own work, though he also claims three French 'masters' belonging to 'the French moment': in 'Tireless Desire', he writes that in the mid-fifties he was 'a complete and total Sartrean', in Alain Badiou, *On Beckett*, ed. and trans. Alberto Toscano and Nina Power (Manchester: Clinamen, 2003), 38; in 'Philosophy as Creative Repetition', he refers to Louis Althusser as 'one of my masters', see Alain Badiou, 'Philosophy as Creative Repetition', *Symptom* 8 (Winter 2007); and in *Conditions*, he writes of Jacques Lacan, 'A contemporary philosopher, for me, is indeed someone who has the unfaltering courage to work through Lacan's anti-philosophy', in Alain Badiou, *Conditions*, trans. Steven Corcoran (London: Continuum, 2008), 129.

14. For a helpful account of this rivalry, see Bruno Bosteels's introduction in Badiou, *The Adventure of French Philosophy*, xii–xvi. Cf. Alain Badiou, *Deleuze: The Clamor of Being*, trans. Louise Burchill (Minneapolis: University of Minnesota Press, 2000).

15 Badiou has written two novels, *Almagestes* (Paris: Seuil, 1964) and *Portulans* (Paris: Seuil, 1967), as well as several plays including recent English translations, *The Incident at Antioch/L'Incident d'Antioche: A Tragedy in Three Acts/Tragédie en trois actes*, trans. Susan Spitzer (New York: Columbia University Press, 2013) and *Ahmed the Philosopher: Thirty-Four Short Plays for Children and Everyone Else*, trans. Joseph Litvack (New York: Columbia University Press, 2014). For a full list of Badiou's novels and plays prior to *The Incident at Antioch*, see Hallward, *Badiou*, 428–429.
16 Ibid., xvii.
17 Alain Badiou *Vocabulaire européen des philosophies: Dictionnaire des intraduisibles*, ed. Barbara Cassin (Paris: Le Robert/Seuil, 2004), 465, cited in Bosteels's introduction to *The Adventure of French Philosophy*, xlviii; my emphasis.
18 Alain Badiou, *Metapolitics*, trans. Jason Barker (London: Verso, 2005), 2–5. Hereafter cited parenthetically in the body of the text using the abbreviation 'M'.
19 Hallward, *Badiou*, xxvi.
20 Jean-Jacques Lecercle insists on Badiou's philosophy being 'read back' by the artworks it encounters in order to produce the 'intraphilosophical effects' Badiou mentions in his epigraph to *Handbook of Inaesthetics*. This is intended in part to dispel potentially reductive critiques of Badiou's inaesthetics that would claim philosophy therein to remain an appropriative force. See Jean-Jacques Lecercle, *Badiou & Deleuze Read Literature* (Edinburgh: Edinburgh University Press, 2010), 139–142.
21 That thought 'punches holes' in knowledge is a Lacanian dictum Badiou consistently references. In *Ethics: An Essay on the Understanding of Evil*, Badiou writes: 'A truth punches a "hole" in knowledges, it is heterogeneous to them, but it is also the source of new knowledges.' See Alain Badiou, *Ethics: An Essay on the Understanding of Evil*, trans. Peter Hallward (London: Verso, 2002), 43.

Chapter 1

1 Alain Badiou, *Logics of Worlds: Being and Event, 2*, trans. Alberto Toscano (London: Continuum, 2009), 548. Hereafter cited parenthetically in the body of the text using the abbreviation 'LW'.
2 See Peter Szondi, *Celan Studies*, trans. Susan Bernofsky and Harvey Mendelsohn (Stanford: Stanford University Press, 2003) and Jacques Derrida, *Sovereignties in Question: The Poetics of Paul Celan*, ed. Thomas Dutoit and Outi Pasanen (New York: Fordham University Press, 2005).
3 See also Hans-Georg Gadamer, *Gadamer on Celan: 'Who Am I and Who Are You?' and Other Essays*, eds and trans Richard Heinemann and Bruce Krajewski

(Albany: State University of New York Press, 1997); essays by Emmanuel Lévinas and Maurice Blanchot, 'Le dernier à parler' and 'De l'être à l'autre', in *Revue des belles lettres* (1972), invoked by Philippe Lacoue-Labarthe in *Poetry as Experience*, trans. Andrea Tarnowski (Stanford: Stanford University Press, 1999), 14.

4   Hallward, *Badiou*, 200.
5   Alain Badiou, 'Age of the Poets', in *The Age of the Poets: And Other Writings on Twentieth-Century Poetry and Prose*, ed. and trans. Bruno Bosteels (London: Verso, 2014), 3–22, 5. Hereafter cited parenthetically in the body of the text using the abbreviation 'AP'.
6   Alain Badiou, *Manifesto for Philosophy*, trans. Norman Madarasz (Albany: State University of New York Press, 1999), 70–71. Hereafter cited parenthetically in the body of the text using the abbreviation 'MP'.
7   Alain Badiou, *The Century*, trans. Alberto Toscano (Cambridge: Polity Press, 2007), 87–88. Hereafter cited parenthetically in the main body of the text using the abbreviation 'TC'.
8   Though, of course, Badiou's 'inaesthetics' seeks to avoid the appropriation of poetry by philosophy, stressing instead local encounters between the two, in which each side retains its autonomy. See Badiou, *Handbook of Inaesthetics*.
9   John Felstiner, *Poet, Survivor, Jew* (London: Yale University Press, 1995), 71.
10 My understanding of Perse's poem is indebted to Bernard Weinberg's helpful fifty-page close-reading from 1962. See Bernard Weinberg, 'Saint-John Perse's "Anabase"', *Chicago Review* 15, no. 3 (Winter–Spring, 1962), 75–124.
11 Alain Badiou, 'Third Sketch of a Manifesto of Affirmationist Art' in *Polemics*, trans. Steven Corcoran (London: Verso, 2006), 133–148, 148.
12 In set-theory there can be no set of all sets so 'the whole', for Badiou, is banned in advance. See John Cleary, 'Subjected to Formalization: Formalization and Method in the Philosophy of Alain Badiou', in *Badiou and His Interlocutors: Lectures, Interviews, Responses*, ed. A.J. Bartlett and Justin Clemens (London: Bloomsbury, 2018), 143–157, 149: 'There is the global real of set theory, namely, the inexistence of the whole.'
13 'Constructivist Thought' asserts the exclusive coextension of language and being, binding the question of being solely to knowledge. Such a schema is unable to tolerate any indeterminate presentation. See Meditation 29, 'Constructivist Thought and the Knowledge of Being', in Badiou, *Being and Event*, 286–294: 'What the constructivist vision of being and presentation hunts out is the "indeterminate", the unnameable part, the conceptless link' (288). More, for the 'constructivist', 'the indiscernible is not. This is the thesis with which nominalism constructs its fortification, and by means of which it can restrict, at its leisure, any pretension to unfold excess in a world of differences' (289). Finally, 'rather than being a distinct and aggressive agenda, constructivist thought is the latent philosophy of all human

sedimentation; the cumulative strata into which the forgetting of being is poured to the profit of language and the consensus of recognition it supports' (294).

14 'Anabasis', in Paul Celan, *Selected Poems*, trans. Michael Hamburger (London: Penguin, 1995), 203.

15 Alain Badiou, *Theoretical Writings*, ed. and trans. Ray Brassier and Alberto Toscano (London: Continuum, 2006), 239. Hereafter cited parenthetically in the main body of the text as 'TW'.

16 Badiou adopts the phrase 'universal reportage' from Stéphane Mallarmé's essay 'Crisis in Verse'. See Stéphane Mallarmé, 'Crisis in Verse', in *Divagations*, trans. Barbara Johnson (Cambridge, MA: The Belknap Press of Harvard University Press, 2007), 201–214, 210: 'To tell, to teach, and even to describe have their place, and suffice, perhaps, in order to exchange human thought, to take or to put into someone else's hand in silence a coin, this elementary use of discourse serving the universal *reporting* in which, except for literature, all genres of contemporary writing participate.'

17 See Michael Hamburger's introduction in Paul Celan, *Selected Poems*, 19–34.

18 J.K. Lyon, *Paul Celan and Martin Heidegger: An Unresolved Conversation (1951-1970)* (Baltimore: The Johns Hopkins University Press, 2006), 26.

19 See 'Death Fugue', in Celan, *Selected Poems*, 63.

20 Paul Celan, 'The Meridian', in *Collected Prose*, trans. Rosmarie Waldrop (Manchester: Carcanet, 2003), 37–55, 47.

21 Lacoue-Labarthe, *Poetry as Experience*, 8.

22 See Lyon, *Paul Celan and Martin Heidegger*, 32–34.

23 'With a Variable Key', in Celan, *Selected Poems*, 91.

24 Felstiner, *Poet, Survivor, Jew*, 73.

25 See Felstiner's examination of Celan's poem 'Homecoming', in Felstiner, *Poet, Survivor, Jew*, 97.

26 Celan, *Selected Poems*, 112–113.

27 Celan's use of the eye as an image follows, Lyon claims, the conflation of the optical, 'that which is seen through discourse', with speech, following Heidegger's *Being and Time*. According to Lyon, 'Celan took this notion a step farther in his poetry by relating human communication normally found in spoken language in the image of communicating through the eye.' Language operates as something which uncovers or makes apparent, presents things to be 'seen', and it is to this Heideggerian idea that the image of 'eyes' bears homage in Celan's poetry. Where 'eyes' are 'slow', there is an implied muffling of speech; 'our eyes' are slow to pick out 'that which is seen through discourse'. See Lyon, *Paul Celan and Martin Heidegger*, 16.

28 Martin Heidegger, 'What Is Metaphysics?' in *Basic Writings*, ed. and trans. David Farrell Krell (Abingdon: Routledge, 2008), 41–57, 51.

29 'The Meridian' in Paul Celan, *Collected Prose*, trans. Rosmarie Waldrop (Manchester: Carcanet, 2003), 37–55, 48.

30   Celan, *Collected Prose*, 48–49.
31   Anthony Mellors, *Late Modernist Poetics: From Pound to Prynne* (Manchester: Manchester University Press, 2005), 190. The Celan quotation is from 'The Meridian', see Celan, *Collected Prose*, 49.
32   Mellors, *Late Modernist Poetics*, 190.
33   Ibid.
34   Martin Heidegger, *Introduction to Metaphysics*, trans. Gregory Fried and Richard Polt (New Haven: Yale University Press, 2000), 23.
35   For an important discussion of Badiou's response to Heidegger's 'Open' in terms of finitude/infinity and 'the God of the Poets', see Christopher Watkin's *Difficult Atheism: Post-Theological Thinking in Alain Badiou, Jean-Luc Nancy and Quentin Meillassoux* (Edinburgh: Edinburgh University Press, 2011), 60–72.
36   This is a charge that, for Badiou, the early Wittgenstein escapes by retaining the importance of an 'act' by which the unspeakable may be 'shown'. The later Wittgenstein of the *Philosophical Investigations*, however, is rejected by Badiou, the emergence of 'language games' consigning Wittgenstein's later work to the realm of the 'sophist'. See Alain Badiou, *Wittgenstein's Antiphilosophy*, trans. Bruno Bosteels (London: Verso, 2011), 116–117. Hereafter cited parenthetically in the body of the text using the abbreviation 'WA'.
37   Ludwig Wittgenstein, *Tractatus Logico-Philosophicus*, trans. D.F. Pears and B.F. McGuinness (London: Routledge Classics, 2001), 89.
38   See Martin Heidegger, 'Metaphysics as History of Being', in *The End of Philosophy*, trans. Joan Stambaugh (London: Harper & Row, Inc., 1973), 1–54.
39   Georg Cantor (1845–1918), creator of transfinite set-theory. For a detailed exposition of his innovations and ideas, see Joseph Warren Dauben, *Georg Cantor: His Mathematics and Philosophy of the Infinite* (Princeton, New Jersey, 1979). Cantor is an absolutely central figure for Badiou; his work constitutes an 'event' for philosophy. See Badiou, *Being and Event*, 2: 'It will be held that the mathematico-logical revolution of Frege-Cantor sets new orientations for thought.' See, as well, Alain Badiou, *Number and Numbers*, trans. Robin Mackay (Cambridge: Polity Press, 2008). Paul Cohen (1934–2007), decisive contributor in the development of Zermelo-Fraenkel Set Theory, especially in his work on the 'axiom of choice' and 'the continuum hypothesis'. See Badiou, *Being and Event*, 355: 'Can ontology produce the concept of a generic multiple, which is to say an unnameable, un-constructible, indiscernible multiple? The revolution introduced by Cohen in 1963 responds in the affirmative: there exists an ontological concept of the indiscernible multiple. Consequently, ontology is compatible with the philosophy of truth.'
40   See Jacques Lacan, *Seminar XX: On Feminine Sexuality, The Limits of Love and Knowledge (1972–1973)*, ed. Jacques-Alain Miller, trans. Bruce Fink (London: W. W. Norton, 1999), 1–55.

41 Mark Hewson, 'Heidegger', in *Alain Badiou: Key Concepts*, ed. A.J. Bartlett and Justin Clemens (Durham: Acumen, 2010), 146–154, 151.
42 Ibid.
43 Martin Heidegger, *On the Way to Language*, trans. Peter. D. Hertz (New York: HarperCollins, 1982), 71.
44 See Martin Heidegger, *Introduction to Metaphysics*, trans. Gregory Fried and Richard Polt (New Haven and London: Yale University Press, 2000), 182.
45 Ibid., 14.
46 Ibid.
47 Ibid., 16.
48 Ibid., 15.
49 Ibid.
50 Gregory Fried and Richard Polt, 'Translators Introduction', in Martin Heidegger, *Introduction to Metaphysics*, trans. Gregory Fried and Richard Polt (New Haven and London: Yale University Press, 2000), vii–xix.
51 Ibid., xiii.
52 Heidegger, *Introduction to Metaphysics*, 15.
53 Martin Heidegger, *Being and Time*, trans. Joan Stambaugh (New York: State University of New York Press, 2010), 33.
54 Heidegger, *Being and Time*, 33.
55 In a discussion of Cartesian ontology in *Being and Time*, Heidegger claims the following, revealing the confusion that results when the traditional adoption of mathematics as relating to ontology is left unchallenged: 'Descartes does not allow the kind of being of innerworldy beings to present itself, but rather prescribes to the world ... its "true" being on the basis of an idea of being (being = constant presence) the source of which has not been revealed and the justification of which has not been demonstrated. [...] his ontology is determined by a basic ontological orientation toward being as constant objective presence, which mathematical knowledge is exceptionally well suited to grasp.' Ibid., 94.
56 Ibid., 93–94.
57 See Badiou, *Being and Event*, 124: 'The Platonic "turn" consisted, at the ambivalent frontiers of the Greek destiny of being, of proposing "an interpretation of φύσις [phusis] as ἰδέα [idea]."'
58 Heidegger, *Introduction to Metaphysics*, 111.
59 Martin Heidegger, *Pathmarks*, ed. William McNeill (Cambridge: Cambridge University Press, 1998), 164.
60 Heidegger, *Introduction to Metaphysics*, 195.
61 Ibid., 194.
62 Plato, *The Republic*, trans. Desmond Lee (London: Penguin Classics, 1987), 326–355.

63 Badiou, *Conditions*, 36. Cited in Hewson, 'Heidegger', 148.
64 Hewson, 'Heidegger', 151.
65 Badiou, *Conditions*, 36. Cited in Hewson, 'Heidegger', 148.
66 Quentin Meillassoux, *After Finitude: An Essay on the Necessity of Contingency*, trans. Ray Brassier (London: Continuum, 2008), 14.
67 For an in-depth account of this statement, see Martin Heidegger, *The End of Philosophy*, trans. Joan Stambaugh (London: Harper & Row, Inc., 1973).
68 Heidegger, *Introduction to Metaphysics*, 27.
69 Ibid., 53.
70 See Heidegger, *Being and Time*, 6, '… to work out the question of being means to make a being – one who questions – transparent in its being', as well as §5, '*The Ontological Analysis of Dasein as Exposing the Horizon for an Interpretation of the Meaning of Being in General*', ibid., 15–19.
71 Heidegger, *Basic Writings*, 47.
72 See Heidegger, *Being and Time*, §40, '*The Fundamental Attunement of Anxiety as an Eminent Disclosedness of Dasein*', 178–184.
73 See Heidegger, *Basic Writings*, 50.
74 Ibid., 52.
75 Heidegger, *Being and Time*, 181.
76 Heidegger, *Basic Writings*, 53.
77 Ibid., 56.
78 Heidegger, *Introduction to Metaphysics*, 89.
79 Heidegger, *Basic Writings*, 143.
80 Ibid., 180.
81 Ibid., 147.
82 Heidegger, *Introduction to Metaphysics*, 15.
83 Richard Polt, *Heidegger: An Introduction* (Abingdon: Routledge Ltd., 1999), 175–176.
84 Ibid.
85 Ibid., 177.
86 Martin Heidegger, 'Language', in *Poetry, Language, Thought*, trans. Albert Hofstadter (New York: Harper & Row, 1971), 187–210, 208.
87 Polt, *Heidegger: An Introduction*, 177.
88 Heidegger, *Being and Time*, 129.
89 Ibid., 161–162.
90 Ibid.
91 Ibid., 162.
92 Ibid., 163.
93 See Mallarmé, 'Crisis in Verse', in *Divagations*, 210.
94 Heidegger, *Introduction to Metaphysics*, 15.
95 Heidegger, *Basic Writings*, 150.

96 Ibid., 147.
97 Ibid., 178.
98 Celan, *Selected Poems*, 101.
99 Ibid.
100 Heidegger, *Basic Writings*, 49–50.
101 Ibid., 52.
102 Heidegger, *Introduction to Metaphysics*, 89.
103 Martin Heidegger, *Poetry, Language, Thought*, trans. Albert Hofstadter (New York: Harper & Row, 1975), 198.
104 Ibid., 196.
105 Ibid., 197.
106 Ibid., 199.
107 Ibid., 198.
108 Albert Hofstadter, introduction to Heidegger, *Poetry, Language, Thought*, ix–xxii, x.
109 See Plato, *Parmenides*, trans. Mary Louise Gill and Paul Ryan, in *Complete Works*, ed. John M. Cooper (Indianapolis: Hackett Publishing Company, 1997), 359–397.
110 Robin Waterfield (trans.), *The First Philosophers: The Presocratics and the Sophists* (Oxford: Oxford University Press, 2000), 60.
111 Alex Ling, 'Ontology', in *Alain Badiou: Key Concepts*, ed. A.J. Bartlett and Justin Clemens (Durham: Acumen, 2010), 48–58, 49.
112 Hallward, *Badiou*, 275.
113 Ibid., 407.
114 Alain Badiou, *Infinite Thought: Truth and the Return to Philosophy*, ed. and trans. Justin Clemens and Oliver Feltham (London: Continuum, 2005), 99. Hereafter cited in the body of the text as 'IT'.
115 See Paul Celan, 'Es Kommt', in *Gesammelte Werke, im fümf Bänden: Dritter Band: Gedichte III, Prosa, Reden* Beda Allemann, Rolf Bücher, Stefan Reichert (Frankfurt: Suhrkamp, 1986), 107. Cf. Pierre Joris's translation in Paul Celan, *Breathturn into Timestead: The Collected Later Poems of Paul Celan*, trans. Pierre Joris (New York: Farrar Straus Giroux, 2014), 442–443: 'There also comes a meaning / down the narrower cut, // it is breached / by the deadliest of our standing marks.' Joris is attentive to the occluded 'I' in the repetition of 'ich' across '*erbricht*' and '*todlichste*', rendering the 'ich' repetition in the 'ea' of 'breached' and 'deadliest'.
116 See Felstiner, *Poet, Survivor, Jew*, 97.
117 Celan, *Selected Poems*, 109–110.
118 See Felstiner, *Poet, Survivor, Jew*, 97. See also Hans-Georg Gadamer, 'Who Am I and Who Are You?' in *Gadamer on Celan: 'Who Am I and Who Are You?' and Other Essays*, eds. and trans. Richard Heinemann and Bruce Krajewski (New York: State University of New York Press, 1997), 67–126, 73: 'So we ask again: what does snow mean here? Is it the experience of writing poetry which is alluded to here?'

119 See also Pierre Joris's gloss on 'erbricht' in *Breathturn into Timestead*, 623: 'The German verb has two meanings, one describing an infraction, a breach, the other referring to the act of vomiting, of expelling like vomit, the word thus subsuming in a very Celanian manner two simultaneous movements in opposite directions.'

120 'Male', in J.B. Sykes, W. Scholze-Stubenrecht, Michael Clark et al. (eds.), *The Oxford-Duden German Dictionary* (Oxford: Oxford University Press, 2001).

121 See Badiou, *Manifesto for Philosophy*, 86: 'Lacoue-Labarthe had the diverted intuition of this request when he deciphered with Celan an "interruption of art". The interruption in my view is not of poetry, but of the poetry *philosophy has handed itself over to*.'

122 See Pierre Joris, 'Celan/Heidegger: Translation at the Mountain of Death', 1988.

123 Celan, *Selected Poems*, 301.

124 See 'Meditation 19: Mallarmé', in Badiou, *Being and Event*, 191–198.

125 Plato, *The Republic*, 429.

126 Ibid., 435.

127 Never mind, of course, the inauguration of structuralist linguistics in Ferdinand de Saussure's work and its radical disavowal of language's direct reference to the world of objects. See Ferdinand de Saussure, *Course in General Linguistics*, trans. Roy Harris (London: Bloomsbury Revelations, 2013).

128 Mallarmé, 'Crisis in Verse', *Divagations*, 210.

Chapter 2

1 See Alain Badiou, *Briefings on Existence: A Short Treatise on Transitory Ontology*, trans. Norman Madarasz (New York: State University of New York Press, 2006). Hereafter cited parenthetically in the main body of the text using the abbreviation 'BOE'.

2 Martin Heidegger, *Hölderlin's Hymns 'Germania' and 'The Rhine'*, trans. William McNeill and Julia Ireland (Bloomington and Indianapolis: Indiana University Press, 2014), xix.

3 Jennifer Gosetti-Ferencei, *Heidegger, Hölderlin and the Subject of Poetic Language: Towards a New Poetics of Dasein* (New York: Fordham University Press, 2004), 71.

4 Heidegger, *Hölderlin's Hymns*, 264–265.

5 Friedrich Hölderlin, *Hölderlin, Friedrich, Hymns and Fragments*, trans. Richard Sieburth (Princeton, NJ: Princeton University Press, 1984), 12. Cf. Friedrich Hölderlin, 'No. 236 to Casimir Ulrich Böhlendorff', in *Friedrich Hölderlin: Essays and Letters on Theory*, trans. Thomas Pfau (Albany, NY: SUNY, 1988), 149–151.

6 Beatrice Hanssen, '"Dichtermut" and "Blödigkeit": Two Poems by Hölderlin Interpreted by Walter Benjamin', *MLN* 112, no. 5 (December 1997), 786–816, 795.

7   Heidegger, *Hölderlin's Hymns*, 264–265.
8   Ibid., 266.
9   See especially Martin Heidegger, 'The Question Concerning Technology', in *Basic Writings*, ed. and trans. David Farrell Krell (Abingdon: Routledge, 2008), 217–238.
10 Heidegger's participation in thinking a new beginning for man is rendered explicitly in Martin Heidegger, *Introduction to Metaphysics*, trans. Gregory Fried and Richard Polt (New Haven: Yale University Press, 2000), and discussed at length by Philippe Lacoue-Labarthe in the prologue to his *Heidegger and the Politics of Poetry*, trans. Jeff Fort (Chicago: University of Illinois Press, 2007), 3–16.
11 Watkin, *Difficult Atheism*, 59.
12 Robert Savage, *Hölderlin after the Catastrophe: Heidegger – Adorno – Brecht* (London: Camden House, 2008), 9.
13 Ibid., 6.
14 For Hölderlin's own interest in the cultural exchange between a new Germany and Ancient Greece, see Hölderlin, 'No. 236 to Casimir Ulrich Böhlendorff', 149–151, and Cyrus Hamlin, 'Hölderlin's Hellenism: Tyranny or Transformation', *Hölderlin-Jahrbuch* 35 (2006–2007), 252–311.
15 '*Die Wanderung*'/'The Journey', in Friedrich Hölderlin, *Selected Poems and Fragments*, trans. Michael Hamburger (London: Penguin Classics, 1998), 182–189, 183–185. Intriguingly, the poem is translated as 'The Migration' in Richard Sieburth's version. See Hölderlin, '*Die Wanderung*'/'The Migration', in *Hymns and Fragments*, 60–67.
16 See Badiou, *Being and Event*, 255: 'There is a paradox of the homeland, in Hölderlin's sense, a paradox which makes an eventual-site out of it.' Hereafter cited parenthetically in the main body of the text using the abbreviation 'BE'.
17 Hölderlin, 'The Journey', 183.
18 Martin Heidegger, *Hölderlin's Hymn 'The Ister'*, trans. William McNeill and Julia Davis (Bloomington and Indianapolis: Indiana University Press, 1996), 7.
19 Ibid., 8.
20 Ibid.
21 See Richard Sieburth's notes in *Hymns and Fragments*, 258: 'Beissner suggests that the journey of the "German tribe" down the Danube and their meeting with the "children of the sun" at the Black Sea may allude to the Swabian settlers who emigrated toward the lower basing of the Danube in 1770; on the other hand, Hölderlin may simply be constructing a genealogical myth in the manner of Hesiod or Pindar.'
22 Hölderlin, *Selected Poems and Fragments*, 185.
23 Ibid.
24 Ibid., 187.
25 Savage, *Hölderlin after the Catastrophe*, 32.

26 Ibid., 9.
27 See Hölderlin, *Hymns and Fragments*, 258.
28 Hölderlin, *Selected Poems and Fragments*, 185–187.
29 Hölderlin, *Hymns and Fragments*, 258.
30 Philippe Lacoue-Labarthe, *Heidegger and the Politics of Poetry*, trans. Jeff Fort (Chicago: University of Illinois Press, 2007), 9.
31 Hölderlin, *Selected Poems and Fragments*, 187.
32 Savage, *Hölderlin after the Catastrophe*, 32.
33 See Gosetti-Ferencei, *Heidegger, Hölderlin …*, 71.
34 Hölderlin, *Selected Poems and Fragments*, 187.
35 See again, Hölderlin, 'No. 236 to Casimir Ulrich Böhlendorff', 149–151.
36 Hölderlin, *Selected Poems and Fragments*, 189.
37 Savage, *Hölderlin after the Catastrophe*, 32.
38 Heidegger, *Being and Time*, 311.
39 Lacoue-Labarthe, *Heidegger and the Politics of Poetry*, 7.
40 The first of these is in Alain Badiou, *Pocket Pantheon: Figures of Postwar Philosophy*, trans. David Macey (London: Verso, 2009). Hereafter cited parenthetically in the main body of the text using the abbreviation 'PP'. The second is included in the recent special issue of *Modern Language Notes* dedicated to Lacoue-Labarthe's thought: see Alain Badiou, 'In Search of Lost Prose', *Modern Language Notes* 132, no. 5 (December 2017): 1254–1266.
41 See Lacoue-Labarthe's various writings on mimesis, especially *Typography: Mimesis, Philosophy, Politics*, trans. Christopher Fynk (Stanford: Stanford University Press, 1998), and especially his essay co-authored with Jean-Luc Nancy, 'The Nazi Myth', trans. Brian Holmes, in *Critical Inquiry* 16, no. 2 (Winter 1990), 291–312. The best account, to my knowledge, of Lacoue-Labarthe's protracted engagement with the question of mimesis is to be found in Alison Ross, *The Aesthetic Paths of Philosophy: Presentation in Kant, Heidegger, Lacoue-Labarthe, and Nancy* (Stanford, California: Stanford University Press, 2007).
42 See Rochelle Tobias, 'From Mythology to Myth: The Courage of Poetry', *Modern Language Notes* 132, no. 5 (December 2017): 1170–1185.
43 Ibid., 1170.
44 See Badiou, 'In Search of Lost Prose', 1254–1266.
45 Lacoue-Labarthe, *Poetry as Experience*, 33.
46 Ibid., 35.
47 See David Macey's translator's note on 'enframing' in the English translation of *Pocket Pantheon*: 'The French term used is *arraisonner* which refers to the boarding of a ship to inspect its cargo for customs purposes. It is used to translate Heidegger's *das Gestell*, normally translated into English as "enframing"', in Badiou, *Pocket Pantheon*, 160.

48 Jeff Fort, 'The Courage of Thought', in Philippe Lacoue-Labarthe, *Heidegger and the Politics of Poetry*, trans. Jeff Fort (Urbana and Chicago: Illinois University Press, 2007), ix–xviii, xiv.
49 Walter Benjamin, 'Two Poems by Friedrich Hölderlin', in *Selected Writings: Vol. 1, 1913–1926*, ed. Marcus Bullock and Michael W. Jennings (Cambridge, Massachusetts: The Belknap Press of Harvard University Press, 1996), 18–36.
50 Élisabeth Décultot, 'Romantic' in *Dictionary of Untranslatables: A Philosophical Lexicon*, ed. Barbara Cassin, translation edited by Emily Apter, Jacques Lezra and Michael Wood (Princeton, New Jersey: Princeton University Press, 2014), 'Romantic', 907–911, 909.
51 I am grateful to David Cunningham for helping me to come to terms with some of these difficulties through his extraordinarily detailed exegesis of the relations between Jena Romanticism, Hegel and the idea of 'genre': see David Cunningham, 'Genre without Genre: Romanticism, the Novel and the New', *Radical Philosophy* 196 (April/May 2016).
52 Walter Benjamin, 'The Concept of Criticism', in *Selected Writings: Vol. 1, 1913–1926*, eds. Marchus Bullock and Michael W. Jennings (Cambridge, Massachusetts: The Belknap Press of Harvard University Press, 2004), 116–200, 173. See also Nicholas Heron, 'Idea of Poetry, Idea of Prose', in *The Work of Giorgio Agamben: Law, Literature, Life*, eds. Justin Clemens, Nicholas Heron and Alex Murray (Edinburgh: Edinburgh University Press, 2008), 97–113, 98.
53 From Novalis's *Briefwechsel*, quoted in Benjamin, 'The Concept of Criticism', 174.
54 G.W.F. Hegel, *Aesthetics: Lectures on Fine Art, volume 1*, trans. T.M. Knox (Oxford: Clarendon Press, 1988), 89.
55 See Justin Clemens, *The Romanticism of Contemporary Theory: Institution, Aesthetics, Nihilism* (Aldershot: Ashgate, 2003), 195: '"Heidegger", for Badiou, serves as a synecdoche for late Romantic theory in general.'
56 Lacoue-Labarthe points to a discussion with Badiou in 1993 after Conférences du Perroquet in the postscript to *Heidegger and the Politics of Poetry*, see Lacoue-Labarthe, *Heidegger and the Politics of Poetry*, 81.
57 Alain Badiou, 'Philosophy and Politics', in *Conditions*, trans. Steven Corcoran (London: Continuum, 2008), 147–176, 147–148.
58 Lacoue-Labarthe, *Heidegger and the Politics of Poetry*, 19.
59 See David Cunningham, 'Genre without Genre', for in-depth accounts of Hegel's 'prose of thought' and 'prose of the world'.
60 Indeed, Lacoue-Labarthe is perennially interested in the proximity between literature and philosophy. See Philippe Lacoue-Labarthe, *The Subject of Philosophy*, ed. Thomas Trezise (Minneapolis, Minnesota: Minnesota University Press, 1993), xvii: Lacoue-Labarthe consistently, in Thomas Trezise's words, 'displac[es] the bar that symbolically separates literature and philosophy (literature/philosophy) in

such a way that on each side literature and philosophy are both crossed out and cancel each other in communicating'.
61 Lacoue-Labarthe, *Heidegger and the Politics of Poetry*, 21.
62 Ibid., 33.
63 Pascal David, 'Heidegger's *Dichtung*: Poetry and Thought', in *Dictionary of Untranslatables: A Philosophical Lexicon*, ed. Barbara Cassin, translation edited by Emily Apter, Jacques Lezra and Michael Wood (Princeton, New Jersey: Princeton University Press, 2014), 219.
64 Lacoue-Labarthe, *Heidegger and the Politics of Poetry*, 10.
65 Cf. Philippe Lacoue-Labarthe, *Musica Ficta (Figures of Wagner)*, trans. Felicia McCarren (Stanford: Stanford University Press, 1994), 93. Lacoue-Labarthe cites Heidegger's claim from *Nietzsche vol. 1*: 'It was their good fortune that the Greeks had no "lived experiences." On the contrary, they had such an original nature and luminous knowledge, such a passion for knowledge, that in their luminous state of knowing they had no need of "aesthetics". He reads Heidegger's claim as follows, emphasizing the contingency of the aesthetic and its imbrication with the originary forgetting enacted in the emergence of metaphysics: 'This *knowledge*, which renders any aesthetic useless and does not find in it anything like philosophy, is nothing else – Heidegger insists on it heavily at this time – than *tekhnè* in its original meaning, this meaning that tragic thinking, in particular Sophocles, still keeps and that philosophy, precisely, begins by forgetting, as if ultimately, somehow, it were born of this very forgetting. The aesthetic, then, only appears with philosophy in the strict sense (metaphysics), that is, "at the moment where the great art, but also the great philosophy that follows the same course, reaches its end."'
66 Cf. Martin Heidegger, 'The Origin of the Work of Art', in *Poetry, Language, Thought*, trans. Albert Hofstadter (New York: Harper & Row, 1971), 15–88.
67 Heidegger, 'The Origin of the Work of Art'. Cited in Lacoue-Labarthe, *Heidegger and the Politics of Poetry*, 10.
68 Ibid., 10.
69 Ibid., 14.
70 From Lacoue-Labarthe and Nancy, 'The Nazi Myth', 291–312. Cited in Mellors, *Late Modernist Poetics*, 94.
71 Cited in Tobias, 'From Mythology to Myth', 1171.
72 Jeff Fort, introduction to *Heidegger and the Politics of Poetry*, ix.
73 Lacoue-Labarthe, *Heidegger and the Politics of Poetry*, 68.
74 Ibid., xiv–xv.
75 Fort, introduction to *Heidegger and the Politics of Poetry*, xv.
76 Lacoue-Labarthe, *Heidegger and the Politics of Poetry*, 69.
77 See Tobias, 'From Mythology to Myth', 1171.
78 Benjamin, 'Two Poems by Friedrich Hölderlin', 20.
79 Lacoue-Labarthe, *Heidegger and the Politics of Poetry*, 70.

80 Ibid., 70.
81 See Benjamin, 'Two Poems by Friedrich Hölderlin', 18: 'Nothing will be said here about the process of lyrical composition, nothing about the person or world view of the creator; rather, the particular and unique sphere in which the task and precondition of the poem lie will be addressed.'
82 Tobias, 'From Mythology to Myth', 1173.
83 Hanssen, '"Dichtermut" and "Blödigkeit"', 789
84 Lacoue-Labarthe, *Heidegger and the Politics of Poetry*, 73.
85 Ibid., 74.
86 Tobias, 'From Mythology to Myth', 1177
87 See Philippe Lacoue-Labarthe, *Heidegger, Art and Politics: The Fiction of the Political*, trans. Chris Turner (Oxford: Basil Blackwell Ltd, 1990), especially chapter 7, 'The Aestheticization of Politics', 61–76.
88 Benjamin, 'Two Poems by Friedrich Hölderlin', 20.
89 Lacoue-Labarthe, *Heidegger and the Politics of Poetry*, 75.
90 Ibid., 104.
91 Alain Badiou, *Conditions* (Paris: Éditions du Seuil, 1992), 216. Badiou of course would claim to have found this 'prose of thought' in the deductions of formal mathematics, see section 1.4, 'The Void and Poetry's Idea'.
92 Cf. Alain Badiou, 'Definition of Philosophy', in *Conditions*, trans. Steven Corcoran (London: Continuum, 2008), 23–25, 25: 'Philosophy is always the breaking of a mirror. This mirror is the surface of language, onto which the sophist reduces all the things that philosophy treats in its act. If the philosopher sets his gaze solely on this surface, his double, the sophist, will emerge, and he may take himself to be one.'
93 Lacoue-Labarthe, *Heidegger and the Politics of Poetry*, 17.
94 Philippe Lacoue-Labarthe, 'Mallarmé', in *Musica Ficta (Figures of Wagner)*, trans. Felicia McCarren (Stanford, California: Stanford University Press, 1994), 41–84.
95 Lacoue-Labarthe, *Figures of Wagner*, 82.
96 Recall in 1.4, the discussion of Mallarmé's claim for verse, 'I say: a flower! And, beyond the oblivion where my voice designs no shape, inasmuch as anything other than the calyxes we know, musically arises, the idea itself, suave, absent from all bouquets.' See also Lacoue-Labarthe, *Figures of Wagner*, 82.
97 Ibid., 83.
98 See 'The Passion for the Real and the Montage of Semblance', in Badiou, *The Century*, 48–57.
99 Lacoue-Labarthe, *Heidegger, Art and Politics*, 5.
100 Lacoue-Labarthe, *Poetry as Experience*, 7.
101 Lacoue-Labarthe, *Heidegger and the Politics of Poetry*, 77.
102 'The Age of the Poets', Badiou's contribution to the 1992 seminar, *La politique des poètes: Pourquoi des poètes en temps de détresse?* organized by Jacques Rancière and

held at the Collège International de Philosophie, collected in English in Badiou, *The Age of the Poets*, 3–22.
103. See Badiou, *Handbook of Inaesthetics*, 23: 'That truth and totality are incompatible is without doubt the decisive – or post-Hegelian – teaching of modernity.'
104. Benjamin, *The Concept of Criticism*, 176.
105. Simon Critchley, 'Re-Tracing the Political: Politics and Community in the Work of Philippe Lacoue-Labarthe and Jean-Luc Nancy', in *The Political Subject of Violence*, ed. David Campbell and Michael Dallas (Manchester University Press, 1993), 73–93, 75.
106. Ibid., 74–77.
107. Ibid., 75.
108. Ibid.
109. See Badiou, *Ethics* and *Metapolitics*.
110. Claude Lefort (1924–2010), a pupil of Maurice Merleau-Ponty, founding member of *Socialisme ou Barbarie* and an early participator in *Les Temps Modernes*. Much of his most important writing, including his essay on totalitarianism, is collected in English translation in Claude Lefort, *The Political Forms of Modern Society*, trans. John B. Thompson (Cambridge, Massachusetts: MIT Press, 1986).
111. Critchley, 'Politics and Community ...', 77.
112. Ibid.
113. For apposite commentary on how Badiou conceives the relation between philosophy and politics, see Bruno Bosteels, *Badiou and Politics*. Discussing Badiou's 'metapolitical' demands for philosophy, Bosteels writes: 'Philosophy must cease to evaluate, in the way of an onlooker at a public spectacle or a judge in the tribunal of historical reason, the essence of the political (*le politique*) and instead ought to put itself under the condition of politics (*la politique*) or rather of *a* politics (*une politique*) so as to investigate which conceptual tools it should develop in order to be able to register in its midst the consequences of a political event.' Bruno Bosteels, *Badiou and Politics* (Durham and London: Duke University Press, 2011), 20.
114. Lacoue-Labarthe, *Typography*, 141–142.
115. Ibid., 175.

Chapter 3

1. Justin Clemens, 'Had we but worlds enough, and time, this absolute, philosopher ...', *The Praxis of Alain Badiou*, ed. Paul Ashton, A.J. Bartlett and Justin Clemens (Melbourne: re.press, 2006), 102–143, 109.
2. Marios Constantinou, 'Forcing Politics: Badiou's Anabasis in the Age of Empire', in *Badiou and the Political Condition*, ed. Marios Consantinou (Edinburgh: Edinburgh University Press, 2014), 1–44, 17.

3   See Xenophon, *The Persian Expedition*, trans. R. Warner (London: Penguin Classics, 1972)
4   See Charles Bambach, *Thinking the Poetic Measure of Justice: Hölderlin-Heidegger-Celan* (New York: State University of New York Press, 2013), 69. See also Heidegger, *Introduction to Metaphysics*.
5   See Heidegger, *Elucidations of Hölderlin's Poetry* and *Hölderlin's Hymn 'The Ister'*.
6   Heidegger, *Hölderlin's Hymn 'The Ister'*, xi.
7   Heidegger, *Elucidations of Hölderlin's Poetry*, 231.
8   Ibid., 48.
9   Bambach, *Poetic Measure*, 67.
10 Ibid., 67-69.
11 See Bambach, *Poetic Measure*, 21. As well, despite his critique of metaphysics, Heidegger remains entrenched, for Badiou at least, within the tradition of metaphysics inaugurated by Plato: 'Heidegger still remains enslaved, even in the doctrine of the withdrawal and the un-veiling, to what I consider, for my part, to be the essence of metaphysics; that is, the figure of being as endowment and gift, as presence and opening, and that the figure of ontology as the offering of a trajectory of proximity.' See *Being and Event*, trans. Oliver Feltham (London: Continuum, 2005), 9.
12 Heidegger, *Elucidations*, 168.
13 Ibid., 161.
14 Bambach, *Poetic Measure*, 71.
15 Ibid., 20.
16 Ibid., 20-21.
17 See Badiou, *Being and Event*, 2: 'Along with Heidegger, it will be maintained that philosophy as such can only be re-assigned on the basis of the ontological question.'
18 For a concise account of Badiou's understanding and mobilization of 'metaphysics', see especially Alain Badiou, 'Metaphysics and the Critique of Metaphysics', *Pli*, 10 (2000), 174-190.
19 Hegel, prefiguring Heidegger, is perhaps the original thinker of homecoming, for his philosophy depends on a reconciliatory return of the spirit to itself, following the integration of what is non-identical to it. See G.W.F. Hegel, *Hegel's Phenomenology of Spirit*, trans. A.V. Miller (Oxford: Oxford University Press, 1977) and Bruno Baugh, *French Hegel: From Surrealism to Postmodernism* (London: Routledge, 2003), 2: 'Spirit's odyssey towards truth is in truth a homecoming, a reconciliation with itself.'
20 See also Emmanuel Lévinas's *Totality and Infinity*, trans Alphonso Lingis (Boston & London: Martinus Nijhoff Publishers, 1979), 82-101.
21 See Badiou's *Ethics*, and 'What Is It to Live?' in Alain Badiou, *Logics of Worlds*, trans. Alberto Toscano (London and New York: Continuum, 2009), 507-514.
22 This is because identity, for Badiou, is never originary but rather prescribed by how a situation structures its elements. The 'one' is only ever the result of this

structuring, the 'count as one' of presentation. See Badiou, *Being and Event*, 81–89.

23 Again, see Badiou, *Being and Event*, 525: 'Undecidability is a fundamental attribute of the event: its belonging to the situation in which its eventual site is found is undecidable. The intervention consists in deciding at and from the standpoint of this undecidability.'

24 'Thought', for Badiou, designates the process via which truth is unfolded by a subject. It opposes both knowledge and opinion, refusing verification by either. As such, it must generate its own momentum. See Badiou, *Being and Event*, and Hallward, *A Subject to Truth*.

25 Pierre Joris highlights a similar negation of Hölderlin in Celan's poem 'Tenebrae' in the introduction to his English translation of Celan's late works. See Joris, introduction to *Breathturn into Timestead*, xxix–lxxix, xlv: 'Most important, some of the poems are clearly what has been called *Widerrufe*: attempts at retracting, countermanding, disavowing previous poetics – those of other poets, but also his own earlier stance. The poem "Tenebrae," for example, is a carefully constructed refutation of Hölderlin's "Patmos" hymn, which, as Götz Wienold has shown, negates the (Christian/pagan) hope for salvation expressed in Hölderlin's lines […] (Close/and difficult to grasp is God./But where danger lurks, that which saves/also grows)'.

26 See Hölderlin, *Selected Poems and Writings*, 159–167 and Celan, *Selected Poems*, 111.

27 Both verbs are commonly used as suffixes to *zurück* (*zurückkommen, zurückkehren*) in order to denote returning, coming back, etc. See Sykes et al. (eds.), *The Oxford-Duden German Dictionary*.

28 'kehren', in Sykes et al., *The Oxford-Duden German Dictionary*, 446.

29 For this formulation, see Theodor W. Adorno, *Negative Dialectics*, trans. E.B. Ashton (London: Routledge, 1996) and Lacoue-Labarthe, *Poetry as Experience*, among many others.

30 'Ankunft', in Sykes et al., *The Oxford-Duden German Dictionary*, 87.

31 Felstiner, *Poet, Survivor, Jew*.

32 Celan, *Collected Prose*, 53.

33 Paul Celan, '[Reply to a Questionnaire from the Flinker Bookstore, Paris, 1958]', in *Collected Prose*, trans. Rosmarie Waldrop (Manchester: Carcanet, 2003), 15–16, 16.

34 This is an explicit rejection of the role of poetry as founding word found in Heidegger. See Martin Heidegger, 'Hölderlin and the Essence of Poetry', in *Elucidations …*, 51–65. See also the 'broadly political' consequences of poetry qua *muthos* in Lacoue-Labarthe, *Heidegger and the Politics of Poetry*, 21.

35 Celan, *Selected Poems*, 111.

36 For evidence of Celan's engagement with Hölderlin, see Bambach, *Poetic Measure*, 204–213.

37 Felstiner, *Poet, Survivor, Jew*, 97.
38 Celan, *Collected Prose*, 53.
39 Hölderlin, *Selected Poems and Fragments*, 161.
40 Ibid.
41 Besides the second strophe mentioned above.
42 Hölderlin, *Selected Poems and Fragments*, 163.
43 Hamburger translates the German word 'Pflock' as 'post', instead of 'stake', which would have been an interesting alternative, for it elects an agent capable of hammering it into the ground, as well as inviting consonance with poetic measuring, waiting, as in 'to stake out', but also risk-taking, as in 'high stakes'.
44 Hölderlin, *Selected Poems and Writings*, 167.
45 See Plato, *The Republic*, 159.
46 Celan, *Collected Prose*, 35.
47 Celan, *Selected Poems*, 202–203.
48 Ibid.
49 See especially Badiou, *Logics of Worlds*, 101: 'Ever since Descartes, this is the essential trait of an *idealist* philosophy: that it calls upon the subject not as a problem but as the solution to the aporias of the One (the world is nothing but formless multiplicity, but there exists a unified *Dasein* of this world). The materialist thrust of my own thought (but also paradoxically of Hegel's, as Lenin remarked in his *Notebooks*) derives from the fact that within it the subject is a late and problematic construction, and in no way the place of the solution to a problem of possibility or unity (possibility of intuitive certainty for Descartes, of synthetic judgements *a priori* for Kant).'

Chapter 4

1 Bruno Bosteels, *Badiou and Politics* (Durham: Duke University Press, 2011), 14.
2 Ibid.
3 See Georg Lukács, *History and Class Consciousness*, trans. Rodney Livingstone (London: Merlin Press, 1968) and Karl Marx, *Grundrisse: Foundations of the Critique of Political Economy* (*Rough Draft*), trans. Martin Nicolaus (London: Penguin, 1993), 156–159.
4 See Theodor W. Adorno, 'Situation', in *Aesthetic Theory*, trans. Robert Hullot-Kentor, eds. Gretel Adorno and Rolf Tiedemann (London: Continuum, 2010), 21–59, 21–22: 'Poetry retreated into what abandons itself unreservedly to the process of disillusionment. It is this that constitutes the irresistibility of Beckett's work.'
5 Adorno, *Negative Dialectics*, 381.

6   Theodor W. Adorno, 'Trying to Understand Endgame', in *The Adorno Reader*, ed. Brian O'Connor (Oxford: Blackwell, 2000), 319–352, 323–324. Cf. Badiou's later imperative from *Conditions*, 21: 'to desire philosophy against history'.
7   See Badiou, *Logics of Worlds*, 548: 'Of all twentieth-century writers, Samuel Beckett is the one who has been my closest philosophical companion. What I mean by this is that thinking "under condition of Beckett" has been, in the register of prose, the counterpart of what, for a long while, thinking "under condition of Mallarmé" has been for poetry.'
8   Badiou, *On Beckett*, 17–18.
9   For this genealogy, see Tzuchien Tho and Giuseppe Bianco (ed.) *Badiou and the Philosophers: Interrogating 1960s French Philosophy*, trans. Tzuchien Tho and Giuseppe Bianco (London: Bloomsbury, 2013), ix–l; Ed Pluth, *Alain Badiou: A Philosophy of the New* (Cambridge: Polity Press, 2010), 108–127. One must also make a distinction between the French reception of Hegel through Alexandre Kojève's lectures and their abiding influence on Sartre and others, and what Bruno Bosteels calls Badiou's 'idiosyncratic' alternative trajectory of the dialectic in French thought, from Pascal and Rousseau to Mallarmé and Lacan. See Bosteels, introduction to Badiou, *Adventures in French Philosophy*, xxxi–xxxiii.
10 Cf. Shane Weller, *A Taste for the Negative: Beckett and Nihilism* (London: LEGENDA, 2005). For an in-depth account of how Badiou's Beckett offers a palliative to orthodoxies in Beckett scholarship, see Andrew Gibson, *Badiou and Beckett: The Pathos of Intermittency* (Oxford: Oxford University Press, 2006), 118–129.
11 Adorno, 'Trying to Understand Endgame', 321.
12 Alain Badiou, 'Affirmative Dialectics: From Logic to Anthropology', *The International Journal of Badiou Studies* 2, no. 1 (2013), 1–13.
13 Ibid., 2.
14 T.W. Adorno, *Minima Moralia: Reflections on a Damaged Life*, trans. E.F.N, Jephcott (London: Verso, 2005), 55.
15 'I saw the Emperor – this world-soul – riding out of the city on reconnaissance. It is indeed a wonderful sensation to see such an individual, who, concentrated here at a single point, astride a horse, reaches out over the world and masters it.' G.W.F. Hegel, 'Letter to Niethammer (74), Jena, Monday, October 13, 1806', in *Hegel: The Letters*, trans. Clark Butler and Christiane Seiler (Bloomington: Indiana University Press, 1984), 114.
16 Adorno, *Minima Moralia*, 55.
17 See Shane Weller, *A Taste for the Negative: Beckett and Nihilism*, 130–131: 'Adorno thinks Beckett's works (and indeed the present as such) principally in relation not to catastrophes in the plural, but to a singular, incomparable catastrophe; namely, the Holocaust, as the very consummation of nihilism. […] Far from being a-historical or non-realist, or even a mere symptom of a certain historical moment, Beckett's art would in its autonomy be a realism far superior to Brecht's

or Mann's because it both responds and corresponds to a new and terrible historical reality.'
18   Adorno, 'Trying to Understand Endgame', 322.
19   Adorno, *Negative Dialectics*, 381.
20   Ibid.
21   Adorno, *Aesthetic Theory*, 221.
22   Cf. Hegel, *Phenomenology of Spirit*, 50–51: 'The scepticism that ends up with the bare abstraction of nothingness or emptiness cannot get any further from there, but must wait to see whether something new comes along and what it is, in order to throw it too into the same empty abyss. But when, on the other hand, the result is conceived as it is in truth, namely, as a *determinate* negation, a new form has thereby immediately arisen, and in the negation the transition is made through which the progress through the complete series of forms comes about of itself.'
23   Adorno, *Negative Dialectics*, xix.
24   Adorno, 'Trying to Understand Endgame', 325.
25   Cf. Adorno, *Negative Dialectics*, 17: 'The power of the status quo puts up the facades into which our consciousness crashes. It must seek to crash through them. This alone would free the postulate of depth from ideology. Surviving in such resistance is the speculative moment: what will not have its law prescribed for it by given facts transcends them even in the closest contact with the objects, and in repudiating a sacrosanct transcendence.'
26   See Lambert Zuidervaart, *Adorno's Aesthetic Theory: The Redemption of Illusion* (Cambridge, MA: MIT Press, 1994), 154: 'When *Endgame* parodies the three Aristotelian unities, it simultaneously pokes fun at existentialist philosophy. Adorno's essay first shows how Beckett reduces various staples of existentialist ontology, such as historicity, the human condition, Heidegger's *Befindlichkeiten*, and Jasper's "situations," to a minimal existence. [...] Adorno demonstrates that Beckett's play does not present the abstract idea of absurdity. Instead it expresses the real absurdity of all culture including existential philosophy, after World War II. By carrying this experience into the details for dramatic form, Beckett raises social critique to the level of aesthetic form.'
27   Adorno, 'Trying to Understand Endgame', 321.
28   Gillian Rose, *The Melancholy Science: An Introduction to the Thought of Theodor W. Adorno* (London: Verso, 2014), 167.
29   Cf. Adorno writing on Brecht, in 'Commitment', 80: 'The process of aesthetic reduction that he pursues for the sake of political truth, in fact gets in the way. For this truth involves innumerable mediations, which Brecht disdains. [...] But the more preoccupied Brecht becomes with information, and the less he looks for images, the more he misses the essence of capitalism which the parable is supposed to present.'
30   There is a distinct Hegelianism in Adorno's thinking here. The artwork's contents are *passed through* and sustained by the form that unifies them. Just as in

Hegel's *Encyclopaedia Logic* that which is other than 'thought' – what Hegel calls 'representations', encompassing intuitions, feelings, the reception of other sensory content, etc. – needs to be integrated and developed in the process of *Nachdenken*, or 'thinking over', for it to be raised to the level of the concept, so too does the manifold and disparate 'content' of the play require its development and unification in 'form' in order to reach an expression adequate to the historical situation from which the work emerges. See G.W.F. Hegel, *Encyclopaedia of the Philosophical Sciences in Basic Outline: Part 1: Logic*, trans. Klaus Brinkmann and Daniel O. Dahlstrom (Cambridge: Cambridge University Press, 2010), §5, 32: 'The true *content* of our consciousness is *preserved* in its translation into the form of thought and the concept, and indeed only then placed in its proper light … in order to learn what is true in objects and events, even feelings and intuitions, opinions, representations, etc., *thinking* them *over* is required. At any rate, thinking them over has at least this effect, namely, that of transforming the feelings, representations, etc., into *thoughts*.'

31 Adorno, 'Trying to Understand Endgame', 321.
32 Adorno, 'Commitment', 78.
33 Cf. Ibid., 77: 'The rudiments of external meanings are the irreducibly non-artistic elements in art. Its formal principle lies not in them, but in the dialectic of both moments – which accomplishes the transformation of meanings within it. The distinction between artist and *litterateur* is shallow: but it is true that the object of any aesthetic philosophy, even as understood by Sartre, is not the publicist aspect of art. Still less is the "message" of a work. The latter oscillates untenably between the subjective intentions of the artist and the demands of an objectively explicit metaphysical meaning.'
34 Zuidervaart, *Adorno's Aesthetic Theory*, 154.
35 Ibid., 155.
36 See Beckett's conversation with Tom Driver, quoted in Claire Locatelli, *Unwording the World: Samuel Beckett's Prose Works after the Nobel Prize* (Philadelphia: University of Pennsylvania Press, 1990), 14: 'When Heidegger and Sartre speak of a contrast between being and existence, they may be right, I don't know, but their language is too philosophical for me. I am not a philosopher. One can only speak of what is in front of him, and that now is simply the mess.'
37 Locatelli, *Unwording*, 13.
38 Ibid., 14.
39 Ibid.
40 Cf. Günther Anders, 'Being without Time: On Beckett's Play *Waiting for Godot*', in *Samuel Beckett: A Collection of Critical Essays*, ed. Martin Esslin (Englewood Cliffs, NJ: Prentice-Hall, 1965), 141: 'Estragon and Vladimir, are clearly men in general; yes, they are abstract in the most cruel, literal sense of the word: they are *abs-tracti*, which means: pulled away, set apart. And as they, having been pulled out of the

world, no longer have anything to do with it, the world has, for them, become empty; hence the world of the play too is an "abstraction": an empty stage, empty but for one prop indispensable to the meaning of the fable: the tree in its center, which defines the world as a permanent instrument for suicide, or life as the non-committing of suicide.'

41 Adorno, 'Trying to Understand Endgame', 325.
42 See Ibid., 320.
43 Adorno, *Aesthetic Theory*, 201. See also Anders, 'Being without Time ...': 140: 'In order to present a fable about a kind of existence, which has lost both form and principle and in which life no longer goes forward, [Beckett] destroys both the form and the principle so far characteristic of fables: now the *destroyed* fable, the fable which does not go forward, becomes the adequate representation of stagnant life; his meaningless parable about man stands for the parable of meaningless man.'
44 Adorno, 'Trying to Understand Endgame', 325.
45 Adorno, 'Commitment', 79.
46 See, for example, Elizabeth Grosz, *Sexual Subversions: Three French Feminists* (Sydney: Allen & Unwin, 1989), 7: 'For Sartre, the human being has at least one immutable, fixed characteristic: its essence is determined by its existence. It is paradoxically forced to be free, to give meaning and value to its existence by its own choices.'
47 Adorno, 'Trying to Understand Endgame', 328.
48 See Zuidevaart, *Adorno's Aesthetic Theory*, 159: 'by presenting the final history of human autonomy in an exchange society, Endgame offers the only fitting reaction to Aushwitz'.
49 Adorno, 'Trying to Understand Endgame', 338. The seminal account of this process of 'reification' is given in Georg Lukács, 'Reification and the Consciousness of the Proletariat', in *History and Class Consciousness*, trans. Rodney Livingstone (London: Merlin Press, 1968), 83–223. For a contemporary account of this process, see Timothy Bewes, *Reification, or The Anxiety of Late Capitalism* (London: Verso, 2002).
50 Adorno, 'Trying to Understand Endgame', 338.
51 Ibid., 321.
52 Ibid., 321–322.
53 Adorno, *Aesthetic Theory*, 24.
54 Jean-Michel Rabaté, 'Unbreakable B's: From Beckett and Badiou to the Bitter End of Affirmative Ethics', in *Alain Badiou: Philosophy and Its Conditions* (New York: State University of New York Press, 2005), 87–108, 101. See also Jean-Michel Rabaté, 'Philosophizing with Beckett: Adorno and Badiou', in *A Companion to Samuel Beckett*, ed. S.E. Gontarski (Malden, MA & Oxford: Wiley-Blackwell, 2010), 97–117, 101: Following a meeting with Beckett, Adorno noted, 'Beckett (after Godot). Not abstraction but subtraction.' Rabaté ties this conviction with Beckett's own

ambivalence towards the philosophical discourses popular throughout the 1940s and 1950s, especially Jean-Paul Sartre's: 'This is linked to what Adorno shrewdly perceives as Beckett's decision to debunk existentialism, to reduce philosophy to meaningless clichés.'

55 See Marx's classic account: Karl Marx, 'The Value-Form, or Exchange Value', in *Capital: A Critique of Political Economy, Volume I*, trans. Ben Fowkes (London: Penguin, 1990), 138–153.
56 Adorno, *Aesthetic Theory*, 201.
57 Adorno, *Negative Dialectics*, xx.
58 Brian O'Connor, introduction to 'Trying to Understand Endgame', 319–352, 319.
59 Zuidevaart, *Adorno's Aesthetic Theory*, 160.
60 Max Horkheimer and Theodor W. Adorno, *Dialectic of Enlightenment: Philosophical Fragments*, ed. Gunzein Schmid Noerr, trans. Edmund Jephcott (Stanford: Stanford University Press, 2002).
61 See especially 'The Concept of Enlightenment', in Horkheimer and Adorno, *Dialectic of Enlightenment*, 1–34.
62 Adorno, *Minima Moralia*, 16.
63 Adorno, 'Trying to Understand Endgame', 325.
64 Ibid.
65 Zuidervaart, *Adorno's Aesthetic Theory*, 158.
66 Adorno, 'Trying to Understand Endgame', 349–350.
67 Ibid., 325.
68 Zuidevaart, *Adorno's Aesthetic Theory*, 158.
69 Adorno, 'Trying to Understand Endgame', 350.
70 Adorno, 'Commitment', 86.
71 See above in the final paragraphs of Chapter 2.
72 Alain Badiou 'Theatre and Philosophy', in *Rhapsody for the Theatre*, trans. Bruno Bosteels with the assistance of Martin Puchner (London: Verso, 2014), 93–110, 102.
73 For Badiou, Theatre's initial 'analytic', the assemblage of its seven 'elements' – place, text, director, actor, décor, costumes and public – becomes a 'productive assemblage' in the moment of its activation on stage. The 'analytic' then becomes a 'dialectic' traversing its elements. The '*dialectic* of Theatre' is 'the singular need for a *spectator* to be summoned to appear in the tribunal of a *morality* under the watchful eye of the *State*'. Badiou continues: 'The productive assemblage of the elements of the analytic is (or is not) the event from which proceed a few truths, by the diagonal movement of the figures of the dialectic.' Badiou, *Rhapsody for the Theatre*, 14–15.
74 Badiou, 'Destruction, Negation, Subtraction: On Pier Paolo Pasolini', in *The Age of Poets*, 83–92, 84.
75 For an incisive account of the complex relationship between affirmation, subtraction and negation in Badiou's recent work, see Benjamin Noys, *The*

Persistence of the Negative: A Critique of Contemporary Continental Theory (Edinburgh: Edinburgh University Press, 2010).

76 Badiou, 'Theatre and Philosophy', 102.
77 The 'generic' is of central importance to Badiou's philosophical project. In his 'inaesthetic' encounter with Beckett's works, the philosophical concept of 'the generic' is subjected to modulation as the consequences of Badiou's reading of Beckett unfold. In *Being and Event*, 'the generic' underpins the subjective unfolding of 'thought', 'truth' and 'truth-procedure', and is to be understood in terms of the relationship between truth and knowledge. It forms the affirmative counterpart to the negative assertion of truth's 'indiscernibility'. Whereas the latter 'indicates … that what is at stake is subtracted from knowledge or from exact nomination', 'the generic' 'positively designates that what does not allow itself to be discerned is in reality the general truth of a situation, the truth of its being'. See Badiou, *Being and Event*, 327–343. Truth is deemed indiscernible but is affirmed too as a generic, predicate-less emergence universally addressed to all. The tie with subtraction is crucial then, for the generic is the positive assertion of what is *subtracted* from the predicates of identification, or 'knowledge'. The set-theoretical underpinning of Badiou's mature philosophy sheds some light on this, for the ontological schema of a 'truth' emergent within a world is precisely a generic set, a set which evades any classification via linguistic predicates.
78 Badiou, *Being and Event*, 327–343.
79 See above in Chapter 3, and Alain Badiou, 'Anabasis', in *The Century*, 81–97.
80 Cf. Power and Toscano's translation notes in *On Beckett*, n.77, 146: 'It is far easier to identify this "conceptual" consistency in Beckett's French work where the name of the place of being is quite consistently *pénombre*. As many quotations here demonstrate, in the English works there is some variation in Beckett's designation of this "place".'
81 Samuel Beckett, 'Malone Dies', in *Three Novels: Molloy, Malone Dies, The Unnamable* (New York: Grove Press, 1991), 171–282, 174.
82 Samuel Beckett, *How It Is* (London: Faber & Faber, 2009), 4.
83 See Samuel Beckett, *Endgame* (London: Faber & Faber, 2009), 21.
84 Beckett, *Three Novels*, 186.
85 Ibid., 180.
86 Ibid., 212.
87 Samuel Beckett, *Lessness*, in *Texts for Nothing and Other Shorter Prose, 1950–1976*, ed. Mark Nixon (London: Faber & Faber, 2010), 127–132, 129.
88 Ibid.
89 Beckett, *How It Is*, 3.
90 Ibid., 15.
91 Ibid., 4.

92 Samuel Beckett, *The Unnamable*, in *Three Novels*, 283–407, 407.
93 Much of Badiou's writing on love appears in the immediate wake of the 1988 publication in France of *L'être et l'événement*. His most lengthy exploration of love, for instance, 'What Is Love?' in *Conditions* is 'a reworked version of a paper [Badiou] gave at a colloquium in 1990 called 'Exercice des savoirs et différence des sexes'. See Badiou, *Conditions*, 179–198. The broader context in which Badiou's writing on love emerges following *Being and Event* is Lacanian psychoanalysis's adoption/rejection by French feminism throughout the 1980s and early 1990s; the respective projects of Julia Kristeva and Luce Irigaray, for example, whose dialogue is perhaps the most persistently cited expression of a French feminism committed to thinking the resources offered by psychoanalysis in the drive to subvert patriarchy. The extent of Lacan's complicity in patriarchy is of course a divisive issue during this time, noted by Elizabeth Grosz throughout her work: 'While a number of feminists have justifiably accused of Lacan of phallocentrism – the representation of two sexes by a single, masculine or sexually neutral model', she writes, 'he is also responsible for the insight of the subject's sexually specific construction.' Elizabeth Grosz, *Sexual Subversions*, 25.
94 Jacques Lacan, 'The Signification of the Phallus', in *Écrits: A Selection*, trans. Alan Sheridan (London: Tavistock, 1977), 281–291, 285.
95 Grosz, *Sexual Subversions*, 20–21.
96 Ibid., 21.
97 The instalment of 'the phallus' at the centre of Lacan's theory of sexual difference follows a complicated trajectory deserving of book-length treatment. The first step is to claim mother and child to be embroiled in a reciprocal quest for identity – a process associated with Lacan's imaginary order. (The most well-known theory relating to the Lacanian imaginary is to be found in Lacan, 'The mirror stage as formative of the function of the I', in *Écrits*, 1–7.) Grosz expresses this relation as one in which 'each strives to see itself reflected in the other; each defines the other's identity, a kind of primordial master-slave dialectic' (Grosz, *Sexual Subversions*, 22). Bruce Fink calls this relation between mother and child 'a potentially dangerous dyadic situation', in which each's desire is unfettered, threatening to engulf the other, see Bruce Fink, *The Lacanian Subject: Between Language and Jouissance* (Princeton: Princeton University Press, 1995, 57). Language intervenes upon this pre-oedipal situation in order to initiate real exchange in place of mere reciprocity. In entering language, the phallus becomes a third term mediating the desires of mother and child. This imposition of the phallus is bound to the symbolic field and often to the father specifically. Writing on this imposition, Elizabeth Grosz surmises that 'through the castration threat the Law demands the sacrifice of the boy's closeness to and pleasure with the mother. In exchange the boy is offered the Name-of-the-Father, a position *like* his father's, a place in the symbolic order as a phallic speaking subject' (Grosz, *Sexual Subversions*, 22).

98 See Elizabeth Grosz, *Jacques Lacan: A Feminist Introduction* (London: Routledge, 1990), 121: 'The penis takes on the function of the phallus only because it is the mark or trace that is able to signify, indeed, produce, the exclusion of half the population. From being a Real organ, the penis becomes an imaginary object dividing the sexes according to its presence or absence, possessed by some, desired by others; it then functions as a symbolic object (an object of exchange or union) between the sexes.'

99 Lacan, 'The Signification of the Phallus', 289.

100 See Lacan, *Seminar XX*, 45: 'What makes up for the sexual relationship is, quite precisely, love'. Badiou introduces his later essay on love, 'The Scene of Two', by declaring it a commentary on Lacan's claim in *Seminar XX* that, in Badiou's paraphrase, 'love comes to supplement the lack of sexual rapport.' Alain Badiou, 'The Scene of Two', trans. Barbara Fulks, *Lacanian Ink* 21 (2003): 42–55, 42.

101 Gillian Rose, *Love's Work: A Reckoning with Life* (New York: New York Review of Books, 1995), 140.

102 See Badiou, *Conditions*, 181: 'Love is not that which from a Two taken as structurally given creates a One of ecstasy. This objection is tantamount to an objection against being-for-death, for the ecstatic One can be inferred to be beyond the Two only as a *suppression of the multiple*. It is from the latter that we owe all the metaphors of the night, of the obstinate sacralising of the encounter, of the terror inflicted by the world. Wagner's *Tristan and Isolde* – in my categories, I call this a figure of disaster, as it is related to the generic amourous procedure.'

103 Alain Badiou and Slavoj Žižek, *Philosophy in the Present*, ed. Peter Engelmann, trans. Peter Thomas and Alberto Toscano (Cambridge: Polity Press, 2009), 11.

104 Ruby Cohn, *A Beckett Canon* (Ann Arbor: Michigan University Press, 2001), 306.

105 Samuel Beckett, *Imagination Dead Imagine*, in *Texts for Nothing*, 85–90, 87.

106 Ibid., 89.

107 The notes on *Lessness* in a recent edition of Beckett's prose offer insight into its creation: 'A set of six thematic groups ("families") of ten sentences are arranged in different permutations', see Beckett, *Texts for Nothing*, xvi. Elizabeth Drew and Mads Haahr helpfully unpack *Lessness*' mathematical underlay in their paper '*Lessness*: Randomness, Consciousness and Meaning', writing that the 'two halves of *Lessness* are two of the 8.3×10^{81} possible orderings of Beckett's 60 sentences'. See Elizabeth Drew and Mads Haahr, 'Lessness: Randomness, Consciousness and Meaning', presented at the 4th International CAiiA-STAR Research Conference 'Consciousness Reframed', Perth, Australia, 1–4 August, 2002, 1–3.

108 Beckett, *Lessness*, 129.

109 Ibid., 131.

110 Ibid.

111 Ibid., 129.

112 'He will make it,' occurs six times in 'Lessness'.

113 Beckett, *Lessness*, 130 and 132: 'Never but imagined the blue in a wild imagining the blue celeste of poesy.'
114 'Celeste' stands out too insofar as it harbours a remainder of Beckett's translation from French to English. Mining the original French text in order to disambiguate the translated English would be a mistake, though in this instance, it is of relevance that 'blue celeste of poesy' is more or less the same in the French: 'Jamais qu'imaginé le bleu dit en poésie celeste qu'en imagination folle.' See Samuel Beckett, *Sans*, in *TÊTES-MORTES: d'un ouvrage abandonné – assez – imagination mort imaginez – bing – sans* (Paris: Les Éditions de Minuit, 1972), 67–77, 76.
115 These are offered extended treatment in Fink, *Lacanian Subject*, 98–125. My presentation of Lacan's theories here closely follows Fink's instructive exegesis.
116 Fink, *Lacanian Subject*, 106.
117 For more on the sexuated positions in relation to love, see Lacan's analysis of courtly love in Jacques Lacan, *The Ethics of Psychoanalysis 1959–1960: The Seminar of Jacques Lacan: Book VII*, trans. Dennis Potter, ed. Jacques-Alain Miller (London: Routledge, 2008), 171–190, and his further elaboration in Lacan, *Seminar XX*, 64–77.
118 Fink, *Lacanian Subject*, 107.
119 Lacan, *Seminar XX*, 74.
120 Grosz, *Jacques Lacan*, 139.
121 For an in-depth account of the philosophical stakes of sexual difference with regard to signification especially, see Joan Copjec's engagement with Judith Butler in Joan Copjec, 'Sex and the Euthanasia of Reason', in *Read My Desire: Lacan against the Historicists* (London: MIT Press, 1994), 201–236.
122 It is as if the 'torture of the cogito', experienced in the solitude of every One's quest for identification, is subjected to further interrogation in this doubled posture: the One subverted from within the Two.
123 Samuel Beckett, *Enough*, in *Texts for Nothing*, 93–98, 96.
124 Ibid.
125 It is interesting in this regard that Lacan suggests towards the end of *Seminar XX* the possible infinitude of Woman's jouissance: 'When I say that woman is not-whole and that that is why I cannot say Woman, it is precisely because I raise the question (*je mets en question*) of a jouissance that, with respect to everything that can be used in the function Φx, is in the realm of the infinite.' Lacan, *Seminar XX*, 103.
126 'When I lean on the shoulder of the woman I love, and can see, let's say, the peace of twilight over a mountain landscape ... the sun about to disappear behind craggy peaks, and know – not from the expression on her face, but from within the world as it is – that the woman I love is seeing the same world, and that this convergence is part of the world and that love constitutes precisely, at that very moment, the paradox of an identical difference, then love exists, and promises to continue to exist. The fact is she and I are now incorporated into this unique Subject, the

Subject of love that views the panorama of the world through the prism of our difference, so this world can be conceived, be born, and not simply represent what fills my own individual gaze.' Alain Badiou with Nicolas Truong, *In Praise of Love*, trans. Peter Bush (London: Serpent's Tail, 2012), 25-26.

127   Sigi Jöttkandt, 'Love', in *Alain Badiou: Key Concepts*, ed. A.J. Bartlett and Justin Clemens (Durham: Acumen, 2010), 73-81, 77.

Conclusion

1   Badiou, 'Affirmative Dialectics', 3.
2   See John Felstiner, 'Paul Celan Meets Samuel Beckett', *American Poetry Review* 4, no. 33 (July/August 2004): 38: 'But hadn't there always been an understanding, hadn't they been meeting all along, those years in Paris – the older man a more-or-less voluntary Irish exile to France and French, the younger man, orphaned, homelandless, reaching Paris but cleaving to German: Beckett chipping away at silence with "this dust of words," Celan with his "gasping words," with the "prayer-sharp knives/of my/silence"?'; 'The years drive on: Celan's charged poems join him with Beckett as Europe's only authentic writers "after Auschwitz," in Adorno's view'; '*Celan me dépasse*', Samuel Beckett will later confide to a friend, 'Celan leaves me behind.'
3   Stefan Müller-Doohm, *Adorno: A Biography*, trans. Rodney Livingstone (Cambridge: Polity Press, 2005), 403-404.
4   In an important early study of Badiou's engagement with literature, Andrew Gibson's *Badiou and Beckett: The Pathos of Intermittency*, Celan and Beckett are often brought together in an interesting way (though our respective emphases are different). My focus has been the kinds of subjectivity that Celan's poems and Beckett's prose 'figure' having come to terms with Badiou's departure from Heidegger. I agree with much in Gibson's book, and our analyses often cohere, for example, 'Celan's poetry explores the possibility for example, of a fragile, aleatory break with stasis, in a manner that begs comparison with Beckett' (ibid., 104). My analysis of Celan's 'Anabasis', however, foregrounds the call, the encounter and the material supplement, rather than, less optimistically, the 'impassable-true', from which Gibson derives the notion that Celan commits to a poetics of the wait not 'in the midst of disaster' but after it, proclaiming that 'in effect, Celan says "not-yet"' (ibid., 107).
5   The best recent account of the difficulties pertaining to the development of Badiou's conceptions of form and formalization is to be found in John Cleary's 'Subjected to Formalization: Formalization and Method in the Philosophy of Alain Badiou', in *Badiou and His Interlocutors*, 143-157.

6   For recent work attending to Badiou, poetry and form, see Tom Eyers's insightful papers, 'Badiou among the Poets', *Boundary 2* (2016) 43 (2), 41–162 and 'Alain Badiou, Wallace Stevens, and the Paradoxical Productivity of Poetic Form', *Textual Practice* 30, no. 5 (2016): 835–855.
7   Alain Badiou, *Philosophy for Militants*, trans. Bruno Bosteels (London: Verso, 2012), 27. Hereafter cited parenthetically in the main body of the text using the abbreviation 'PM'.
8   See the first two sections of Chapter 4 in particular.
9   See Louise Burchill, 'Woman, the Feminine, Sexual Difference', in *The Badiou Dictionary*, ed. Steven Corcoran (Edinburgh: Edinburgh University Press, 2015), 390–395, 394: 'There are several indices from the very end of the 1990s of a major inflection in Badiou's stance on sexuation and the universal, with this being linked more broadly to the question of the "immanence of truths" insofar as that which is basically involved here is a truth's relation to its originating site – which is, of necessity, a "particularity."'
10 Louise Burchill, 'Woman's Adventures with/in the Universal', in *Badiou and His Interlocutors*, eds A.J. Bartlett and Justin Clemens (London: Bloomsbury, 2018), 105–125, 125.
11 See Louise Burchill, 'Feminism', in *The Badiou Dictionary*, ed. Steven Corcoran (Edinburgh: Edinburgh University Press, 2015), 126–132.
12 Burchill, 'Feminism', 130.
13 See Jöttkandt, 'Love', 73–81.
14 See Philippe Lacoue-Labarthe, *Phrase*, trans. Leslie Hill (Albany, NY: SUNY Press, 2018).
15 Michael Hamburger's English translation of 'Les Globes' is used in both *Poetry as Experience* and 'In Search of Lost Prose'.
16 Alain Badiou, 'In Search of Lost Prose', trans. Jacob Levi and Lucy Bergeret, *MLN* 132, no. 5 (December 2017), 1254–1266, 1255. Hereafter cited parenthetically in the body of the text using the abbreviation 'ISLP'.
17 Christopher Fynsk, *Lacoue-Labarthe's Phrase: Infancy, Survival* (New York: SUNY press, 2017), 15.

Bibliography

Adorno, T.W. (1974), 'Commitment', trans. F. McDonagh, *New Left Review* 1: 75–89.
Adorno, T.W. (1996), *Negative Dialectics*, trans. E.B. Ashton, London: Routledge.
Adorno, T.W. (2000), 'Trying to Understand Endgame', in *The Adorno Reader*, ed. B. O'Connor, 319–352, Oxford: Blackwell.
Adorno, T.W. (2005), *Minima Moralia: Reflections on a Damaged Life*, trans. E.F.N. Jephcott, London: Verso.
Adorno, T.W. (2010), *Aesthetic Theory*, trans. R. Hullot-Kentor, London: Continuum.
Anders, G. (1965), 'Being without Time: On Beckett's Play Waiting for Godot', in *Samuel Beckett: A Collection of Critical Essays*, 140–151, Englewood Cliffs, NJ: Prentice-Hall.
Apter, E., and B. Bosteels. (2014), 'Introduction', in A. Badiou *The Age of Poets: And Other Writings on Twentieth-Century Poetry and Prose*, ed. and trans. B. Bosteels, with an introduction by E. Apter and B. Bosteels, xx–xxv, London: Verso.
Badiou, A. (1992), *Conditions*, Paris: Éditions de Seuil.
Badiou, A. (1999), *Manifesto for Philosophy*, trans. N. Madarasz, New York: SUNY.
Badiou, A. (2000), *Deleuze: The Clamor of Being*, trans. L. Burchill, Minneapolis: University of Minnesota Press.
Badiou, A. (2000), 'Metaphysics and the Critique of Metaphysics', *Pli*, 10: 174–190.
Badiou, A. (2001), *Ethics: An Essay on the Understanding of Evil*, trans. P. Hallward, London: Verso.
Badiou, A. (2003), *On Beckett*, trans. A. Toscano and N. Power, Manchester: Clinamen.
Badiou, A. (2003b), 'The Scene of Two', trans. B.P. Fulks, *Lacanian Ink*, 21: 42–55.
Badiou, A. (2005a), *Being and Event*, trans. O. Feltham, London: Continuum.
Badiou, A. (2005b), *Handbook of Inaesthetics*, trans. A. Toscano, Stanford, CA: Stanford University Press.
Badiou, A. (2005c), *Infinite Thought: Truth and the Return to Philosophy*, trans. J. Clemens and O. Feltham, London: Continuum.
Badiou, A. (2005d), *Metapolitics*, trans. J. Barker, London: Verso.
Badiou, A. (2006a), *Briefings on Existence: A Short Treatise on Transitory Ontology*, trans. Norman Madarasz, New York: SUNY.
Badiou, A. (2006b), *Theoretical Writings*, trans. R. Brassier and A. Toscano, London: Continuum.
Badiou, A. (2006c), 'Third Sketch of a Manifesto of Affirmationist Art', in *Polemics*, trans. S. Corcoran, 133–148, London: Verso.
Badiou, A. (2007), *The Century*, trans. A. Toscano, Cambridge: Polity Press.

Badiou, A. (2007b), 'Philosophy as Creative Repetition', *Symptom*, 8 (Winter), Available online: www.lacan.com/newspaper8.htm (accessed 1 December 2018).
Badiou, A. (2008), *Conditions*, trans. S. Corcoran, London: Continuum.
Badiou, A. (2008b), *Number and Numbers*, trans. R. Mackay, Cambridge: Polity Press.
Badiou, A. (2009a), *Logics of Worlds: Being and Event, 2*, trans. A. Toscano, London: Continuum.
Badiou, A. (2009c), *Pocket Pantheon*, trans. D. Macey, London: Verso.
Badiou, A. (2009d), *Theory of the Subject*, trans. B. Bosteels, London: Continuum.
Badiou, A. (2010a), *Five Lessons on Wagner*, London: Verso.
Badiou, A. (2010b), *Second Manifesto for Philosophy*, trans. L. Burchill, Cambridge: Polity Press.
Badiou, A. (2011), *Wittgenstein's Antiphilosophy*, trans. B. Bosteels, London: Verso.
Badiou, A. (2012a), *Philosophy for Militants*, trans. B. Bosteels, London: Verso.
Badiou, A. (2012b), *The Adventure of French Philosophy*, ed. and trans. B. Bosteels, London: Verso.
Badiou, A., with N. Truong (2012c), *In Praise of Love*, London: Peter Bush.
Badiou, A. (2013a), 'Affirmative Dialectics: From Logic to Anthropology', *The International Journal of Badiou Studies*, 2 (1): 1–13.
Badiou, A. (2013b), *Rhapsody for the Theatre*, trans. B. Bosteels and M. Puchner, London: Verso.
Badiou, A. (2014), *The Age of Poets: And Other Writings on Twentieth-Century Poetry*, trans. B. Bosteels, introduction by E. Apter and B. Bosteels, London: Verso.
Badiou, A. (2017), 'In Search of Lost Prose', *MLN*, 132 (5): 1254–1266.
Badiou, A., and S. Žižek. (2009b), *Philosophy in the Present*, trans. P. Engelmann, P. Thomas and A. Toscano, Cambridge: Polity Press.
Badiou, A., with N. Truong (2012c), *In Praise of Love*, London: Peter Bush.
Bambach, C. (2013), *Thinking the Poetic Measure of Justice: Hölderlin-Heidegger-Celan*, New York: SUNY.
Bartlett, A.J., and J. Clemens (2010), *Alain Badiou: Key Concepts*, Durham: Acumen.
Baugh, B. (2003), *French Hegel: From Surrealism to Postmodernism*, London: Routledge.
Beckett, S. (1972), *TÊTES-MORTES: d'un ouvrage abandonné – assez – imagination mort imaginez – bing – sans*, Paris: Les Éditions de Minuit.
Beckett, S. (1983), 'Dante ... Bruno. Vico. Joyce', in *Disjecta: Miscellaneous Writings and a Dramatic Fragment*, ed. R. Cohn, 19–33, London: Calder.
Beckett, S. (1991), *Three Novels: Molloy, Malone Dies, The Unnamable*, New York: Grove Press.
Beckett, S. (2009), *Endgame*, London: Faber & Faber.
Beckett, S. (2009b), *How It Is*, London: Faber & Faber.
Beckett, S. (2010), *Texts for Nothing and Other Shorter Prose, 1950–1976*, ed. M. Nixon, London: Faber & Faber.
Benjamin, W. (1996), 'Two Poems by Friedrich Hölderlin', in *Selected Writings, Vol. 1 1913–1926*, ed. M. Bullock and M.W. Jennings, 18–36, Cambridge, MA: The Belknap Press of Harvard University Press.

Benjamin, W. (2004), 'The Concept of Criticism', in *Selected Writings, Vol. 1 1913–1926*, ed. M. Bullock and M.W. Jennings, 116–200, Cambridge, MA: The Belknap Press of Harvard University Press.

Betteridge, T. (2012), 'Silence Being Thought: Badiou, Heidegger, Celan', *Evental Aesthetics*, 1 (2): 17–48.

Betteridge, T. (2016), 'Alain Badiou's Anabasis: Rereading Paul Celan against Heidegger', *Textual Practice*, 30 (1): 45–68.

Bewes, T. (2002), *Reification, or the Anxiety of Late Capitalism*, London: Verso.

Birns, N. (2010), *Theory after Theory: An Intellectual History of Literary Theory from 1950 to the Early 21st Century*, New York: Broadview Press.

Bosteels, B. (2011), *Badiou and Politics*, Durham: Duke University Press.

Bosteels, B. (2012), 'Introduction', in A. Badiou, *The Adventure of French Philosophy*, ed. and trans. B. Bosteels, xxxi–xxxiii, London: Verso.

Burchill, L. (2015a), 'Feminism', in *The Badiou Dictionary*, ed. S. Corcoran, Edinburgh: Edinburgh University Press. 126–132.

Burchill, L. (2015b), 'Woman, the Feminine, Sexual Difference', in *The Badiou Dictionary*, ed. S. Corcoran, Edinburgh: Edinburgh University Press. 390–395.

Burchill, L. (2018), 'Woman's Adventures with/in the Universal', in *Badiou and His Interlocutors*, ed. A.J. Bartlett and J. Clemens, 105–125, London: Bloomsbury.

Celan, P. (1986), *Gesammelte Werke, im fümf Bänden: Dritter Band: Gedichte III, Prosa, Reden*, Frankfurt: Suhrkamp.

Celan, P. (1995), *Selected Poems*, trans. M. Hamburger, London: Penguin.

Celan, P. (2003), *Collected Prose*, trans. Rosmarie Waldrop, Manchester: Carcanet.

Celan, P. (2014), *Breathturn into Timestead: The Collected Later Poems of Paul Celan*, trans. P. Joris, New York: Farrar Straus Giroux.

Cleary, J. (2018), 'Subjected to Formalization: Formalization and Method in the Philosophy of Alain Badiou', in *Badiou and His Interlocutors*, ed. A.J. Bartlett and J. Clemens, 143–157, London: Bloomsbury.

Clemens, J. (2003), *The Romanticism of Contemporary Theory: Institution, Aesthetics, Nihilism*, Aldershot: Ashgate.

Clemens, J. (2006), 'Had We but Worlds Enough, and Time, This Absolute, Philosopher …', in *The Praxis of Alain Badiou*, ed. A.J. Bartlett, P. Ashton and J. Clemens, 104–143, Melbourne: re.press.

Constantinou, M. (2014), 'Forcing Politics: Badiou's Anabasis in the Age of Empire', in *Badiou and the Political Condition*, ed. M. Consantinou, 1–44, Edinburgh: Edinburgh University Press.

Cohn, R. (2001), *A Beckett Canon*, Ann Arbor: Michigan University Press.

Copjec, J. (1994), *Read My Desire: Lacan against the Historicists*, London: MIT Press.

Corcoran, S. (2015), *The Badiou Dictionary*, Edinburgh: Edinburgh University Press.

Critchley, S. (1993), 'Re-Tracing the Political: Politics and Community in the Work of Philippe Lacoue-Labarthe and Jean-Luc Nancy', in *The Political Subject of Violence*, ed. D. Campbell and M. Dallas, 73–93, Manchester: Manchester University Press.

Cunningham, D. (2016), 'Genre without Genre: Romanticism, the Novel and the New', *Radical Philosophy*, 196 (April/May).
Dauben, J.W. (1979), *Georg Cantor: His Mathematics and Philosophy of the Infinite*, Princeton, NJ: Princeton University Press.
David, P. (2014), 'Heidegger's *Dichtung*: Poetry and Thought', in *Dictionary of Untranslatables: A Philosophical Lexicon*, ed. B. Cassin, trans. E. Apter, and J. Lezra and M. Wood, 219, New Jersey: Princeton University Press.
Décultot, E. (2014), 'Romantic,' in *Dictionary of Untranslatables: A Philosophical Lexicon*, ed. B. Cassin, trans. E. Apter, and J. Lezra and M. Wood, 907–911, Princeton, NJ: Princeton University Press.
Derrida, J. (2005), *Sovereignties in Question: The Poetics of Paul Celan*, ed. T. Dutoit and O. Pasanen, New York: Fordham University Press.
de Saussure, F. (2013), *Course in General Linguistics*, trans. R. Harris, London: Bloomsbury.
Drew, E., and M. Haahr (2002), '"Lessness" : Randomness, Consciousness and Meaning', presented at the 4th International CAiiA-STAR Research Conference, 'Consciousness Reframed', Perth, Australia, 1–4 August, 2002. Available online: http://www.random.org/lessness/paper (accessed 5 July 2014).
Eyers, T. (2015), ''Badiou among the Poets', *Boundary 2*, 43 (2): 141–162.
Eyers, T. (2016), 'Alain Badiou, Wallace Stevens, and the Paradoxical Productivity of Poetic Form', *Textual Practice*, 30 (5), 835–855.
Felstiner, J. (1995), *Paul Celan: Poet, Survivor, Jew*, London: Yale University Press.
Felstiner, J. (2004), 'Paul Celan Meets Samuel Beckett', *American Poetry Review*, 33 (4): 38.
Feltham, O. (2006), 'Translator's Preface,' in A. Badiou, *Being and Event*, trans. O. Feltham, xvii–xxxiii, London: Continuum.
Fink, B. (1995), *The Lacanian Subject: Between Language and Jouissance*, Princeton, NJ: Princeton University Press.
Fort, Jeff. (2007), 'The Courage of Thought', in P. Lacoue-Labarthe, *Heidegger and the Politics of Poetry*, trans. Jeff Fort, Urbana and Chicago: Illinois University Press. ix–xviii.
Fynsk, C. (2017), *Lacoue-Labarthe's Phrase: Infancy, Survival*, New York: SUNY.
Gadamer, H. (1997), *Gadamer on Celan: "Who Am I and Who Are You?" and Other Essays*, ed. and trans. R. Heinemann and B. Krajewski, Albany, NY: SUNY.
Gibson, A. (2006), *Beckett and Badiou: The Pathos of Intermittency*, Oxford: Oxford University Press.
Gosetti-Ferencei, J. (2004), *Heidegger, Hölderlin and the Subject of Poetic Language: Towards a New Poetics of Dasein*, New York: Fordham University Press.
Grosz, E. (1989), *Sexual Subversions: Three French Feminists*, Sydney: Allen & Unwin.
Grosz, E. (1990), *Jacques Lacan: A Feminist Introduction*, London: Routledge.
Hallward, P. (2003), *Badiou: A Subject to Truth*, London: University of Minnesota Press.
Hallward, P., ed. (2004), *Think Again: Alain Badiou and the Future of Philosophy*, London: Continuum.

Hamburger, M. (1995), 'Introduction', to P. Celan, *Selected Poems*, trans. M. Hamburger, 19–34, London: Penguin.

Hamlin, C. (2006), 'Hölderlin's Hellenism: Tyranny or Transformation', *Hölderlin-Jahrbuch*, 35: 252–311.

Hanssen, B. (1997), '"Dichtermut" and "Blödigkeit": Two Poems by Hölderlin Interpreted by Walter Benjamin', *MLN*, 112 (5): 786–816.

Hegel, G.W. (1984), *Hegel: The Letters*, trans. C. Butler and C. Seiler, Bloomington: Indiana University Press.

Hegel, G.W. (2010), *Encyclopaedia of the Philosophical Sciences in Basic Outline: Part 1: Logic*, ed. and trans. K. Brinkmann and D.O. Dahlstrom, Cambridge: Cambridge University Press.

Hegel, G.W.F. (1977), *Hegel's Phenomenology of Spirit*, ed. and trans. A.V. Miller, Oxford: Oxford University Press.

Hegel, G.W.F. (1988), *Aesthetics: Lectures on Fine Art*, 1, trans. T.M. Knox, Oxford: Clarendon Press.

Heidegger, M. (1971), *Poetry, Language, Thought*, trans. Albert Hofstadter, New York: Harper & Row.

Heidegger, M. (1973), *The End of Philosophy*, trans. Joan Stambaugh, London: Harper & Row, Inc.

Heidegger, M. (1982), *On the Way to Language*, ed. and trans. P.D. Hertz, New York: HarperCollins.

Heidegger, M. (1996), *Hölderlin's Hymn "The Ister"*, ed. and trans. W. McNeill and J. Davis, Bloomington and Indianapolis: Indiana University Press.

Heidegger, M. (1998) *Pathmarks*, ed. and trans. W. McNeill, Cambridge: Cambridge University Press.

Heidegger, M. (2000), *Elucidations of Hölderlin's Poetry*, trans. K. Hoeller, New York: Humanity Books.

Heidegger, M. (2000b), *Introduction to Metaphysics*, trans. G. Fried and R. Polt, New Haven, CT: Yale University Press.

Heidegger, M. (2008), *Basic Writings*, trans. D.F. Krell, Abingdon: Routledge.

Heidegger, M. (2010), *Being and Time*, trans. J. Stambaugh, New York: State University of New York Press, or SUNY Press.

Heidegger, M. (2014), *Hölderlin's Hymns "Germania" and "The Rhine"*, trans. W. McNeill and J. Ireland, Bloomington and Indianapolis: Indiana University Press.

Heron, N. (2008), 'Idea of Poetry, Idea of Prose', in *The Work of Giorgio Agamben: Literature Law, Life*, ed. J. Clemens, N. Heron and A. Murray, 97–113, Edinburgh: University Press.

Hewson, M. (2010), 'Heidegger', in *Alain Badiou: Key Concepts*, ed. A.J. Bartlett and J. Clemens, Durham: Acumen. 146–154.

Hofstadter, A. (1971), 'Introduction', in M. Heidegger, *Poetry, Language, Thought*, ix–xxii, New York: Harper and Row.

Hölderlin, F. (1984), *Hymns and Fragments*, trans. R. Sieburth. Princeton, NJ: Princeton University Press.
Hölderlin, F. (1988), 'No. 236 to Casimir Ulrich Böhlendorff', in *Friedrich Hölderlin: Essays and Letters on Theory*, trans. T. Pfau, Albany, NY: SUNY.
Hölderlin, F. (1998), *Selected Poems and Fragments*, ed. J. Adler, trans. M. Hamburger, London: Penguin.
Horkheimer, M., and T.W. Adorno. (2002), *Dialectic of Enlightenment: Philosophical Fragments*, ed. G. Schmid Noerr, trans. E. Jephcott, Stanford: Stanford University Press.
Joris, P. (1988), *Celan/Heidegger: Translation at the Mountain of Death*. Available online: http://wings.buffalo.edu/epc/authors/joris/todtnauberg.html (accessed 1 January 2017).
Joris, P. (2014), 'Introduction', in *Paul Celan, Breathturn into Timestead: The Collected Later Poetry*, trans. Pierre Joris, xxix–lxxix, New York: Farrar, Straus, Giroux.
Jöttkandt, S. (2010), 'Love', in *Alain Badiou: Key Concepts*, ed. A.J. Bartlett and J. Clemens, 73–81, Durham: Acumen.
Kristeva, J. (1989), *Black Sun: Depression and Melancholia*, New York:
Lacan, J. (1999), *The Seminar of Jacques Lacan Book XX, Encore 1972–73: On Feminine Sexuality; the Limits of Love and Knowledge* ed. J. Miller, trans. B. Fink, London: W. W. Norton.
Lacan, J. (2008), *The Ethics of Psychoanalysis 1959–1960: The Seminar of Jacques Lacan: Book VII*, ed. J. Miller, trans. D. Potter, London: Routledge.
Lacoue-Labarthe, P. (1990), *Art, Heidegger, and Politics*, trans. C. Turner, Oxford: Basil Blackwell.
Lacoue-Labarthe, P. (1993), *The Subject of Philosophy*, ed. T. Trezise, Minneapolis: Minnesota University Press.
Lacoue-Labarthe, P. (1994), *Musica Ficta (Figures of Wagner)*, trans. F. McCarren, Stanford: Stanford University Press.
Lacoue-Labarthe, P. (1998), *Typography: Mimesis, Philosophy, Politics*, trans. C. Fynsk, Stanford: Stanford University Press.
Lacoue-Labarthe, P. (1999), *Poetry as Experience*, trans. A. Tarnowski, Stanford: Stanford University Press.
Lacoue-Labarthe, P. (2007), *Heidegger and the Politics of Poetry*, trans. J. Fort, Chicago: University of Illinois Press.
Lacoue-Labarthe, P. (2018), *Phrase*, trans. L. Hill, Albany, NY: SUNY.
Lacoue-Labarthe, P., and J. Nancy (1988), *The Literary Absolute: The Theory of Literature in German Romanticism*, trans. P. Barnard and C. Lester, New York: SUNY.
Lacoue-Labarthe, P., and J. Nancy (1990), 'The Nazi Myth', trans. B. Holmes, *Critical Inquiry*, 16 (2): 291–312.
Lecercle, J. (2010), *Badiou and Deleuze Read Literature*, Edinburgh: Edinburgh University Press.
Lefort, C. (1986), *The Political Forms of Modern Society*, trans. J.B. Thompson, Cambridge, MA: MIT Press.

Lévinas, E. (1979), *Totality and Infinity*, trans. A. Lingis, London: Boston.
Ling, A. (2010), 'Ontology', in *Alain Badiou: Key Concepts*, ed. A.J. Bartlett and J. Clemens, 48–58, Durham: Acumen.
Locatelli, C. (1990), *Unwording the World: Samuel Beckett's Prose Works after the Nobel Prize*, Philadelphia: University of Pennsylvania Press.
Lukács, G. (1968), *History and Class Consciousness*, trans. R. Livingstone, London: Merlin Press.
Lyon, J.K. (2006), *Paul Celan and Martin Heidegger: An Unresolved Conversation*, Baltimore: The Johns Hopkins University Press.
Mallarmé, S. (2007), 'Crisis in Verse', in *Divagations*, trans. B. Johnson, Cambridge, MA: The Belknap Press of Harvard University Press. 201–211.
Marx, K. (1990), *Capital: A Critique of Political Economy, Volume I*, ed. and trans. Ben Fowkes, London: Penguin.
Marx, K. (1993), *Grundrisse: Foundations of the Critique of Political Economy (Rough Draft)*, trans. M. Nicolaus, London: Penguin.
Meillassoux, Q. (2008), *After Finitude: An Essay on the Necessity of Contingency*, trans. R. Brassier, London: Continuum.
Mellors, A. (2005), *Late Modernist Poetics: From Pound to Prynne*, Manchester: Manchester University Press.
Michelson, A. (1980), 'Bayreuth: The Centennial "Ring"', *October*, 14: 65–70.
Müller-Doohm, S. (2005), *Adorno: A Biography*, trans. R. Livingstone, Cambridge: Polity Press.
Norris, C. (2012), *Badiou, Derrida and the Formal Imperative*, London: Continuum.
Norris, C. (2012), 'Diagonals: Truth-Procedures in Derrida and Badiou', in *Speculations, a Journal of Speculative Realism, Speculations III*, 150–188, New York: Punctum Books.
Noys, B. (2010), *The Persistence of the Negative: A Critique of Contemporary Continental Theory*, Edinburgh: Edinburgh University Press.
O' Connor, B. (2000), Introduction to 'Trying to Understand Endgame', in *The Adorno Reader*, ed. B. O'Connor, 319–352, Oxford: Blackwell.
Plato. (1987), *The Republic*, trans. D. Lee, London: Penguin Classics.
Plato. (1997), *Parmenides*, ed. and trans. M.L. Gill and P. Ryan in Plato, *Complete Works*, ed. J.M. Cooper, 359–397, Indianapolis: Hackett Publishing Company.
Pluth, E. (2010), *Alain Badiou: A Philosophy of The New*, Cambridge: Polity Press.
Polt, R. (1999), *Heidegger: An Introduction*, Abingdon: Routledge Ltd.
Power, N., and A.Toscano. (2003), 'Think Pig!', Introduction to *On Beckett*, ed. and trans. N. Power and A. Toscano, xi–xxxiv, Manchester: Clinamen Press.
Rabaté, J. (2005), 'Unbreakable B's: From Beckett and Badiou to the Bitter End of Affirmative Ethics', in *Alain Badiou: Philosophy and Its Conditions*, ed. G. Rierra, 87–108, New York: SUNY.
Rabaté, J. (2010), 'Philosophizing with Beckett: Adorno and Badiou', in *'A Companion to Samuel Beckett*, ed. S.E. Gontarski, 97–117, Oxford: Wiley-Blackwell.

Rose, G. (1995), *Love's Work: A Reckoning with Life*, New York: New York Review of Books.
Ross, A. (2007), *The Aesthetic Paths of Philosophy: Presentation in Kant, Heidegger, Lacoue-Labarthe, and Nancy*, Stanford, CA: Stanford University Press.
Rose, G. (2014), *The Melancholy Science: An Introduction to the Thought of Theodor W. Adorno*, London: Verso.
Savage, R. (2008), *Hölderlin after the Catastrophe: Heidegger – Adorno – Brecht*, London: Camden: House.
Sykes, J.B., W. Scholze-Stubenrecht and M. Clark., eds. (2001), *The Oxford-Duden German Dictionary*, Oxford: Oxford University Press.
Szondi, P. (2003), *Celan Studies*, trans. S. Bernofsky and H. Mendelsohn, Stanford, CA: Stanford University Press.
Tho, T., and G. Bianco., eds. (2013), *Alain Badiou and the Philosophers: Interrogating 19602 French Philosophy*, trans. T. Tho and G. Bianco, London: Bloomsbury.
Tobias, R. (2017), 'From Mythology to Myth: The Courage of Poetry,' *Modern Language Notes*, 132 (5): 1170–1185.
Waterfield, R. trans. (2000), *The First Philosophers: The Presocratics and the Sophists*, Oxford: Oxford University Press.
Watkin, C. (2011), *Difficult Atheism: Post-Theological Thinking in Alain Badiou, Jean-Luc Nancy and Quentin Meillassoux*, Edinburgh: Edinburgh: University Press.
Weinberg, B. (1962), 'Saint-John Perse's "Anabase"', *Chicago Review*, 15 (3): 75–124.
Weller, S. (2005), *A Taste for the Negative: Beckett and Nihilism*, London: LEGENDA.
Wittgenstein, L. (2001), *Tractatus Logico-Philosophicus*, ed. and trans. D.F. Pears and B. F. McGuinness, London: Routledge Classics.
Xenophon. (1972), *The Persian Expedition*, trans. R. Warner, London: Penguin Classics.
Zuidervaart, L. (1994), *Adorno's Aesthetic Theory: The Redemption of Illusion*, Cambridge, MA: MIT Press.

Index

abstraction 1, 58, 63, 138, 140–52, 189 n.2
absurd (-ity) 143–6, 150–1, 209 n.26
Adorno, Theodor W. 138–54, 185, 209–10 n.30
   Badiou on 152–4, 181–2
   on Beckett 139, 142–53
   on Beckett and Celan 181, 217 n.2
   critique of existentialism/Sartre 141–52
   dialectic of enlightenment 150–1
   Hegel 209–10 n.30
   identity 139, 150
   negative dialectics 143, 150–1, 153
   negative image 151–2
   Proust and death 151
   reification 151
   the subject and history 149–51
affirmation 13–17, 24–5, 107, 138, 140–3, 181
   the generic 155, 168, 213 n.77
   generic prose 140, 155
   identity 168
   meaning 145
   and negation 120, 212 n.75
   negative dialectics 143
   poem 53–4, 63–7
   'Third Sketch of a Manifesto for Affirmationist Art' 24
Age of Poets 20–2, 45, 53, 60–2, 88, 108
   and subject/figure 181–2
alterity. *See* difference
Althusser, Louis 190 n.13
anabasis 113–21, 129–35, 181–2, 217 n.4
   in Badiou's philosophy 113
   dialectics 137
   as distinct from homecoming 116
   encounter 129–35
   immanence 12, 134
   negated homecoming 111, 113, 129–35, 184
   as political subject 111, 113, 134–5, 181–2
   Saint-John Perse 24–5

   same and other 116–19
   and the Two 138, 156
   thought 120
   undecidability 119, 134
analytic philosophy 4, 20, 49
antiphilosophy 35
appear (-ing) (-ance) 42–5, 68
Apter, Emily 182
artifice 66, 96
Auschwitz 10, 29, 89, 138
   Beckett 139, 142, 171, 209 n.26
   Celan 2, 11, 22, 26, 120, 122
   and the end of philosophy 10, 89, 96, 103, 142
   impact on language 31–2, 61, 91
   meaning 142–4, 171
   nihilism 208 n.17
   rupture in thought/history 2, 10, 122, 147, 152
   and the subject 12, 150
authenticity
   Being and Time 88
   identity 77–8, 115
   poetic language 74, 94, 115
   political violence 89–90
   purification 76
   subject 134

Bambach, Charles 115–17
Beckett, Samuel
   Adorno on 139, 142–53
   Badiou on 19, 137–80, 208 n.7
   and Celan 11–12, 138, 154, 217 n.2
   encounter 139, 155, 170
   Endgame 141–53, 158, 209 n.26, 211 n.48
   Enough 171–80, 188
   formal transition 156, 170
   generic prose 92–3, 139, 154–62
   generic truth 139, 153
   grey black 157–64, 170–1, 175–6
   How it is 156–8, 162–4

Imagine Dead Imagine 169
latent poem 12, 92–3, 156, 163–80, 184, 186–8
Lessness 157–8, 161–2, 169–71, 215 n.107
and Mallarmé 19, 208 n.7
Malone Dies 158–61
subject 154–80, 184, 188 (*see also* The Two)
subtraction 140–52, 159–60
Theatre of the Absurd 140
The Unnamable 156, 164, 174
Benjamin, Walter 71, 92–108
body 6, 160. *See also under* subject
dancing body 14–16
and Lacan 173
subject body 120, 160, 172, 178, 180, 182
thought body 18
Bosteels, Bruno 137, 182, 204 n.113
Burchill, Louise 12, 185–8, 218 n.9

Cantor, Georg 4–5, 189 n.6, 194 n.39
Cavaillès, Jean 10
Celan, Paul 19–20, 22–3, 53–4, 57, 61–2, 185–8
'Anabasis' 113–21, 129–35, 217 n.4 (*see also under* anabasis)
Badiou on 134, 137, 182
and Beckett 11–12, 138, 154, 181, 217 n.2
'Below' 30–2
burden under suture 20, 61–2, 68
Celan completes Heidegger 23, 45, 60–2, 103
'*Es Kommt*' 58–60
German language 28–9
and Heidegger/meeting at Todtnauberg 22, 62, 91, 103, 114
'Homecoming' 121–9
as interface between Badiou and Heidegger 2, 11–12, 60–2, 68, 113–14, 184
poetics 23–8, 33, 51, 58–60, 91, 93, 107, 121–35, 193 n.27
politics/subject 134, 137, 182
'Speak, You Also' 51
'Todtnauberg' 61, 90–2, 114
'With a Changing Key' 29–30

communism 78, 134
conditions 3, 5, 20, 110, 134, 139
compossibility 20–1, 111
Critical Theory 92, 140

dance 13–19, 182. *See also under* subject
restrained intensity 15–16, 182
deconstruction 7, 10, 110
Deleuze, Gilles 6–8
Derrida, Jacques 7–9, 19, 115
desacralization 69–77
(dis)enchantment 72–5, 140
God of Poets 71–4
versus transcendence 75
Descartes, Jacques 36, 41, 73, 190 n.13, 195 n.55
diagonal (-ality) 4, 109, 189 n.6, 212 n.73
dialectic(s) 78, 120, 137–8, 208 n.9
affirmative dialectics 141–2
antidialectics (-al) 138, 145, 154, 162
Badiou on 137–8, 141–2, 153–4, 162
Bosteels on 137
Celan 127–8
of enlightenment 150–1
French dialecticians 2, 154
Hegelian 7, 154
Hölderlinian 71, 78, 87
Logics of Worlds 137
materialist 137, 207 n.49
negative dialectics 143, 150–1, 153
same and other 117
subject 132
of the *dictamen* 101
difference 115–18, 163, 171, 178–80, 182–8
Adorno 152
alterity 32, 114–21, 129–35
Celan 32–3, 121, 132–4, 187
constitutive for the subject 133, 185–8
Lévinas 114–19
love 177–8
minimal difference 132, 141, 159–63
as the Same 133
Same/Other 32, 33, 80, 114–21, 135

epistemology 26
ethics 99–100, 116–18, 120
event
Badiouian 3–5, 12, 17–18, 44, 74, 141, 194 n.39

Beckett 159, 170
  as encounter 93, 129, 133–5, 138, 166–7, 174–8
  Hölderlin 80
  latent poem 93
  Mallarmé 62
  poem 184
  subject 18, 111, 120, 134–5, 154, 170, 174–8, 183–4, 188
  undecidability 17, 206 n.23
existentialism 139–51

figure 65–9, 98, 101–11, 118, 171, 183. *See also* subject
  figure without figure 107–11, 183
  generic figures 172–8
Felstiner, John 23, 30, 51, 58–9, 122, 125, 217 n.2
feminism 214 n.93
  Burchill's reading of Badiou 185–8
  liberal 185
  phallocentrism 164–5, 172–80
finitude 74, 117, 167, 175, 187
French philosophy 2–10, 190 n.13, 208 n.9, 214 n.93

George, Stefan 76, 83–4, 88
German philosophy 2, 5–8
Gibson, Andrew 217 n.4
Greece
  and Germany's emergence 69, 78
  Greek event 37, 43, 74–5, 190 n.10
  Hölderlin on 71, 78–89, 115
  myth 114–15
  philosophy 39, 115, 117, 190 n.10
Grosz, Elizabeth 165, 173, 214 n.93, 214 n.97

Hallward, Peter 5, 9, 12, 20, 57, 120
Hamburger, Michael 29–30, 58, 79, 84, 121, 123, 130–1, 207 n.43
Hanssen, Beatrice 71, 101
Hegel, Georg 7, 8, 20, 36, 93, 95, 117, 141–2, 154, 209–10 n.30
Heidegger, Martin 4, 5–10
  Badiou's critique 22, 34, 36–45, 51–2, 67–8, 69–71, 74–5, 88, 104, 113–17, 190 n.10 (*see also* ontology)
  Critchley on 109
  Dichtung 37, 49, 91–3, 97–8, 100–3
  homecoming 113, 117, 125–8, 134
  idle-talk 32, 48–50
  inauguration/German people 70–1, 83–5, 89, 95, 98, 114–15, 183
  influence on Celan 29, 61–2
  Lacoue-Labarthe on 89–103, 110
  on language 48–9, 51–4, 61
  the Nothing 45–52
  oblivion of Being 46
  open 33
  phusis 36–45, 68
  reading of Hölderlin 23, 72, 81, 83–5, 88, 114–15
  Savage on 83
Hofstadter, Albert 53–4
Hölderlin, Friedrich 21, 23, 43, 69–74. *See also* Lacoue-Labarthe; Heidegger
  Badiou on 73–4, 79
  Benjamin on 71, 92–108
  exchange and alterity 71, 82, 87, 115
  Heidegger on 88, 99
  '*Heimkunft*'/'Homecoming' 121–9
  'The Ister' 81, 114–15
  'The Journey' 78–89
  letter to Ulrich Bohlendorff 71
  native/foreign 87, 115
  Savage on reception of 75–6
  'Timidity' 92, 99, 107
Holocaust, the. *See* Auschwitz
homecoming 111, 113–29, 133–4, 184, 205 n.19

idea, the 36, 39–44, 58, 63, 67–8. *See also* poetic idea
idealism 133, 207 n.49
immanence 12–15, 134, 167, 182. *See also* subject
inaesthetics 8, 13, 21, 191 n.20
infinite, the 69, 72, 77, 88, 118, 120, 187–8, 189 n.6
  infinite knowledge 175–8
Irigaray, Luce 214 n.93

Jena Romanticism 92, 95, 108, 201 n.51
Joris, Pierre
  on Celan 197 n.115, 198 n.119, 206 n.25
Jöttkandt, Sigi 178, 186

Kant, Immanuel 100, 120, 140
Kierkegaard, Søren 140
knowledge 14–18, 27–8, 34, 41, 45, 66, 118, 183
Kristeva, Julia 214 n.93

Lacan, Jacques 2, 4, 7, 120, 164–6, 185, 190 n.13, 191 n.21
 phallocentrism 164–5, 172–80
 the phallus 179, 214 n.93, 214 n.97
 sexual difference 172–7, 214 n.93
Lacoue-Labarthe, Philippe 4. See also poem becoming-prose
 on Auschwitz 29, 93, 103
 Badiou on 61, 75, 93–5, 103–6, 109–10, 183, 186–8
 becoming-prose 89–102, 108
 on Benjamin 92–108
 on Celan 61, 90–1, 187, 198 n.121
 dialogue with Badiou 90, 93, 105–6, 184, 200 n.40
 dictamen/das Gedichtete 99–108
 end of philosophy 75, 103, 107, 109, 152
 on Heidegger/Hölderlin 68, 85, 88–9, 89–102, 202 n.65
 on Mallarmé 105–6
 mimesis 200 n.41
 mytheme/myth 95–7, 102
 philosophy and poetry/suture 61, 90, 96, 104, 201 n.60
 phrase 186–8
 triangulation of philosophy and poetry by politics 94–9, 102, 109–10
latent poem 156, 163–80, 184, 186–7
Lautman, Albert 10
Lévinas, Emmanuel 115–18
Locatelli, Clara 145
love 12, 68, 138, 155, 163–80, 185, 216 n.126
 and collective 179
 context of Badiou's writing on 214 n.93
 the novel 164
 and subject (*see* The Two)

Malevich, Kazimir 141, 159–60, 163. See also minimal difference
Mallarmé, Stéphane 2, 19–20, 50, 52, 65–6, 139, 141, 193 n.16, 208 n.7. See also poetic idea

Badiou and Lacoue-Labarthe 105–6, 110
Marx, Karl 4, 20, 72, 137, 212 n.55
materialism 20, 133, 137, 140, 207 n.49
mathematics 2–10, 34–8, 41–4, 60, 64, 74–5, 189 n.6
 matheme 37–8, 43, 62–5
 Plato 64–7
 prose of thought 104
 set-theory (*see* ontology)
Meillassoux, Quentin 45
Michelson, Annette 189 nn.2–3
minimal difference. *See* difference
Mizoguchi, Kenji 167–8
multiple (-icity). *See* ontology
myth (-ology)
 Dichtung 93
 Fascism 77, 89, 98
 Greek 85–7
 Hölderlin 79, 84–7
 Lacoue-Labarthe on 90–1, 102, 107
 mytheme 95–6
 and politics 76–8, 89, 134–5
 and transcendence 69–76
 Wagner 1, 106

Nancy, Jean-Luc 98, 109, 152
Nazism 1–2, 10, 76, 98, 103
 Goebbels 76
 Heidegger 2, 22
 Hölderlin 'field edition' 76
Nietzsche, Friedrich 13–7, 35, 71, 117
nihilism 6, 24, 55, 72, 140, 143–6, 208 n.17
Novalis 92–3, 100–1, 108

ontology. See thought of being
 Adorno on 150–1
 Badiouian 5, 36–45, 117
 Badiouian in relation to Heideggerian 34, 36–45, 51–2, 190 n.10
 being qua being 2–3, 5, 34, 36–8, 45, 52
 and epistemology 26
 Existential 144–51
 'Jewish critique' of 115–16
 mathematics equals ontology 2–3, 36
 multiplicity/inconsistency 52, 55–6, 194 n.39
 nothing, the 45–52
 Parmenides and the One 55–7

phenomenological 47
of presence/poetic ontology 37–41, 43, 55, 60, 64, 67
set-theory/set-theoretical discourse 5, 36–8, 44, 55, 60, 64, 190 n.8
subtractive 34, 36–7, 45, 55, 96
withdrawal of the object 28, 44, 64–8, 108
other. *See* difference

performance 153
Perse, Saint-John 23–7, 62, 113, 121, 133, 192 n.10
Pessoa, Fernando 21, 108
phenomenology 7, 40–1, 47, 166
Plato 37, 43, 65–8, 190 n.13
  idea against *phusis* 36–43
  The 'Platonic Turn' 44, 195 n.57
  The Republic 6, 63–5, 129
poem becoming-prose 89–103, 108–9, 111, 183–4, 187
poetic idea 11, 65–8, 72, 105. *See also* thought of being
  figure without figure 108, 111
  'the idea of poetry is prose' 92
  withdrawal of the object 28, 44, 64–8, 108
poetic language
  affirmative 53–4, 63–7, 168
  Auschwitz 29, 91
  Badiou on 20, 25, 55, 60
  Celan on 29, 33, 62, 182, 187
  central silence 28–33, 35–6, 51–2, 68, 95, 184
  contra communication 27, 51–2
  Dichtung 45, 48–9, 91–3, 97–8, 100–3
  figure 68, 156
  Heideggerian 49–51, 53–4
  incapacity 26, 59, 61–2
  ineloquence 25–7
  inheritance and German heritage 59
  interruption by the matheme 36–45, 64
  'modern' relation to mathematics 65
  mystery/enigma 21, 37, 44, 53, 62–4, 68
  naming 39, 44, 174
  narrow path/impassable-true 58–9, 131, 217 n.4
  and the nothing 45–8, 50–3
  opposition to openness 33–4, 53, 107

paronomasia 27, 58, 131
poetics of the wait 75, 78, 88–9, 217 n.4
prose. *See also* poem becoming-prose
  generic prose 139–40, 156–7
  Jena Romanticism 92–3, 95
  lost prose 94, 186
  prose of thought 93, 95, 103–4, 203 n.91
  prosodic set-up 155–6, 164, 168, 171
prosody 26–7, 125–6, 133
psychoanalysis 4, 164–5, 186, 214 n.93

Rabaté, Jean-Michel 149, 211 n.54
real, the 5, 22, 60–1, 73, 120, 144, 163, 190 n.8
  passion for the real 71–2, 77, 137, 159–60
  semblance and identity 77–8, 89, 160
  subtraction 163
Rose, Gillian 144, 167

Sartre, Jean-Paul 6, 10, 48, 140–52, 190 n.13
Savage, Robert 75–6, 83
Schlegel, Friedrich 92
sexual difference. *See also* The Two
  Badiou's critique of Lacan 164–6, 172–4
  Grosz's critique of Lacan 165, 173–4, 214 n.97
  immanence 167
  love as truth of 166
  'masculine'/'feminine' roles 174–5, 178–80
  non-biological conception of 165
  and Two of love 177, 185
sophistry 34–6, 54, 64, 103–4
Stevens, Wallace 183
subject, the
  affirmation 120, 154, 171
  of anabasis 119–21, 134, 182
  autonomy 150
  body 120, 160, 172, 178, 180, 182
  cogito 156–7, 162
  collective 84, 138, 179, 182
  dance 16–18
  encounter 129, 132, 154, 155–6
  figure without figure 107–11, 183
  generic, the 155
  generic humanity 140, 155, 165
  idealist 133

immanence 12–15, 134, 167, 182
inner dynamism 13–17, 120, 134–5
interruption 135
material(ism) 120, 133–4, 207 n.49
and philosophy 111
poetic figure 111, 156
of politics 70, 111, 134–5, 181–2
practical processes 5, 166–7, 174
subtraction 154–5
Two of love 155, 163–80
without object 108–9, 182–4
subtraction 12, 14–15, 154, 159–60
Adorno 140, 142–51, 154, 211 n.54
Adorno and Badiou 141
and affirmation 66, 140–1, 154
Badiou 43–5, 60, 104, 140–1
in Beckett 139–51, 158–60
of being from appearance/presence 43–5, 60, 68, 70, 104
of being from language 108, 158–60
contra destruction 138, 154
event 162
and Existential ontology 142–50
generic, the 213 n.77
and generic prose 140, 156–7
from identity 159, 179
Malevich 159–60
and matheme 43–5, 104
and minimal difference 159–63
negativity/negation 138, 140, 154
and poem 57, 60, 66–7, 107–8, 159
and subject 132–3, 138, 154–5, 172, 181
thought of being 64, 67
withdrawal of the object 66–7
suture (d) (s) 20–2, 61, 93, 184. *See also* Age of Poets
Badiou's critique of Lacoue-Labarthe 93–6, 104
philosophy to poetry 20–2, 104
Szondi, Peter 19, 71

thought of being 23, 33–6, 45, 50, 52, 57
Celan/'the modern poem' 57, 59–64, 66–7, 70, 95
Tobias, Rochelle 90, 101–2

Trakl, Georg 21, 53–4, 97
truth(s) 3, 8, 12, 20–1, 75, 153, 165, 188, 191 n.21, 194 n.39
and antiphilosophy 35
Badiou and Heidegger on 40–4, 53–5, 68, 70, 104
Celan 51, 59–61
and the generic 19, 155, 213 n.77
immanence 134, 218 n.9
and inaesthetics 13
indiscernible 155, 213 n.77
material emergence 111, 118, 120, 135, 141
and myth 76
nihilism 72
and the poem 20, 26–7, 33, 36, 51, 53–5, 59–61, 70, 101–3, 106
of sexual difference 174
and sophistry 34–5
subject 118, 120–1, 133, 172–4, 177–80, 184
suture 21
truth procedure 53, 106, 138–41, 155, 166–8, 172–4, 177–80, 185, 188
Two, the 12, 138–9, 154–80, 184, 188. *See also* subject; love
Rose 167
Tristan and Isolde 167

void, the 44, 52–68, 175–8
set 54, 57
von Hellingrath, Norbert 75–6, 88

Wagner, Richard 1–2, 105–6, 189 n.2, 189 n.3, 215 n.102
Watkin, Christopher 74
Webern, Anton 140
whole, the 24, 45–7, 52–4, 62, 108, 111, 179
sets 192 n.12
Wittgenstein, Ludwig 28, 34–5, 194 n.36

Xenophon 114, 119

Žižek, Slavoj 167

www.ingramcontent.com/pod-product-compliance
Lightning Source LLC
Chambersburg PA
CBHW052035300426
44117CB00012B/1828